BEST
シグマベスト

最高水準問題集

中学英作文

佐藤誠司　著

文英堂

本書のねらい

▶みなさんは，“定期テストでよい成績をとりたい”とか，“希望する高校に合格したい”と考えて毎日勉強していることでしょう。そのためには，**どんな問題でも解ける最高レベルの実力**を身につける必要があります。では，どうしたらそのような実力がつくのでしょうか。それには，よい問題に数多くあたって，自分の力で解くことが大切です。

▶この問題集は，最高レベルの実力をつけたいという中学生のみなさんの願いに応えられるように，次の3つのことをねらいにしてつくりました。

1 出題形式・内容ごとに自分の弱点が確かめられるようにする。

2 おさえておかなければならない内容をきめ細かく分析し，問題を1問1問練りあげる。

3 最高レベルの良問を数多く収録し，より広い見方や深い考え方の訓練ができるようにする。

▶この問題集を大いに活用して，どんな問題にぶつかっても対応できる最高レベルの実力を身につけてください。

本書の特色と使用法

1 すべての章を「標準問題」→「最高水準問題」で構成し，段階的に無理なく問題を解いていくことができる。

▶本書は，「標準」と「最高水準」の２段階の問題を解いていくことで，各章の学習内容を確実に理解し，無理なく最高レベルの実力を身につけることができるようにしてあります。
▶本書全体での「標準問題」と「最高水準問題」それぞれの問題数は次のとおりです。

標準問題 ……55 題　　最高水準問題 ……32 題

豊富な問題を解いて，最高レベルの実力を身につけましょう。
▶さらに，学習内容の理解度をはかるために，章ごとに「**実力テスト**」を設けてあります。ここで学習の成果と自分の実力を診断しましょう。

2 「標準問題」で，各章の学習内容を確実におさえているかが確認できる。

▶「標準問題」は，各章の学習内容のポイントを１つ１つおさえられるようにしてある問題です。１問１問確実に解いていきましょう。

▶どんな難問を解く力も，基礎学力を着実に積み重ねていくことによって身についてくるものです。まず，「標準問題」を順を追って解いていき，基礎を固めましょう。

▶その章の学習内容として絶対におさえておくべき重要な問題に 重要 のマークをつけています。じっくり取り組んで，解答の導き方を確実に理解しましょう。

3 「最高水準問題」は各章の最高レベルの問題で，最高レベルの実力が身につく。

▶「最高水準問題」は，各章の最高レベルの問題です。総合的で，幅広い見方や，問題への取り組み方が身につくように，難問・奇問ではなく，各章で勉強する基礎的な事項を応用・発展させた質の高い問題を集めました。

▶特に難しい問題には， 難 マークをつけて，解答でくわしく解説しました。

4 「標準問題」にある〈ガイド〉や，「最高水準問題」にある〈解答の方針〉で，基礎知識をおさえたり適切な解き方を確認したりすることができる。

▶「標準問題」には， ガイド をつけ，学習内容の要点や注意すべきポイントなどを示しました。

▶「最高水準問題」の下の段には， 解答の方針 をつけて，問題を解く糸口を示しました。ここで，解法の正しい道筋を確認してください。

5 くわしい〈解説〉つきの別冊解答。どんな難しい問題でも解き方が必ずわかる。

▶別冊の「解答と解説」には，各問題のくわしい解説があります。答えだけでなく， 解説 もじっくり読みましょう。

▶ 解説 には 文法 注意！ 暗記 Q&A ［参考］ といった項目を設け，知っているとためになる知識や高校入試で問われるような情報などを満載しました。難関校ならではの難しい英作文問題への取り組み方もていねいに解説しています（くわしくは次ページ）。

6 難関校の英作文問題の“書き方”がわかる。

▶英作文の学習では，自分で書いた答えが本当に正しいのかどうかわからなかったり，あるいは，「ＡとＢのどちらの表現を使うべきだろう？」と悩んだりするでしょう。こういったもっともな疑問への答えを曖昧にしたままでは，いつまでたっても「適切な文」を書くことはできません。本書では，別冊の「解答と解説」に 文法 注意！ 暗記 Q&A ［参考］といったコーナーを設け，中学生のみなさんがそれらの疑問への答えを見つけ，やがてどんな難問にもひとりで太刀打ちできるように，くわしくていねいな解説を心がけました。

▶「解答と解説」で扱う文法事項，暗記事項には，一般の中学生が学校で習わない内容も多く含まれていますが，難関校入試ではこのレベルまで出題される可能性もあり，むしろ今の時期に押さえておけば，この先の英語学習で確実に役立つものばかりです。もしよくわからなかった問題があれば，解説をじっくり読んで，もう一度問題に取り組んでください。

7 ［付録］：「英作文の勉強の仕方」と「暗記用例文100」。

▶本書では，別冊に［付録］として「英作文の勉強の仕方」をつけました。自力ではなかなか取り組みにくい「和文英訳」や「自由英作文」について，どのように勉強すれば効果的な学習ができるのか，具体的なアプローチの仕方を紹介しています。

▶英作文問題への対策としては，あらかじめ自分の頭の中に，使える英語表現をたくさんストックしておくことも大いに有効です。「暗記用例文 100 」は，英作文での利用価値が高いとっておきの 100 例文ですので，ぜひしっかり覚えて，実際の入試で解答を書く際の土台として活用してください。

▶なお，「暗記用例文 100 」には，タイトル右の QR コードからアクセスできる英語音声も用意しています。ネイティブスピーカーが読んだ英語音声を聞きながら，自分でも声を出して覚えるのがおすすめです。目で字面を追うだけより記憶に残りやすくなります。

【音声の利用方法】

以下の方法で，簡単に再生することができます。

1．紙面の QR コードを，スマートフォンやタブレットで読みとります。

2．表示される URL にアクセスすると，プレーヤーの画面が表示されます。

3．タップして再生を開始してください。

●音声は無料でご利用いただけますが，通信料金はお客様のご負担となります。●すべての機器での動作を保証するものではありません。●やむを得ずサービス内容に予告なく変更が生じる場合があります。●QR コードは㈱デンソーウェーブの登録商標です。

もくじ

1 整序英作文問題

注意　文頭に来る語も小文字で与えられている場合がある。解答欄には文頭の語は大文字で書くこと。

標準問題

（解答）別冊 p.2

001 ［　］内の語(句)を並べ替えて，日本語の内容に合う英文を完成しなさい。

① スマートフォンはとても便利だと私は思いました。（東京・城北高）

[smartphones / I / very / found / useful].

② とても天気がよいので駅まで歩きたい。（東京・城北高）

[I / walk / is / nice / the weather / so / want / that / to] to the station.

③ 日本から韓国までどれくらいの距離があるか知っていますか。（東京・城北高）

[do / Japan / from / far / how / is / it / know / to / you] Korea?

④ マンボウを見たかったのですが，そこにはいませんでした。（東京・城北高）

The sunfish [there / wanted / was / to / not / see / I].

⑤ 1か月にどれくらい本を読みますか。（大阪・追手門学院大手前高）

[do / many / read / how / you / books / a] month?

⑥ ケンジは妻に誕生日ケーキを作ってあげました。（大阪・追手門学院大手前高）

Kenji [cake / birthday / made / a / wife / his].

⑦ ケーキのおかわりはいかがですか。（京都・大谷高）

[another / cake / have / like / piece of / to / would / you]?

⑧ 金閣寺は今まで私が訪れた中で最も美しい寺です。（京都・大谷高）

Kinkaku-ji is [beautiful / ever / I've / most / temple / that / the / visited].

①

②

③

④

⑤

⑥

⑦

⑧

重要 002 ［　］内の語(句)を並べ替えて，日本語の内容に合う英文を完成しなさい。

① 私の先生によって与えられた宿題は，英語でエッセイを書くことです。 （東京・中央大杉並高）
[my teacher / an essay / is / in / the homework / by / English / write / given / to].

② 東京でオリンピックが開催されてからずいぶんたちます。 （東京・中央大杉並高）
[the Olympic Games / time / has / a / it / since / held / long / been / were] in Tokyo.

③ 私は，新宿へ行くにはどの電車に乗ればよいのか，隣の人に尋ねました。 （東京・中央大杉並高）
I [the person / which / take / to / to / asked / next / train / me] to go to Shinjuku.

④ その工場の全従業員は，自社製品が世界中でもっと人気が出てほしいと思っている。
All [be / around / their products / the workers / popular / in the factory / more / the world / want / to]. （東京・中央大杉並高）

⑤ 明日も寒い日になりそうだ。 （愛知・滝高）
[another / day / be / there / going / to / cold / is] tomorrow.

⑥ この本を読んだおかげで，江戸時代の生活がいくらかわかった。 （愛知・滝高）
[idea / some / life / this book / me / gave / of / in] the Edo period.

⑦ 私はまだマミほどたくさんの本は読んでいない。 （東京農業大第一高）
[Mami / as / as / I / read / books / not / many / have] yet.

⑧ 将棋を好む子どもたちの数は増加している。 （東京農業大第一高）
[is / like / children / increasing / the / shogi / who / of / number].

①

②

③

④

⑤

⑥

⑦

⑧

ガイド 整序作文問題の対策としては，この形式でよく問われる文法事項を一通り頭に入れておくことが大切。まとまった意味を表す構文や連語も問われやすい。②④⑦⑧などはその例。

重要 **003** ［ ］内の語(句)を並べ替えて，日本語の内容に合う英文を完成しなさい。

① 何か温かい食べ物を食べたい。 (神奈川・鎌倉学園高)

I [to / to / would / something / like / have / hot] eat.

② その新しい図書館は古い図書館の2倍の広さになります。 (大阪・開明高)

The new library [twice / as / will / the / one / large / be / old / as].

③ もう何年もこの木には実がつかない。 (近畿大附和歌山高)

There [no / on / has / been / this / fruit] tree for many years.

④ 沖縄に行くのはこれが2回目です。 (熊本・真和高)

This [been / have / I / is / the second / time / to] Okinawa.

⑤ この図書館には，私が必要としている本はありません。 (熊本・真和高)

[I / in / is / need / not / the book / this library].

⑥ 福岡は多くの外国人が訪れる都市です。 (福岡・西南学院高)

Fukuoka is [visited / countries / from / people / a city / many / by / foreign].

⑦ 留学にいくら必要か調べるつもりだ。 (福岡・西南学院高)

I'm going to check [to / need / study / how / money / I / much / abroad].

⑧ 最初にしなければならないのは，部屋を掃除することだ。 (福岡・西南学院高)

[to / to do / have / clean / thing / is / you / the first] your room.

① ______________________________

② ______________________________

③ ______________________________

④ ______________________________

⑤ ______________________________

⑥ ______________________________

⑦ ______________________________

⑧ ______________________________

ガイド ①②④⑧は，日本語を見ただけで，「文全体の形」や「意味のまとまりを作る語の組み合わせ」がある程度頭に浮かぶのが望ましい。

004 ［ ］内の語（句）を並べ替えて，日本語の内容に合う英文を完成しなさい。

① 向こうで泣いている女の子は誰ですか。 （大阪・関西大第一高）
[girl / over / there / is / the / crying / who]?

② 40を8で割ると5です。 （大阪・関西大第一高）
[forty / eight / divided / is / by] five.

③ 誰かがその犬の世話をしないといけない。 （大阪・関西大第一高）
[should / taken / the dog / be / by / care / someone / of].

④ このソファはとても重いので，リビングルームに運び込むのに4人必要だ。 （東京・明治大付中野高）
This sofa is [move / so / four people / need / that / to / heavy / we / it] to the living room.

⑤ 空気を循環させるために窓を開けたままにしておいた方がよい。 （東京・明治大付中野高）
You should leave [in / the air / keep / open / order / the windows / to] circulating.

⑥ 日本では，ウナギは水がきれいな川で捕れる高価な魚として知られている。 （東京・明治大付中野高）
In Japan, *unagi*, or eel, is [in / expensive / an / known / caught / as / fish] clean rivers.

⑦ 先生は生徒全員に聞こえるように大きい声で話した。 （東京・中央大高）
The teacher [hear / loud / all the students / for / spoke / to / enough].

① ______________________________

② ______________________________

③ ______________________________

④ ______________________________

⑤ ______________________________

⑥ ______________________________

⑦ ______________________________

ガイド ①⑦は語順を誤りやすいので注意。

005 [ ]内の語(句)を並べ替えて，会話を完成しなさい。

① Masaki: I [been / the book / have / for / which / looking] I borrowed. Did you see it? (山形県)
Lily: No. I'll help you find it.

② Yoshie: [use / can / you / do / your father / think] this computer? (山形県)
David: Yes. He often writes e-mails with it.

③ A: Do you know what we should put in this emergency kit? (福島県)
B: Look at this list. I think [what / will / you / it / show] you should put.

④ A: Hello. May I speak to Tom, please? (宮崎県)
B: Sorry. He's out now. I'll [you / him / call / to / tell] back.

⑤ A: [be / what / like / the weather / will] tomorrow? (宮崎県)
B: It'll be sunny.

⑥ A: You have a nice camera. (沖縄県)
B: Thanks. This [the camera / gave / is / me / my father] on my birthday.

⑦ A: I have not seen that man before. [that / who / you / person / know / is / do]? (東京・青山学院高等部)
B: I think he is our new English teacher.
A: Oh, you must be right!

⑧ A: Can you guess the answer? It [like / star / animal / is / an / shaped / a]. It lives under the sea. What is it? (東京・青山学院高等部)
B: It is *Hitode*!
A: Yes, that's right. We call it a starfish in English.

① ______________________

② ______________________

③ ______________________

④ ______________________

⑤ ______________________

⑥ ______________________

⑦ ______________________

⑧ ______________________

ガイド 日本語が与えられていないので，会話の状況をたどりながら解く必要がある。⑤⑦は語順を誤りやすいので注意。

006 [ ]内の語(句)を並べ替えて，会話を完成しなさい。

① A: [you / this / to / how / going / weekend / spend / are]? (兵庫・関西学院高等部)
B: I am planning to go shopping with my sister.

② A: How did you find my house? (兵庫・関西学院高等部)
B: A woman [enough / me / kind / show / was / the way / to].

③ A: She speaks Japanese well. She has a lot of Japanese friends.
B: Do you know [in / has / long / been / how / Japan / she]? (兵庫・関西学院高等部)

④ A: Why are you going to the other library? (兵庫・関西学院高等部)
B: The [I / in / not / need / library / book / this / is].

⑤ A: I heard that you stayed in Japan for another week. Why is that?
B: I didn't [visiting / Japan / to / without / Kyoto / leave / want].
(兵庫・関西学院高等部)

⑥ A: Who is that man? (東京・錦城高)
B: I think you know. He [living / this town / all / is / in / the people / to / known].

⑦ A: This book is really wonderful. Did you read this? (東京・錦城高)
B: Yes. I [read / an / book / never / interesting / have / such].

⑧ A: The question [the teacher / was / too / us / asked / which / difficult].
B: No one can answer that. (東京・錦城高)

①

②

③

④

⑤

⑥

⑦

⑧

ガイド ①③⑧のように疑問詞や関係詞があるときは，それを先頭に置いた意味のかたまりを作る。

007 サトル(Satoru)と留学生のアイシャ(Aisha)，フェイロン(Fei Long)の３人が，休日にあおい町(Aoi Town)に出かける話をしています。下の２つのポスターを見ながら，［　］内の語(句)を並べ替えて会話を完成しなさい。ただし，それぞれ不要な語(句)が１つ含まれています。 (茨城県)

Aoi Art Museum

【場所】 あおい駅から歩いて５分

【今月の特別企画】

＊有名漫画家の原画を展示

＊地元ゆかりの画家による絵画作品を郷土史とともに紹介

Aoi Science Museum

【場所】 あおい駅から歩いて20分

【今月の特別企画】

＊サイエンスショー「エネルギー問題について考える」(世界の現状を3D映像で)

＊写真展「海の不思議」(世界で活躍する写真家の作品を展示)

Satoru: Please look at the posters. We will go to Aoi Station by train, then walk to one of the museums. ①[how / want to / you / which museum / do / visit]? Aisha, you like the Aoi Art Museum, right?

Aisha: Yes, because ②[famous cartoonists / taken / many pictures / by / there are / drawn] in this museum.

Fei Long: I see. Actually, my idea is different. I am interested in the science museum.

Satoru: Why?

Fei Long: Because we can learn many things about ③[that / have to / the amazing ocean / energy problems / solve / we].

Aisha: But we can learn many things in the art museum, too. For example, the history of Aoi Town .... Oh, also, ④[takes / to walk / it / only 5 minutes / only 20 minutes / from] Aoi Station to the museum.

Satoru: Umm .... It's very hard to decide.

① ＿＿＿＿＿＿＿＿＿＿＿＿＿＿＿＿＿＿＿＿

② ＿＿＿＿＿＿＿＿＿＿＿＿＿＿＿＿＿＿＿＿

③ ＿＿＿＿＿＿＿＿＿＿＿＿＿＿＿＿＿＿＿＿

④ ＿＿＿＿＿＿＿＿＿＿＿＿＿＿＿＿＿＿＿＿

ガイド 名詞を後ろから修飾する形に注意。④の形の文はよく使われる。

008 [ ]内の語(句)を並べ替えて，英文を完成しなさい。

① It's [not as / week / as / it / cold / was / last]. (東京・青稜高)

② [has / always / blue / the cat / looks / eyes / which] lonely. (東京・青稜高)

③ I [teacher / buy / asked / my / dictionary / which / to]. (東京・青稜高)

④ To [took / around / hours / the lake / me / two / walk]. (東京・青稜高)

⑤ What [fruit / called / small / English / this / is / in]? (東京・青稜高)

⑥ Do you know [the exam / has / he / for / prepared / how / hard]? (奈良・西大和学園高)

⑦ Your friends are coming soon. Clean [as / as you / your / can / quickly / room]. (東京・中央大附高)

⑧ Tom [all / had / that / he / spent / the money], so he couldn't buy anything. (東京・中央大附高)

⑨ Mary really likes listening to classical music. She has [as / do / many / I / CDs / twice / as]. (東京・青山学院高等部)

⑩ I would like [meet / the / joined / you / to / who / man] our project team last week. He has a lot of experience in business. (東京・青山学院高等部)

①

②

③

④

⑤

⑥

⑦

⑧

⑨

⑩

ガイド ⑤⑥⑧⑨は語順を誤りやすいので注意。

重要 **009** [ ]内の語(句)を並べ替えて，日本語の内容に合う英文を完成しなさい。ただし，③～⑧の[ ]には不要な語(句)が1つ含まれています。

① 私は君と遊びに来たのではなく試験を受けるためにここに来たのだ。 (東京・中央大高)
I came here [but / to play / to take / with / you / not / the examination].

② たくさんの興味深い授業があるので学校生活は楽しい。 (東京・中央大高)
[make / school life / interesting / enjoyable / classes / my / a lot of].

③ あなたは今日，何回宿題をするように言われたか覚えている？ (千葉・専修大松戸高)
Do you remember [to / did / you / many / were / how / told / times] do your homework today?

④ 残念だけど，私は次に何をしたらよいかわからないわ。 (千葉・専修大松戸高)
I'm [to / that / what / know / don't / of / afraid / I] do next.

⑤ 今朝の地震で妹たちが泣いちゃったんだ。 (千葉・専修大松戸高)
My sisters [happened / because / the earthquake / this / cried / that / for / of] morning.

⑥ あなたはそのコーチからどのくらい水泳を教わっているの？ (千葉・専修大松戸高)
How [swimming / have / learned / long / from / you / been / learning] the coach?

⑦ あれはぼくが今までに見た中で2番目に高い塔だよ。 (千葉・専修大松戸高)
That is [have / I / tower / taller / the second / that / tallest / ever] seen.

⑧ 姉は今朝父が捕った魚を料理する予定なのよ。 (千葉・専修大松戸高)
My sister [cook / the fish / caught / this / by / morning / will / my father].

① ______________________________

② ______________________________

③ ______________________________

④ ______________________________

⑤ ______________________________

⑥ ______________________________

⑦ ______________________________

⑧ ______________________________

ガイド ①は but，②は make，⑤は that をどう使うかを考える。⑧は「不要なものが1つ含まれている」という点に注意。

重要 **010** [ ]内の語(句)を並べ替えて，英文を完成しなさい。ただし，それぞれの[ ]には不要な語(句)が1つ含まれています。

① 朝食のとき，母は私に放課後すぐに帰ってきてと言った。 (神奈川・桐蔭学園高)
At breakfast, [as / asked / come / home / me / my mother / please / soon / to] as school was over.

② 私は，そのアメリカ人女性に聞かれた質問に答えられなかった。 (神奈川・桐蔭学園高)
[answer / asked / by / couldn't / I / lady / the American / the questions / was].

③ 草があまりにぬれていて，座れなかった。 (神奈川・桐蔭学園高)
The grass [we / it / on / so / that / too / was / couldn't sit / wet].

④ 私が会ったフランス人の学生たちは，富士山の美しさに感動していた。 (神奈川・桐蔭学園高)
The [the beauty / I / with / impressed / them / French students / met / that / were] of Mt. Fuji.

⑤ 子どものころによい友人を持つことほど大事なことはない。 (神奈川・桐蔭学園高)
[anything / as / in / is / good / having / as important / friends / nothing] childhood.

⑥ [known / five / other / with / for / we / each / years / have]. (愛知・中京大附中京高)

⑦ [injured / people / were / have / accident / the / in / many]. (愛知・中京大附中京高)

⑧ [first / will / abroad / my / to / it / trip / be]. (愛知・中京大附中京高)

⑨ [childhood / remind / remember / photos / me / my / these / of]. (愛知・中京大附中京高)

① ______________________________

② ______________________________

③ ______________________________

④ ______________________________

⑤ ______________________________

⑥ ______________________________

⑦ ______________________________

⑧ ______________________________

⑨ ______________________________

ガイド ③⑤⑨は定型的な表現。⑥⑦はどの語が不要かに注意。

最高水準問題

解答 別冊 p.16

011 [ ]内の語(句)を並べ替えて，日本語の内容に合う英文を完成しなさい。

① 君はこの制服を着て，彼らと一緒に歩くだけでいい。 (埼玉・慶應義塾志木高)
[and walk / all / do / have / is / this uniform / to / wear / with them / you].

② 私の両親は北海道に行くと必ずそのホテルに泊まります。 (埼玉・慶應義塾志木高)
My [at the hotel / go / Hokkaido / parents / never / staying / to / without].

③ 僕は3年ぶりにバスケットボールをしました。 (埼玉・慶應義塾志木高)
I [basketball / the first / for / in / time / three years / played].

④ 探すようにお願いしておいた本は見つかりましたか。 (埼玉・慶應義塾志木高)
[asked / for / found / have / I / look / the book / you to / you]?

⑤ いつスマートフォンを買い替えるかを決めるのは，想像より難しい。 (東京・明治大付中野高)
[upgrade / is / our / deciding / to / than / when / smartphones / harder] we imagine.

⑥ トムはいくつなぞなぞを解けるかを数えて，自分がどのくらい賢いかを判断している。
Tom judges how [of / clever / is / riddles / the number / counting / he / by / that] he can solve. (東京・明治大付中野高)

⑦ 学びの素晴らしい点は，誰もそれを奪うことができないということだ。 (東京・明治大付中野高)
The beautiful thing [take / no / is / about / away / learning / can / one / that / it] from you.

① ______________________________

② ______________________________

③ ______________________________

④ ______________________________

⑤ ______________________________

⑥ ______________________________

⑦ ______________________________

解答の方針

①②③は定型的な表現。⑤はどの語で文を始めるかを考える。⑦は語順を誤りやすいので注意。

012 [ ]内の語(句)を並べ替えて，それぞれの文章を完成しなさい。ただし，それぞれの[ ]には不要な語(句)が1つ含まれています。

① [to / doesn't / one / what / do about / no / understands] the problem.

(奈良・西大和学園高)

② The old man [as / me / ran away / next / sitting / soon / to / was] as the train stopped at Shibuya Station.

(奈良・西大和学園高)

③ Bears sleep through winter, for about six months. Even though they do not move much for such a long time, they can walk and run around without any trouble soon after they come out in spring. However, people cannot do that. When a patient has to stay in bed and does not move at all, after a week or so the patient will [fast / not / as / to / as before / be able / need / walk]. Someday, scientists may find out more about the bear's amazing body to help people who need special care after staying in bed for a long time.

(東京・都立国際高)

④ When the World Cup came to Africa for the first time in 2010, a photographer from Europe went to Africa. She traveled to ten countries there and talked to people working for local soccer teams. One of the soccer coaches said that people really love soccer and it brings them together. Anyone can play this sport because they only need a field, a ball, and a goal. Children make their soccer balls from garbage and play with them. Even when people do not have much, they can have happy lives. It depends [their / how / of / looking / on / the things / at / way] they have.

(東京・都立国際高)

⑤ Can you imagine a life without computers and the Internet? For about the last 50 years, we have been developing this technology, and it has really changed our lives. By using a computer, people can look for information, send messages, and even talk without leaving their desks. This is true at schools and offices. Information [been / convenient / has / in / made / more / technology / our lives] many ways. Today students can learn outside the classroom, and also people can work at home.

(東京・都立国際高)

① ______________________________

② ______________________________

③ ______________________________

④ ______________________________

⑤ ______________________________

013 [ ]内の語(句)に1語を補って並べ替え，日本語の内容に合う英文を完成しなさい。

① 今から作るなら，何が一番簡単に作れると思いますか。 (福岡・久留米大附設高)

[the easiest / cook / is / what / you / to / think] from now?

② 野球のルールはソフトボールとはあまり違わないと思います。 (福岡・久留米大附設高)

I think the rules of baseball [of / aren't / different / softball / very / from].

③ あなたが有名になればなるほど，もっと本が売れるでしょう。 (福岡・久留米大附設高)

[become / more / you / famous], the more books of yours will be sold.

④ どうして怒っていたのか教えてほしい。 (福岡・久留米大附設高)

[me / made / know / you / angry / let].

⑤ 本を買ってきてくれるなんて，優しいね。 (福岡・久留米大附設高)

It was nice [buy / for / to / the books / me / you].

⑥ 試験が終わったら，何をするのが楽しみですか。 (東京・開成高)

[after / are / exam / forward / is / looking / the / to / what / you] over?

難 ⑦ 私たちはその国の人口がいかに多いのかに驚きました。 (東京・開成高)

[at / country's / how / population / surprised / the / was / we / were].

難 ⑧ このガソリンスタンドに寄っておきましょう。ここから先はしばらく見つけられないかもしれませんから。 (東京・開成高)

Let's stop by this gas station. [a / able / be / find / for / from / here / might / not / to / we / while].

① ______________________________

② ______________________________

③ ______________________________

④ ______________________________

⑤ ______________________________

⑥ ______________________________

⑦ ______________________________

⑧ ______________________________

解答の方針

①③は語順を誤りやすいので注意。④は let と make の使い方がポイント。⑥は forward に着目する。

014 [ ]内の語(句)を並べ替えて，日本語の内容に合う英文を完成しなさい。ただし，①～⑤の下線の語は必要に応じて適切な形に変えなさい。また，⑥・⑦は[ ]内の語に1語を補って並べ替えなさい。

① 私が一昨日買ったかばんは彼女のものとは違います。 (東京・江戸川女子高)
The bag [the day / different / hers / yesterday / before / buy / I / is / from].

② 彼女はまだその宿題をやり終えていません。 (東京・江戸川女子高)
[finish / the / have / homework / yet / do / she / not].

③ 世界で富士山ほど美しい山はありません。 (東京・江戸川女子高)
There [other / so / be / beautiful / Mt. Fuji / mountain / no / as] in the world.

④ そのドアを開けっぱなしにしてはいけません。 (東京・江戸川女子高)
[open / must / door / leave / not / be / the].

⑤ とても美しい朝だったので，彼女たちは散歩に行きました。 (東京・江戸川女子高)
It [that / beautiful / a / go / be / morning / they / for / such] a walk.

難 ⑥ 充電できるときに充電しておかないと，こうなるんですよ。 (東京・開成高)
[battery / charge / don't / happen / things / this / when / you / your] when you can.

難 ⑦ あなたはうそをつかれているってどうしてわかったのですか。 (東京・開成高)
[did / how / know / lied / were / you / you]?

①

②

③

④

⑤

⑥

⑦

解答の方針

①～⑤では，たとえばbeは，is，am，are，was，were，been，beingのどれかに変える。to beのような(2語以上に変えた)形は想定されていない。

015 [ ]内の語(句)を並べ替えて，それぞれの文章を完成しなさい。 (東京工業大附科学技術高)

① Rachel Carson is known as a nature writer. Her book *Silent Spring* tells us the dangers of pollution and its *impact on the environment surrounding us. She (1)[surrounded / grew / a house / up / by / in] woods in western *Pennsylvania. Every morning she (2)[hearing / looked / the birds / to / forward] outside her window. On her way to school she often talked to the birds just like friends. She developed a sense of wonder about the natural world. In her books, she teaches children to listen to the voices of the earth.

(注) impact 影響 Pennsylvania 米国ペンシルベニア州

② Are you interested in volunteer work? Doing volunteer work is a wonderful way to see new places and meet new people. Volunteers also help many children and adults to learn information that can help them through their life. Around the world, there are volunteer teachers. They work in different ways. Some volunteers (1)[teach / go / the people / to / abroad] there for a few months or years. Other volunteers stay in their own country. Maybe they go to a school for just one or two hours a week (2)[help / reading / children / young / to / with] and math. Maybe they teach their country's language, for example, French, Spanish, or English, to people who move there from another country.

③ All plants and animals die, but when every plant or animal in a species dies, the species is *extinct. This means that it's lost forever. When one species dies, maybe (1)[it / other / that / species / need] will die, too. People need to protect all the plants and animals on the earth. If they don't, many species will become extinct in the future. We can all protect plants and animals in small ways. When we take a walk, we should always (2)[are / leave / they / flowers / as]. Then, in the future, more plants will grow from the seed. In gardens and parks, we can grow plants that animals need for food and for their homes. All these things will help to protect important species.

(注) extinct 絶滅した

① (1) ______________________________

(2) ______________________________

② (1) ______________________________

(2) ______________________________

③ (1) ______________________________

(2) ______________________________

016 宇宙飛行士(astronaut)に関する次の英文を読み，[ ]内の語(句)を並べ替えて，それぞれの文章を完成しなさい。

(東京・巣鴨高)

Have you ever wondered what it would be like to look out the window of a spaceship and see the Earth below? Can you imagine what the *zero-gravity environment would be like? If you were an astronaut in the International Space Station, this might be part of your daily schedule. Clearly, an astronaut's average day is light years different ①[everyday / from / of / office worker / that / the].

To begin with, a day in the life of an astronaut might include as many as 15 sunrises as the space station goes around the Earth. Because of this, astronauts often lose sense of time. However, they still try to stay on a regular schedule and ②[a / five hours / get / of / sleep / about] night. It is the best that they rest next to a fan. Because the hot air people breathe out doesn't rise in space, they need to make sure they get enough fresh oxygen instead of breathing in their own *exhaled carbon dioxide. They also ③[get / have / sleeping / to / to / used] in a noisy environment—some say the sounds inside a space station are like a *vacuum cleaner that is always turned on. After waking up, astronauts eat the first of their three daily meals. They have to be careful ④[away / from / keep / to / their food / going] because that might damage the station's machines. For this reason, astronauts drink through straws.

The zero-gravity environment can cause people to lose muscle and bone, so astronauts need to get lots of exercise. They tie themselves into an exercise bike so they can work out and keep their bodies feeling strong.

(注) zero-gravity environment 無重力環境
exhaled carbon dioxide (呼吸により)吐き出された二酸化炭素
vacuum cleaner 掃除機

① ______________________________

② ______________________________

③ ______________________________

④ ______________________________

解答の方針

読解力と文法・作文の力の両方を問う問題。①～④のすべてに，よく問われる文法的なポイントが含まれている。

第1回 実力テスト

▶解答→別冊 p.26

時間 30 分　目標 70 点

得点
／100

1 [ ]内の語(句)を並べ替えて，日本語の内容に合う英文を完成しなさい。

(①～⑤各 7 点，⑥～⑧各 10 点，計 65 点)

① 私が昨日食べたアップルパイは私の兄が作りました。 (京都・立命館宇治高)

[ate / by / my brother / I / made / the apple pie / was / yesterday].

② この地図があればパーティーの場所をすぐに見つけることができます。 (京都・立命館宇治高)

[to find / the party / help / the place / this map / for / will / you] quickly.

③ 成田空港で見知らぬ人に英語で話しかけられました。 (奈良・帝塚山高)

[to / a stranger / I / spoken / at / by / was] Narita Airport.

④ ドアを開けっぱなしにしておくとは君はとても不注意だった。 (奈良・帝塚山高)

[open / you / leave / it / the door / careless / to / of / was].

⑤ 500人を超える乗客を乗せた船が行方不明です。 (奈良・帝塚山高)

[is / than / more / missing / a ship / passengers / carrying / five hundred].

⑥ 赤色のコートは茶色のコートの 3 倍の値段だ。 (奈良・帝塚山高)

[as much / the brown / costs / the red coat / times / as / three] coat.

⑦ 急いで食べなさい。そうしないと列車に乗り遅れてしまうよ。 (奈良・帝塚山高)

[or / in / eat / miss / you / better / you'll / had / a hurry,] the train.

⑧ キャシーは母が買ってくれた指輪をなくしてしまった。 (奈良・帝塚山高)

[has / ring / her mother / the / her / lost / bought / Cathy / for].

①

②

③

④

⑤

⑥

⑦

⑧

2　[　]内の語(句)を並べ替えて，文章を完成しなさい。

（千葉・渋谷教育学園幕張高）　（各7点，計35点）

On December 5, 1901, Walter Elias Disney was born in an upstairs bedroom of a two-story cottage on North Tripp Avenue in Chicago.

Walt's parents and older brothers were ①[busy / farm jobs / take / to / to school / too / Walt / with]. So he didn't start until he was almost seven. By then, his younger sister Ruth, who was five, was ready for school, too. Walt said that starting school with his younger sister "②[could / embarrassing / happen / most / that / the / thing / was] to a boy."

Walt always wanted to entertain people, to make them have a good time. Once a group of actors came to town to perform Peter Pan. ③[a boy / about / grows / it / never / up / was / who]. Walt loved the play and played Peter in his school performance. His brother Roy used wires to lift Walt into the air. To the audience it looked like he was flying.

Almost as soon as he could hold a pencil, Walt spent hours and hours drawing. He told everybody that he was an artist. He really had talent. His neighbor Doc Sharwood thought that Walt ④[a picture / asked / for / good / he / so / that / was] of his horse. Doc Sharwood and his wife praised the picture. It made Walt very proud.

One day he discovered a barrel of black *tar. He and Ruth dipped big sticks into the tar and drew pictures all over the side of their white house. ⑤[all happy / at / not / saw / their parents / they / were / when] the artwork. The tar couldn't be removed!

（注）　tar　タール（黒い粘着性物質で，主に道路舗装などに用いる）

①

②

③

④

⑤

2 和文英訳問題

標 準 問 題

(解答) 別冊 p.28

017 英語に直しなさい。

① 彼女はどれくらいの間そこに住んでいますか。 (東京・桜美林高)

② このかばんは3つの中で一番重いです。 (東京・桜美林高)

③ バスを待っている生徒たちは眠そうでした。 (東京・桜美林高)

④ 彼は眠かっただけでなく空腹でした。 (東京・桜美林高)

⑤ 私はその寺がいつ建てられたか知りません。 (東京・桜美林高)

⑥ 私は人形を集めることに興味があります。 (東京・京華高)

⑦ Ken は始発電車に乗るために，早起きをしなければならなかった。 (東京・京華高)

⑧ 彼と知り合って3年になる。 (奈良・帝塚山高)

⑨ 話し相手がほしいなあ。 (奈良・帝塚山高)

① ______________________

② ______________________

③ ______________________

④ ______________________

⑤ ______________________

⑥ ______________________

⑦ ______________________

⑧ ______________________

⑨ ______________________

ガイド ①⑧は時制，⑤は語順に注意。また，③の「眠そうでした」，⑨の「話し相手」は，どんな形で表現するかを考える。

重要 **018** 英語に直しなさい。

① 私にあなたの辞書を貸してもらえませんか。 （大阪・追手門学院大手前高）

② 父は私にソーシャルメディア(social media)を使うのをやめなさいと言った。 （東京・城北高）

③ リコ(Riko)はちょうど歯磨きを終わらせたところです。 （東京・城北高）

④ 風邪をひいてしまって，今日は一緒に出かけられない。 （東京・錦城高）

⑤ ぼくは，彼女ほどうまくギターを弾けない。 （東京・錦城高）

⑥ おととい，彼は疲れているように見えた。 （東京・錦城高）

⑦ 父は30分ずっとめがねを探している。 （広島・修道高）

⑧ もしぼくが君なら，彼女にその花は買わないよ。 （神奈川・法政大第二高）

⑨ 料理の仕方を学ぶことは，人生において最も重要なことの１つです。 （東京・中央大杉並高）

⑩ 日本へあなたが戻ってくるときに私はあなたに再び会うことを希望しています。 （東京・中央大杉並高）

① ______________________________

② ______________________________

③ ______________________________

④ ______________________________

⑤ ______________________________

⑥ ______________________________

⑦ ______________________________

⑧ ______________________________

⑨ ______________________________

⑩ ______________________________

ガイド ②③は不定詞と動名詞の使い方に注意，⑦⑩は時制，⑧は仮定法がポイント。

重要 **019** 英語に直しなさい。ただし，(　)内に与えられた語をそのままの形で順に用いること。

① あなたの立場なら，何をすべきか彼女に伝えるだろうね。(were, tell, she)　(京都教育大附高)

② このドレスを選ぶのを誰かが手伝ってくれましたか。(anyone, help, dress)　(京都教育大附高)

③ この新聞によると，明日京都は大雨になるようです。(says, it, hard)　(京都教育大附高)

④ この動物は英語で何と呼ぶか知っていますか。(you, called)　(神奈川・桐光学園高)

⑤ 道路を横断する際は気をつけたほうがよいですよ。(had, be, in)　(神奈川・桐光学園高)

①

②

③

④

⑤

ガイド　①は仮定法を使う。④は語順に注意。

020 英語に直しなさい。ただし，(　)内に与えられた語で文を始めること。

① その少女がなぜ泣いているのか私に教えてください。(Please)　(神奈川・法政大第二高)

② あなたにとって若いときに夢を持つことは大切です。(It)　(近畿大附和歌山高)

③ 君の質問に答える前に，なぜ知りたいのかを私に教えてください。(Before)　(近畿大附和歌山高)

④ どうして君はそのパーティーに参加したのですか。(What)　(広島・修道高)

①

②

③

④

ガイド　②は不定詞を含む基本構文を使う。④は頻出表現。

021 下線部の日本語を英語に直しなさい。②は関係代名詞を用いて書くこと。（大阪・プール学院高）

Masao: Hi, Aiko. Your pencil case looks nice. I like the color.

Aiko: Thank you, Masao. This is very old. ①私は8歳からずっとそれを持っているのよ。 My brother gave it to me for my birthday. The next year, he bought me a bag. This is the bag.

Masao: That looks nice, too. I like the picture of the cat on it.

Aiko: I like cats. It's my sixteenth birthday next Sunday, and my father is going to buy a real cat. ②ネコは私が一番好きな動物なの。 I've wanted a cat for a long time, so I can't wait!

Masao: Good for you. ③あなたのお父さんはよくあなたをペットショップに連れて行ってくれるの？

Aiko: Of course. I love my father. I'd like to be a teacher like him, too.

① ______________________________

② ______________________________

③ ______________________________

ガイド ③「よく」に当たる語を正しい位置に置くこと。

重要 **022** 下線部の日本語を英語に直しなさい。ただし，(　)内の語を必ず使い，動詞の場合は必要に応じて適当に形を変えなさい。（千葉・昭和学院秀英高）

① A: What an elegant castle it is! The people who built it must have worked hard!

B: それを建てるのに20年かかったんだ。 (it, them)

② A: Didn't you break your watch yesterday?

B: あの店で直してもらった。 (I, repair)

① ______________________________

② ______________________________

ガイド どちらも重要な形。

023 下線部が[ ]内の日本語の意味になるよう，空所に5語の英語を補いなさい。 （東京・巣鴨高）

① A: (　　　　　　　　　　) Tokyo to Kyoto?
B: Well, maybe about 300km? I'm not sure. You should look on the Internet.
[東京から京都までどれくらいだっけ。]

② A: (　　　　　　　　　　) tomorrow's homework? I can't get the answer.
B: Sure. What question?
A: Thanks. Question 2, please.
[明日の宿題，手伝ってくれないかな。]

③ A: What's wrong? You look sick.
B: I have a terrible headache today.
A: (　　　　　　　　　　) rest? You've studied so much today.
[少し休んだらどう。]

④ A: What's that tall tower over there?
B: Don't you know? It's Tokyo Skytree. It's 634 meters tall.
It's (　　　　　　　　　　) Tokyo Tower.
[東京タワーの倍くらいあるんだよ。]

① ＿＿＿＿＿＿＿＿＿＿＿＿＿＿＿＿＿＿＿＿ Tokyo to Kyoto?

② ＿＿＿＿＿＿＿＿＿＿＿＿＿＿＿＿＿＿＿＿ tomorrow's homework?

③ ＿＿＿＿＿＿＿＿＿＿＿＿＿＿＿＿＿＿＿＿ rest?

④ It's ＿＿＿＿＿＿＿＿＿＿＿＿＿＿＿＿＿＿＿＿ Tokyo Tower.

ガイド ①「どれくらい」は，この会話では距離を尋ねている。 ②helpの使い方がポイント。
④「(2)倍」の表し方がポイント。

最高水準問題

解答 別冊 p.37

024 英語に直しなさい。

① ここから遠く離れた町へ引っ越したなつかしい友だちから電話をもらった。（東京・桐朋高）

② ぼくたちは幼なじみなので，思い出話に花が咲いた。（東京・桐朋高）

③ 自分の将来のために何をすべきかわかっている若者はどれくらいいるのだろうか。（岡山白陵高）

④ 昨夜，祖父がしてくれた話に感動して涙を流しました。（智弁学園和歌山高）

難 ⑤ 母親は午後からいそいそと買い物に出かけたが，結局何も買わずに帰ってきた。（智弁学園和歌山高）

⑥ 日本人のほとんどは自分の意見をはっきりと述べないと言われるが，私はそうは思わない。（智弁学園和歌山高）

⑦「すてきな帽子ね。それ，誰にもらったの。」「名古屋のおばさんがくれたんだ。」（智弁学園和歌山高）

①

②

③

④

⑤

⑥

⑦

025 下線部を英語に直しなさい。（兵庫・灘高）

① 電車の中がそれほど混んではいなかったので，つり革を持って立って文庫本を読んでいた。席が空いたので座って読み出すと，放課後の部活でくたくたに疲れていたのか，眠ってしまった。

② 家より，図書館の方がずっと勉強しやすい。私に話しかける人も，うるさいテレビをつける人もいない。

①

②

解答の方針

024 ②「幼なじみ」の訳し方がポイント。

025 ①「疲れていたのか」の訳し方がポイント。

026 **下線部を英語に直しなさい。**

① マイク(Mike)はもっとゆっくり仕事をすれば間違えないのに。あわてるから彼はいつも間違う。

(広島・修道高)

② A: (1)この前教えてくれた例の美術館に行ってきたよ。 (福岡・久留米大附設高)

B: 本当？ どうだった？ 絵本展，素敵だったでしょ？

A: うん。(2)世界中から集まった絵本がたくさんあっておもしろかったよ。1日じゃ全部見て回れなかった。

B: そうなの？ 私ももう一度見に行きたいと思ってたの。よかったら今度の日曜に一緒に行かない？

A: いいね！

①

② (1)

(2)

難 **027** **下線部①・②については，日本語の内容を表す英語を書きなさい。下線部③・④については，[ ]内の語(句)を並べ替えて英文を完成しなさい。** (愛媛・愛光高)

ハチが元気に外を舞う季節になってきた。かつては「ブンブンブン」などと口ずさみながら眺めていたものだが，昨今は孫娘のことが心配でならない。①彼女はハチを見ると，捕まえて口に入れようとするのである。②その光景はとても恐ろしいので，私がハチを見つけたときはハチを触らないように彼女に頼む。しかし，幼い孫娘は聞く耳を持たない。③彼女はハチに危害を加えようと思っているわけではないのだが，ハチは攻撃されたと思い，そして彼女を刺そうとするのだ。家族で対策を考える毎日だ。④彼女を守るのに一番良いのは，ハチについてもっと多くを学ぶことかもしれない。

③ [it / it / a bee, / got / doesn't / thinks / though / to / she / has / attack / attacked / want] and tries to sting her.

④ [be / about bees / way / learn more / to / to / her / may / the best / protect].

①

②

③

④

028 下線部を英語に直しなさい。 （奈良・西大和学園高）

誰にでも締め切りの直前になって，ようやく事の重大さに気づき，後悔したことが一度や二度あるだろう。私自身にも忘れられない苦い思い出がある。学生のころ，大事なレポートがあった。①時間は十分にあったにもかかわらず，書き始めなかったのだ。というのも，当時の私は，オンライン授業ということもあり，生活習慣が乱れきっていたからだ。気が付いたころには後の祭り。締め切り前日となり，付け焼き刃のレポートを完成させた。返却時，②たくさん助言をくださった，ある先生が私のレポートはコウジ(Kouji)のものほどよくないとおっしゃった。コウジと比べられたことよりも，結果として先生の期待に応えられなかった自分の情けなさが身に染みた。だから③考え方を変えた。時間は皆に平等に与えられている。これからも，優先順位を見定めて，自ら律していきたい。

① ______________________________

② ______________________________

____

③ ______________________________

難 **029** 下線部を英語に直しなさい。 （東京・筑波大附高）

① A: Where's Yoko?
B: She's in the library. 君が先週勧めた本を読んでいるよ。

② A: Is Hiroshi in his room?
B: Yes. 朝から飲まず食わずで勉強しているのよ。

③ A: How many days a week do you practice tennis at school?
B: Only two days. That's our school rule, and we can't change it.
もっと練習時間があればうまくなれるんだけど。

④ A: You look very busy with your studies this week.
B: Yes, but 先週ほど宿題は多くないよ。

① ______________________________

② ______________________________

③ ______________________________

④ Yes, but ______________________________.

解答の方針

029 時制・仮定法の使い方に注意。

第2回 実力テスト

▶解答→別冊 p.41

時間40分　目標70点　得点　／100

1 英語に直しなさい。

（京都・立命館宇治高）（各6点，計30点）

① なぜあなたが昨日学校に来なかったのか私に教えてもらえますか。
② このゾウ(elephant)は，この動物園の開園以来一番人気のある動物の1つです。
③ 旅行をしている間の犬の世話を彼は私に頼んだ。
④ この問題はとても難しかったので，何人かの生徒は答えることができなかった。
⑤ 将来のために何かをすることは，何もしないよりもずっとよい。

①
②
③
④
⑤

2 下線部を英語に直しなさい。

（大阪桐蔭高）（各5点，計10点）

Kana: I want to be a cabin attendant on an international flight because I love to fly, and ①長期休みが来ると今度はどの国に行こうかといつも考えます。

Robert: You have a nice dream! To become a cabin attendant, you must learn about different cultures, traditions, *social customs, and people's ways of thinking, *as well as improving your English.

Kana: Thank you for your advice, Mr. Robert. ②たくさん学ぶのは大変ですが，キャビン・アテンダントになるために勉強するのは楽しみです。

Robert: Go for it, Kana.

（注） social custom 社会的慣習　as well as ～ ～だけでなく

①
②

3 ①・②の問いに答えなさい。

（①各6点，②(1)(2)各7点，(3)8点，計40点）

① あなたは，オーストラリアから来た外国語指導助手(ALT)のMr. Greenと，学校の廊下で話しているところです。(1)〜(3)の状況で使う英文を，それぞれ6語以上で書きなさい。（三重県）

(1) 日本の文化に興味があるか尋ねるとき。

(2) 日本には訪れる場所がたくさんあると伝えるとき。

(3) オーストラリアで撮った写真を見せてほしいと伝えるとき。

② Ryotaは，英語の授業で，自分が住むあおぞら町(Aozora Town)について紹介することになり，下の原稿を準備しました。あなたがRyotaなら，(1)〜(3)の内容をどのように英語で表しますか。それぞれ4語以上の英文で書きなさい。

【原稿】

> Hello, everyone. I am going to tell you about Aozora Town.
> (1) あおぞら町はひかり山(Mt. Hikari)で有名だということ。
> (2) 春にひかり山に登ったら，多くの美しい花を見ることができるということ。
> (3) ひかり山の近くのレストランはあおぞら町で一番人気があるということ。
> Thank you.

① (1) ______________________________

(2) ______________________________

(3) ______________________________

② (1) ______________________________

(2) ______________________________

(3) ______________________________

4 英語に直しなさい。

（東京・明星高）（20点）

電車やバスに友だちと乗ると，つい友だちとの会話がはずんで，ふだんより声が大きくなる学生が多い。他の乗客とのトラブルを防ぐためにも，公共のマナーには気をつけたいものである。

____

____

____

____

3 状況に応じて会話を完成する問題

注意　英文の語数が指定されている問いでは，短縮形(I'm，don't など)やハイフンを使った語(e-mail など)は 1 語と数える。また，符号(，.！？“ ” など)は語数に含めない。なお，特に指定がない限り，文の数はいくつでもよい。

標 準 問 題

(解答) 別冊 p.44

030 イラストを見て，問いに答えなさい。与えられた〈語〉を参考にしてもよい。　(愛知県)

[A] 買い物に行く途中のあなたは，困っている様子の外国人を見かけ，手助けを申し出ました。下線部①・②にそれぞれ 4 語以上の英語を書き，対話を完成させなさい。ただし，①には I(私は，私が)，②には way(道，道筋)を必ず使うこと。

〈対話文〉(A ＝あなた，B ＝外国人)

A: Excuse me, ①__________________?

B: Oh, yes, please. I'm looking for Asahi Station. Do you know the station?

A: Yes, ②__________________. I'll take you there.

B: Thank you. You're so kind!

〈語〉 ～を助ける，助け　help　　～を知っている　know

① ______________________________

② ______________________________

[B] 2 週間の海外研修の最終日に，あなたはこれまで使用していた机を掃除しています。そこに親しくなった外国人の同級生がやって来て，あなたに話しかけました。下線部①・②にそれぞれ 4 語以上の英語を書き，対話を完成させなさい。ただし，①には desk(机)，②には last(最後の)を必ず使うこと。

〈対話文〉(A ＝外国人の同級生，B ＝あなた)

A: What are you doing?

B: I ①__________________.

A: Why?

B: Because ②__________________. I'll go back to Japan tomorrow.

A : Oh, really? I feel so sad, but I hope to see you again.

〈語〉 ～を掃除する，きれいな　clean　　～を使う，使用　use

① ______________________________

② ______________________________

重要 031 それぞれの絵の2人の会話が成り立つよう，①・②の質問に対する答えを，主語と動詞を含む1つの英文で書きなさい。

（北海道）

①

②

① ________________________________

② ________________________________

重要 032 次の①・②がそれぞれ自然な会話となるよう，(a)・(b)に入る適切な英語を3語以上で書きなさい。会話は(1)～(4)の順に行われています。

（島根県）

①

②

① ________________________________

② ________________________________

033 次の会話が下のチラシの内容に合うよう，下線部①～③の空所に適切な語を１つずつ入れなさい。 （兵庫県）

A: Look! They want high school students to take ①(　　　　) (　　　　) the fashion contest.

B: How can we join it?

A: We have to send a design. They welcome students who ②(　　　　) (　　　　) in fashion.

B: Do you have any ideas about the design?

A: Yes, I got an idea from my grandmother's kimono.

B: That's so cool!

A: If we win the first contest in May, we'll be able to walk ③(　　　　) the (　　　　) in the final contest in August.

B: Sounds good!

① (　　　　) (　　　　)　　② (　　　　) (　　　　)

③ (　　　　) the (　　　　)

ガイド チラシ中のどの言葉に相当する英語が空所に入るかを考える。

重要 034 友子(Tomoko)さんは，留学生のウェンディ(Wendy)さんと話をしています。それぞれの場面に合うよう，(　)内に 3 語以上の英語を入れなさい。会話は①から⑪の順に行われています。

（富山県）

（注） Mozart　モーツァルト

（注） bonus CD　特典 CD

（注） classical concert
クラシックのコンサート

④ ________________________________

⑧ ________________________________

⑪ ________________________________

ガイド　④は相手の応答とつながる発言を考える。⑧⑪はひとまとまりの会話の最後の発言なので，自由な発想で考えてよい。

重要 035 次の(1)〜(4)は，ミホ(Miho)がアメリカを訪れたときの出来事を描いたイラストです。(3)の場面で，ミホは何と言ったと思いますか。[　　　] に入る言葉を25語程度の英語で書きなさい。(千葉県)

ガイド 空所に短い言葉を入れるのは難しくないが，「25語程度」という条件があるので，発言内容をある程度ふくらませる必要がある。

036 高校生の果歩(Kaho)と，果歩の高校に留学しているマイク(Mike)が話しています。2人の会話が成り立つよう，①には1つの英文を，②には3つ以上の英文を入れなさい。 (宮城県)

Kaho: A new *exchange student is going to come to our class next month.

Mike: I know! Her name is Alice, right? I'm very excited.

Kaho: Do you know anything about her?

Mike: Yes, a little. I heard about her from our English teacher. She is interested in Japanese culture.

Kaho: ①＿＿＿＿＿＿＿＿

Mike: She likes Japanese comics. So she studies Japanese.

Kaho: Oh, really? Then, let's have a welcome party for her.

Mike: That will be nice. Kaho, what do you want to do for her at the party?

Kaho: ②＿＿＿＿＿＿＿＿

(注) exchange student 交換留学生

① ＿＿＿＿＿＿＿＿＿＿＿＿＿＿＿＿

② ＿＿＿＿＿＿＿＿＿＿＿＿＿＿＿＿

＿＿＿＿＿＿＿＿＿＿＿＿＿＿＿＿

重要 037 留学生のティム(Tim)とホストファミリーのあなた(You)とが，次のような会話をするとします。これを読んで，下の問いに答えなさい。 (大阪府)

You: Hi, Tim. Next summer, you and I will *go on a trip with my family, right? ①＿＿＿＿＿＿＿＿

Tim: Yes. Now, I have two ideas: going to the beach, or going to the mountain. Both sound good to me, but I can't decide. Which place is better, the beach or the mountain? Please choose the better place and tell me what we can enjoy there.

You: OK. ②＿＿＿＿＿＿＿＿

Tim: I see. I understand why it is better. I am excited.

(注) go on a trip 旅行に行く

① 下線部①に，「その計画を一緒に作りましょう。あなたは何か考えがありますか」と伝える10語程度の英文を書きなさい。

② 下線部②に，前後のやり取りに合う内容を20語程度の英語で書きなさい。

① ＿＿＿＿＿＿＿＿＿＿＿＿＿＿＿＿

② ＿＿＿＿＿＿＿＿＿＿＿＿＿＿＿＿

＿＿＿＿＿＿＿＿＿＿＿＿＿＿＿＿

最高水準問題

解答 別冊 p.47

038 下線部に適切な英語を補い，会話を完成しなさい。 （埼玉・立教新座高）

① ハナとティムが趣味について話しています。

Hana: What do you like to do in your free time?
Tim: Well, I like exercising. I like going to the gym. And sometimes, I enjoy reading books.
Hana: I also enjoy reading books when I have time.
Tim: But these days, I often listen to books instead. I listen to audiobooks.
Hana: Oh, do you?
Tim: Yeah, I like listening to audiobooks.
Hana: Why?
Tim: Because ____________________.
Hana: So, you mean you can do two things together.
Tim: Right. It is called "Multitasking." I love multitasking.

② ケンジとジョンが昨日の出来事について話しています。

Kenji: Hi, John. What's up?
John: Hey, Kenji. I went to a movie with Aya yesterday.
Kenji: That sounds fun. How was the movie? Did you enjoy it?
John: Not really. I had an argument with her.
Kenji: I'm sorry to hear that. What ____________________?
John: Well, the movie was OK, but I said the main actor Bob Depp wasn't cool. But she was a big fan of him.
Kenji: Oh, you didn't know that she was a fan? She is always talking about him with her friends.
John: Oh no, I didn't know that.

① ____

② ____

解答の方針

① ハナの返答に合う内容を考える。 ② ジョンの返答に合う内容を考える。

難 039 下線部に指示された英語を使い，会話を完成しなさい。 （愛知・東海高）

Teacher: Today we will talk about how to protect ourselves from *COVID-19 in our daily lives. First, when we go out, there is something important to do. Do you know what it is?

Student A: ①[rememberを用いて6語以上の英語を書きなさい].

Teacher: Exactly. You should take it off only when you eat. Next, think about our classroom. We need to make sure it has a lot of fresh air all the time. How can we do that?

Student B: I think that ②[keepを用いて6語以上の英語を書きなさい].

Teacher: You're right. If you do that, the air can move around. Next, let's turn to lunch time. What should we do before we eat?

Student C: ③[soapを用いて6語以上の英語を書きなさい].

Teacher: That's right. And don't forget to use a clean towel to dry them. Also, we usually have big *gatherings and ceremonies in the gym, but in this school year, we have canceled all of them. Do you know why?

Student D: We mustn't stand too close to each other, but ④[enoughを用いて6語以上の英語を書きなさい].

Teacher: You got it. Unfortunately, our gym is too small. Finally, there is a lot of information about COVID-19 and other things on the Internet. But some information is not true. So ⑤[believeを用いて6語以上の英語を書きなさい].

Everyone, stay safe and stay healthy.

（注） COVID-19 新型コロナウイルス感染症 gatherings and ceremonies 集会や式典

①

②

③

④

⑤

解答の方針

①②⑤については，与えられた動詞が主にどのような形で使われるかを知っておく必要がある。④は，enoughには副詞（「十分に」）と形容詞（「十分な」）の意味があるので，入れる場所に注意する。

040 次の絵を見て，あとの問いに答えなさい。 （東京・国際基督教大高）

① ［　］内の語を並べ替えて，絵(2)の男の子の願い事を表す英文を完成しなさい。

He ［ visit / travel / and / wishes / he / world / could / famous / around / the / many / that ］ places.

② ［　］内の語を並べ替えて，絵(3)の ア に入る英文を完成しなさい。

I want ［ because / sound / feelings / never / to / she / my / made / turtle's / understand / has / a ］ before.

③ 絵(4)の イ に入る英文を，10語で書きなさい。ただし，wish を使うこと。2文になってもかまいません。

④ 絵(6)の下線部ウを英語に直しなさい。

① ______________________________

② ______________________________

③ ______________________________

④ ______________________________

難 041 自動販売機(a vending machine)の前で外国人旅行者があなたに話しかけている。下線部にそれぞれ8語以上の英語を入れて，会話を完成しなさい。 （愛知・滝高）

Tourist: Excuse me. What are these?
You: Oh, they're vending machines.
Tourist: What is a vending machine?
You: In Japan ①__________________.
Tourist: Wow! It's very convenient. Well, I'll try some drinks. Could you tell me how to use this machine?
You: Sure. ②__________________
Tourist: Sounds easy. Thank you very much.
You : You're welcome. Have a good time in Japan!

① In Japan ______________________________.

② ______________________________

第3回 実力テスト

▶解答→別冊 p.51

時間 20 分　目標 70 点　得点 ／100

1 中学生の Takuya は，京都(Kyoto)を旅行中の Leo と電話で会話をしています。Leo は，Takuya の家にホームステイしている留学生です。会話中の①～③に，Takuya から Leo への質問を 3 語以上の英語で書きなさい。ただし，次の［　　］内からそれぞれ 1 語を使用すること。
（群馬県）（各 15 点，計 45 点）

how	what	where	who	why

Takuya

① ______________________

It's sunny here. It's a wonderful day for the trip.

Leo

Oh, you're so lucky. ② ______________________

I am going to visit a castle and a famous temple today.

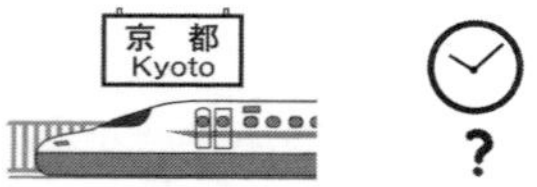

That sounds great. You'll come home tomorrow, right?
③ ______________________

At two. It will take about four hours by *Shinkansen*.
So I'll come home at about six o'clock.

① ______________________

② ______________________

③ ______________________

2　下の絵を参考にして下線部に5語以上の英語を補い，会話を完成させなさい。

（大阪女学院高）　（① 15 点，②③各 20 点，計 55 点）

Yuka:　I'm going to the movies next week. Would you like to come?

Jenny:　Yes, of course. When do you want to go?

Yuka:　On Tuesday. There's a good action movie.

Jenny:　I see. ① ______________________________?

Yuka:　At three fifteen.

Jenny:　Oh, I'm sorry. My last class finishes at four. Are there any evening shows?

Yuka:　Yes, there are a few. They start at about seven.

② ______________________________?

Jenny:　I like love stories.

Yuka:　Oh, there's a good one at seven fifteen. It is "Osaka Love Story."

Jenny:　Great! Let's watch that. By the way, can we eat before the movie?

Yuka:　Yes. There's a nice restaurant next to the theater.

③ ______________________________.

Jenny:　OK. See you then.

①

②

③

① ______________________________

② ______________________________

③ ______________________________

4 与えられた情報を使って英文を書く問題

標 準 問 題

(解答) 別冊 p.52

重要 **042** 次の英文とグラフ(graph)をもとに，①・②の問いに答えなさい。 （宮崎県）

Our ALT asked us a question in English class. She asked, "____________________ at home?" I'm going to talk about our answers.

Please look at the graph. A lot of students study English by reading English books or by writing something in English at home. The number of students reading English books is the largest. It's three times as large as the number of students listening to English CDs. I often speak in English with my family. But there are not many students doing that. Only two students do other ways.

Our ALT said, "Listening, reading, speaking, and writing are all important. Please study English in many ways."

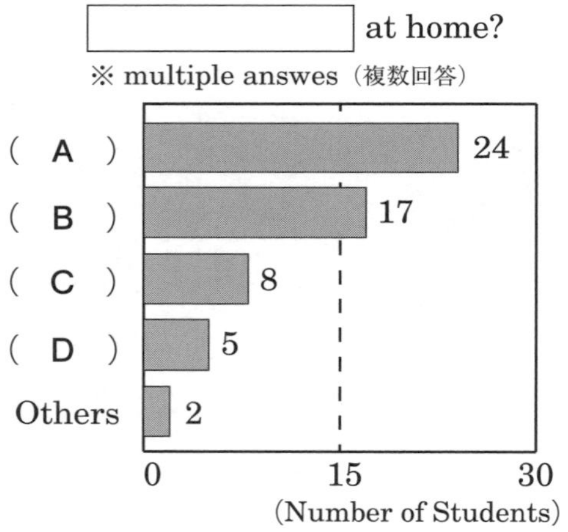

① 英文の下線部とグラフの[　　　]に共通して入る語句を答えなさい。

② グラフのA～Dに入る適切なものを，次の中から1つずつ選びなさい。

ア Listening to English CDs　　イ Reading English books

ウ Speaking in English　　エ Writing something in English

① ______________________________ at home?

② A (　　) B (　　) C (　　) D (　　)

ガイド ①は表現力を，②は読解力を問う問題。①は疑問文なので，どんな疑問詞を使うか(あるいはYes / Noで答える質問にするか)を考える。

043 次のA～Cのひとつづきの絵と英文は，ある日の出来事についてのユキコ(Yukiko)とレイカ(Reika)の会話を表しています。英文が絵の説明となるよう，下の【条件】に従って，Bの下線部に適する英語を書きなさい。

（神奈川県）

A

Yukiko said, "I visited my grandfather last Sunday. He lives in Kamome *Village." Reika said, "I have never been to that village. How did you get there?"

B

Yukiko said, "I usually go to my grandfather's house with my family by car. But this time I went *by myself by train and bus." Reika asked, "____________________ get there when you used the train and the bus?"

C

Yukiko said, "Two hours. I enjoyed seeing the beautiful mountains from the bus. I talked about my trip with my grandfather. Next time, we can visit Kamome Village together." Reika said, "Oh, I'd like to!"

（注） village 村　by myself 1人で

【条件】

(1) it と long を必ず用い，この2語を含めて6語以上を下線部に入れること。

(2) 下線部を含む文が完成した英文となるように書くこと。

____ get there when you used the train and the bus?

ガイド 定型的な形の文を使う。時制に注意。

044 中学生のEmiは，あるレストランの前で見かけた看板に書かれていた内容を留学生のJimに紹介するための英文をノートに書いています。Emiが考えている内容を参考にしながら，書き出しに続けて，①に2語の英語を，②に4語以上の英語を書き，Emiのノートを完成させなさい。（岡山県）

【看板】

「人気ナンバーワン」の部分をnumber oneで書いてみたけれど，この表現では「人気である」ということが伝わらないかもしれないな。別の表現で書いてみよう。

[Emi]

「おすすめ」の部分は，シェフが私たちにどうしてほしいのかを考えると，知っている単語で表現できそう。

【Emiのノート】

「当店人気ナンバーワン」

This is the number one food at this restaurant.

This is the [①] food at the restaurant.

「シェフRui本日のおすすめ」

It is the food that Chef Rui [②] today.

① This is the (　　　　) (　　　　) food at this restaurant.

② It is the food that Chef Rui ＿＿＿＿＿＿＿＿＿＿＿＿ today.

重要 045 健司(Kenji)は留学生のマーク(Mark)を誘ってボランティア活動に申し込んだ後，マークから【メール１】を受け取った。健司は【広告】を見ながら返信として【メール２】を作成した。下線部①・②が意味の通る文になるよう，(　)に入る６語以上の英語を書きなさい。ただし，(　)内に与えられた語を使うこと。

(佐賀県)

【メール１】

Hi, Kenji. I want to ask you about the volunteer work at Blue Park. You told me that I should take a bus to the park, but how long does it take to walk there from Tamahama Station? If it is sunny, I want to walk. If it rains, I'll take a bus.

Mark

【メール２】

Hi, Mark. I will answer your question. ①(walk), so it's a long way. ②And if it rains, (park). We will learn about sea animals at Tamahama Station Hall. It's near the station!

Kenji

【広告】

ボランティア募集！
海辺の清掃で，地域に貢献してみませんか？

日時：6月25日（日曜日）10:00 ～ 12:00
場所：ブルーパーク
　▲玉浜駅から市営バス「ブルーパーク行き」で約10分
　▲玉浜駅から徒歩で約40分

募集人数：約30名（小学生以上）

☆雨天時は，ブルーパークでのボランティア活動の代わりに，玉浜駅ホール（南口を出てすぐ）で，海の生物についての勉強会を行います。

① ______________________________, so it's a long way.

② And if it rains, ______________________________.

重要 **046** 由美(Yumi)は，友人のルーシー(Lucy)にメールを送ることにしました。伝えたいことは，来月，英語を勉強している子どもたちに英語の歌を歌ってあげるつもりなので，ルーシーも私の部屋に来てピアノを弾いてくれないかということです。下線部に英語を補い，メールを完成しなさい。(静岡県)

Hello, Lucy.

____

____

____

____

Bye,
Yumi

047 あなたは英語の授業で，友人のマーク(Mark)にメッセージを伝える方法について，次のワークシートに自分の考えとその理由を書いています。 (岩手県)

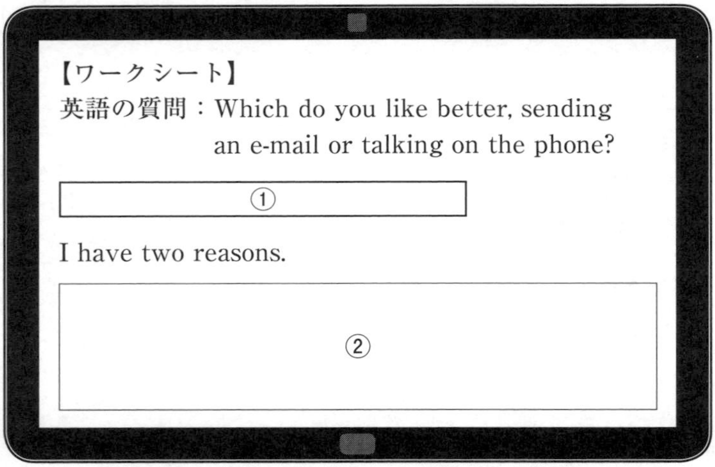

① 「アメリカに帰国したマークが，ある試合に勝利した」という状況で，あなたはどちらの方法を選びますか。①に入る適切な英語を6語以上で書きなさい。
② ①で選んだ理由となるように，②に入る適切な英語を20語以上で書きなさい。

① ______________________________

② ______________________________

____

____

048　高校生の健太はある日曜日の午後に駅前で２人の外国人観光客から宿泊予定のホテルへの行き方を尋ねられました。あなたが健太なら，次の【地図】中のアとイの道順のうち，どちらを案内しますか。下の【２人の外国人観光客から得た情報】も参考にしてどちらか１つを選び，①にその記号を書きなさい。②には，それを選んだ理由を20語程度の英文で書きなさい。（広島県）

【地図】

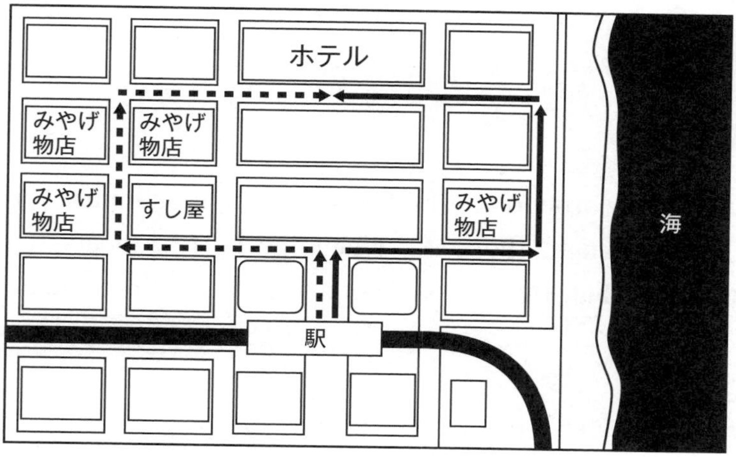

（注）　みやげ物店　souvenir shop

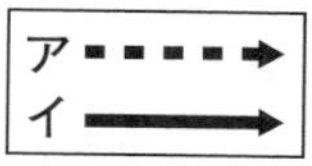

【２人の外国人観光客から得た情報】

・ホテルまでは徒歩で移動する。

・この町を訪れるのは初めてである。

・ホテルへの到着時刻は決めておらず，途中で観光などをしたい。

①（　　　）

②

ガイド　「正しい方の道順を選べ」という問いではない。「自分ならこちらの道順を勧める」という選択に基づいて，①にはどちらかの道順を入れ，②にはその道順を選んだ理由を入れる。

049 英文の説明がイラストの内容に合うよう，空所に適切な１語を入れなさい。 （兵庫県）

This picture shows how water goes around. When it rains on mountains, the water will go into a (①), and then to the sea. When the (②) heats the water, it will go up in the air. After that, the water becomes (③). From them, it will rain again.

① (　　　　) ② (　　　　) ③ (　　　　)

重要 050 岡山白陵中学校で英語のスピーチコンテストが開催されることになった。その件で，あなたの知り合いのジョーンズさんに手紙を出さなければならない。下線部に下記の内容を伝える英文を20～30語で書いて，依頼の手紙を完成させなさい。なお，数字も英語で書くこと。 （岡山白陵高）

開催日	２月25日
参加者生徒	12名
お願い	審査員(judge)の１人になってほしい。

Dear Mr. Jones,

How are you doing? We're going to have an English speech contest at Okayama Hakuryo Junior High School.

I'm waiting for your good answer.

Sincerely yours,

(Your name)

051 あなたは留学生のMaryと，英語の授業で「身の回りにある便利なもの」について発表するため，ショッピングセンター(shopping center)に調べに来ています。2人の会話を読んで，問いに答えなさい。 (大分県)

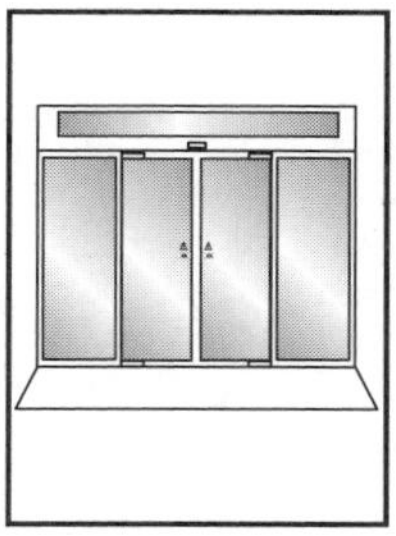
the automatic door
自動ドア

the elevator
エレベーター

the shopping cart
ショッピングカート

Mary: I think a lot of things are convenient in this shopping center.
You: Yes. Look at that. ______________________
Mary: I think so too. Let's find more.

(問) 下線部に適切な英語を補いなさい。第1文は，下の(　)内に，the automatic door，the elevator，the shopping cartのどれかを入れて作りなさい。それに続いて，そのものの便利な点を説明する文(2つ以上でもよい)を，主語と動詞を含む10語以上の英語で書きなさい。

I think (　　　　　　　　　　) is convenient.

____

____

052 下線部に3語以上の英語を補い，会話や文章を完成しなさい。 (大阪・関西大倉高)

① A: ______________ age?
B: I'm sorry. I don't want to tell you about it.
A: Then I have to guess it .... Forty-five?
B: No! I'm only thirty!

② My father, mother, and brother are Osaka Tigers fans, and they think I'm an Osaka Tigers fan, too, but I support Tokyo Lions. I've never shown that to anyone because I don't want to look different. Nobody knows I am happy when my team wins. I can't put my team's posters on my bedroom wall. On my birthday, my family members ______________, and I am sad.

① ______________________

② ______________________

最高水準問題

解答 別冊 p.56

053 留学生の Linda があなたに SNS 上で相談しています。添付されたカタログを参考にして，下の問いに答えなさい。 （鹿児島県）

	X	Y

価格	~~8,600円~~ 4,300円	2,900円
特徴	化学繊維（防水）	綿（天然素材）
重さ	970g	590g
容量	30L	20L

（問） （　）には，X・Y のうちであなたが Linda に勧めたい方を選び，その記号を入れなさい。下線部には，その理由を２つ，合わせて25～35語の英語で書きなさい。

You should buy (　　　) because ______________________________

____

____

____

解答の方針

２つの品物には，価格・素材・重さ・容量の点で違いがあるが，全部の情報を入れる必要はない。自分が知っている単語を使って書ける内容の英文を考える。

難 **054** 下線部①，②を英語に直しなさい。また，[A]に入る内容を考え，書き出し(However)に続けて10〜20語の英語を書きなさい。

（奈良・東大寺学園高）

1980年代のグルメブーム以来，日本において①旅の醍醐味の１つは食べ物だ，と多くの人々が考えてきた。その地の味を楽しむのは旅の大きな目的だった。ところが，[　A　]。たとえば，近所のスーパーの一角では遠い地方の食品を集めて販売することがあるし，今や家にいても日本中から食べ物のお取り寄せが可能だ。ただ私にしてみれば，②旅先でその土地の人とともに楽しむ料理は格別だ。

①

②

[A] However,

055 次の会話は，Kenta と，来日したばかりの ALT である Smith 先生との授業中のやり取りの一部である。自然な会話となるよう，下線部に20語以上30語以内の英語を入れなさい。内容的なまとまりを意識して，具体的に書くこと。

（山口県）

Ms. Smith: It's very hot in Japan now, but I know Japan has other seasons, too. Can anyone tell me about the seasons in Japan?

Kenta: Yes. I'll tell you about the next season. It's *autumn. It's a good season for *going out.

Ms. Smith: OK. What can I enjoy when I go out in autumn?

Kenta: ______________________________

Ms. Smith: Thank you. I'm *looking forward to going out in autumn in Japan!

（注） autumn 秋　go(ing) out 外出する　look(ing) forward to 〜 〜を楽しみにする

解答の方針

054 ①の「醍醐味」，②の「格別」などはそのまま訳すのが難しいので，易しい日本語に置き換えて考える。

056 Akiko は学校の授業で，海外から来た観光客向けに日本のおすすめ観光地を紹介するプレゼンテーションをすることになりました。Akiko が作ったメモの内容に合うように下線部①・②を補い，英文の原稿を完成させなさい。ただし，①は 9 語～14語，②は10語～15語で書きなさい。

（千葉・渋谷教育学園幕張高）

～メモ～

・紹介するところ：高尾山

・高尾山へのアクセス：都心から電車で 1 時間弱

・紹介したいこと

1）2009年にミシュラン旅行ガイドで 3 つ星を獲得。

2）年間260万人以上の観光客が世界中から訪れる人気の山。

3）猿園，野生植物園，薬王院(創建1000年以上)など見どころが多く，子どもから大人まで楽しめる。

4）桜やスミレなどいろいろな種類の花が見られる。

5）四季折々に変化する美しい自然を味わってほしい。

6）天気の良い日には山頂からきれいな富士山が見える。

I'd like to talk about Mt. Takao. ① ________________________ by train. Mt. Takao has become very popular with people all over the world since it received three stars from the Michelin Travel Guide in 2009. More than 2.6 million tourists visit the mountain every year. Mt. Takao is full of amazing places such as the monkey park, the wild plant garden and Yakuo-in Temple with a history of more than 1000 years, and they attract not only children but also adults. Mt. Takao is also a good place to see cherry blossoms, violets and many other kinds of flowers. ② ________________________. When the weather is fine, you can see a wonderful view of Mt. Fuji from the top of the mountain. Why don't you visit Mt. Takao?

① ____

____

② ____

____

解答の方針

それぞれの下線部に入る英語が，メモのどの部分に対応しているかを考える。①は定型的な表現を利用できる。

難 057　Hibiya市では，市民が余暇を過ごすための新しい公共施設の建設を計画している。資料1を参考にして，資料2にイラストで示された施設の「よい点」と「問題となる点」を1つずつ挙げ，それぞれの理由を，合わせて50語以上の英語で説明しなさい。　（東京・都立日比谷高）

資料1：Chart

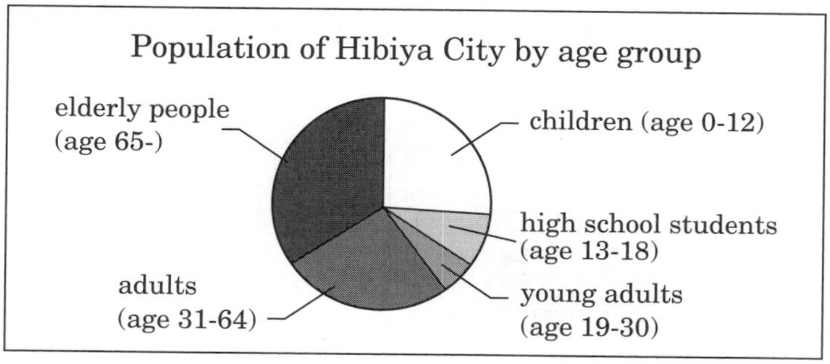

資料2：Plan

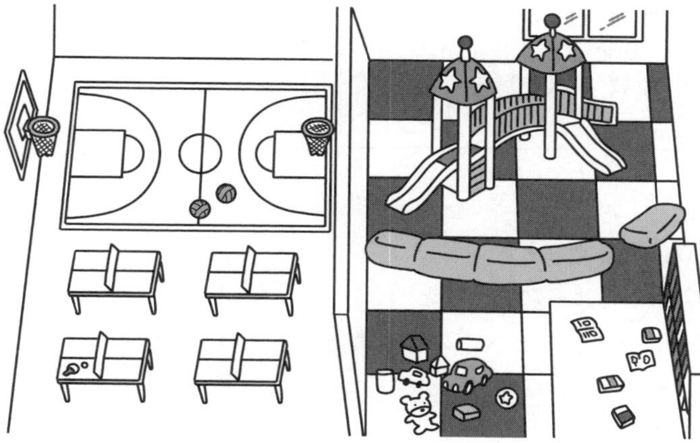

解答の方針

問題文の指示に忠実に従うことが大切。「よい点とその理由」「問題となる点とその理由」の両方を，2つの資料から考える必要がある。

第4回 実力テスト

▶解答→別冊 p.59

時間 30 分　目標 80 点　得点　／100

1 あなたの学校に来ているALTのジョシュ(Josh)先生が，春休みに離島への旅行を計画しています。ジョシュ先生は，離島への移動のために飛行機(airplane)と船(ship)のどちらを利用したらよいか迷っています。どちらかの方法をジョシュ先生に勧める英文を，下の【条件】に従って書きなさい。

（沖縄県）　（40点）

飛行機（airplane）	船（ship）

⑴ 所要時間：50分 ⑵ 便数：1日3便 （出発時刻：8 a.m. / 12 p.m. / 6 p.m.） ⑶ 運賃：12,000円	⑴ 所要時間：8時間 ⑵ 便数：1日1便 （出発時刻：8 a.m.） ⑶ 運賃：4,000円

【条件】

[1]　主語・動詞を含む英文を，3文以内で書くこと。

[2]　どちらの移動方法を勧めたいかがわかるように書くこと。

[3]　その移動方法を勧めたい具体的な理由を，イラストに示された⑴～⑶の情報に基づいて，2つ書くこと。

[4]　示された英文(書き出し)に続けて書くこと。

Mr. Josh,

I would like to give you advice for your trip.

____

____

____

I hope you have fun on your trip!

2 あなたは英語の授業で，「思い出の写真」について発表を行うことになった。次の【写真】をもとに，【スピーチ原稿】を完成しなさい。下線部①・②は，写真の内容と状況に合うように英語を書きなさい。下線部③にはあなた自身の考えを英語で書きなさい。①～③はそれぞれ5語以上使用し，下線部を含む文がまとまった意味になるように書くこと。（佐賀県）

（各20点，計60点）

【写真】

【スピーチ原稿】

I'm going to talk about a picture of my family. I went to a mountain in Kumamoto with my family last year. Please look at this. At this moment, we saw a big bird which was flying in the sky, and my father was so excited. ①____________________ because he likes bird watching. However, my sister began to cry when she saw the bird. My mother took care of her and said, "②____________________." After that, we had lunch on the top of the mountain. It was a great time.

This year, I'm going to go to the sea because ③____________________.

Thank you for listening.

① ____

② ____.

③ ____.

5 自分の考えを英語で書く問題

注意　英文の語数が指定されている問いでは，短縮形(I'm，don't など)やハイフンを使った語(e-mail など)は１語と数える。また，符号(，．！？“ ”など)は語数に含めない。なお，特に指定がない限り，文の数はいくつでもよい。

標 準 問 題

解答　別冊 p.60

058　**下のイラストがあなたの部屋だとしたら，そこにあったらいいと思うものを１つ考え，次の指示に従って３文以上の英文で書きなさい。**　（宮城・東北学院高）

(1)　あったらいいと思うものを具体的に１つ挙げること。

(2)　あったらいいと思う場所を書くこと。

(3)　あったらいいと思う理由を書くこと。

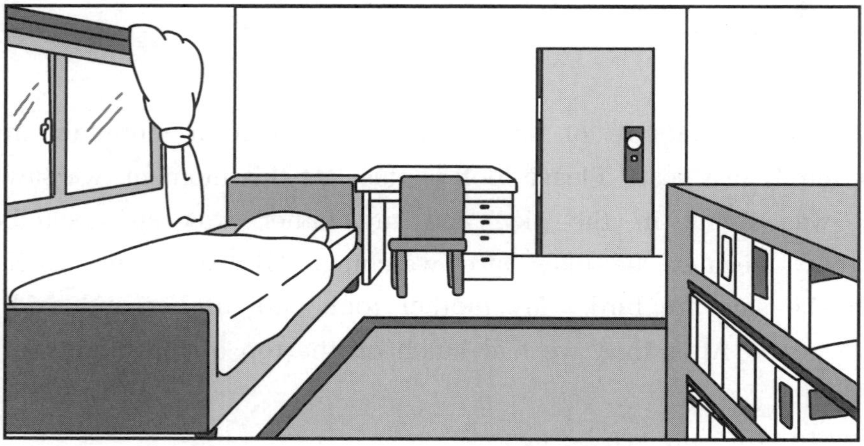

ガイド　「３文以上の英文で」という条件があるので，(1)～(3)をそれぞれ１文で答えれば書きやすい。

059　あなたは英語の授業で，『地球のためにできること』というタイトルでスピーチをすることになり，次のメモを作成しました。【メモ】をもとに【スピーチ原稿】を完成しなさい。①〜③にはメモに即した適切な英語を書き，④にはあなたの考えを書くこと。　（大阪・四天王寺高）

【メモ】

(1) ゴミをたくさん出さない
- 買い物をするときは自分のバッグを使う
- できるだけ紙をリサイクルする
- 壊れたものは修理する

(2) 二酸化炭素を減らす
- あなたの考え

【スピーチ原稿】

What can we do to save the earth?

Now there are a lot of environmental problems on the earth. One of them is trash. The easiest way to make less trash is to ①__________ when we go shopping. It is good to recycle ②__________ possible. To ③__________ is another good way. I also think we should do something to reduce CO_2. For example, ④__________

One person can only do little things, but if we try together, we can do big things. I want everyone to remember this to save the earth.

①____________________

②____________________

③____________________

④____________________

ガイド　「環境を守るために何ができるか」という問いはよく見られるので，具体的な例を英語で表現できるよう練習しておくとよい。

重要 060 それぞれの質問に対するあなた自身の考えを，10語以上の英語で述べなさい。

（北海道・函館ラ・サール高）

① What do you want to do during your high school days? And why?
② What do you want to be in the future? And why?
③ Why do you want to study English?

①

②

③

061 以下の英文は，あなたが友人のボブ（Bob）からもらったメールの一部です。ボブの質問に対するあなたの答えを，30語以上の英語で書きなさい。

（茨城・常総学院高）

【あなたがボブからもらったメールの一部】

Hello. Last Wednesday, my English teacher, Ms. Green, asked her students, "Who is the most important person for you?" First, she told us about herself. The most important person for her is her grandfather. He was also an English teacher, and he worked in Japan many years ago. She heard his stories many times when she was small, and she became interested in working as an English teacher in Japan. His stories had a great *influence on her life. The most important person for me is my guitar teacher. I want to be a musician, and her lessons and support are very important for me. Who is the most important person for you? And why do you think so?

（注） influence 影響

ガイド 「○○語以上」という条件がある問いでは，その語数に満たない答案は減点されるので注意。

062 あなたは英語の授業で，自分の関心のあることについて発表することになり，次のメモを作成しました。メモをもとに，原稿の①・②に適切な英語を入れなさい。また③の(　　)には【あなたが参加したいボランティア活動】をＡまたはＢから１つ選んで符号で入れ，下線部にはその理由を10語以上20語以内の英語で書きなさい。

（岐阜県）

〈メモ〉

（導入）　先週，ボランティア活動についてのポスターを見た。
長い間ボランティア活動に興味があったので参加したい。

（活動内容）　Ａ　公園でゴミを拾う。
Ｂ　図書館で，子どもたちに本を読む。
【あなたが参加したいボランティア活動とその理由】
あなたの考え

（まとめ）　参加の呼びかけ

〈原稿〉

Last week, I saw a poster about volunteer activities. I'd like to join one of them because ①________________ volunteer activities for a long time.

In the poster, I found two different activities, A and B. If I choose A, I will *pick up trash in the park. If I choose B, I will ②________________.

③ I want to join (　　) because ________________.

Would you like to join me?

（注） pick up trash　ゴミを拾う

① ________________________________

② ________________________________

③ I want to join (　　) because ________________________

____

ガイド　「○○語以上○○語以内」のように制限語数が明示されている場合は，その語数の範囲内に収まっていない答案は減点されるので注意。

063 次の英文は，地球規模の社会問題を扱った高校生向けの講演会(lecture)の【案内】の一部と，それについて，あなたとオリバー(Oliver)が話をしている会話です。①・②の問いに答えなさい。【会話】の＊＊＊の部分には，あなたの名前が書かれているものとします。 （新潟県）

【案内】

Lecture A: Safe Water for Everyone	About 2,200,000,000 people cannot drink *clean and safe water, and many of them become sick. Safe water is necessary for their *healthy lives.
Lecture B: Studying at School	About 1,600,000,000 children do not go to school. Many of them hope to learn how to read, write, or *calculate, and improve their lives.
Lecture C: Don't Waste Food	About 2,000,000,000 people cannot eat enough food, but more than 30% of the world's food is wasted. How can we stop wasting food?
Lecture D: Forests Will Be Lost	*By 2030, 60% of *the Amazon rainforest may be lost. Then, many animals and plants living there will lose their home.

（注） clean きれいな　healthy 健康的な　calculate 計算する　by ～までには
the Amazon rainforest アマゾンの熱帯雨林

【会話】

＊＊＊: Wow, all the lectures look interesting. Which one will you listen to?

Oliver: I will listen to (A). My mother works at a restaurant and she often says a lot of food is wasted. I want to learn how to stop that. How about you? Which lecture are you interested in the most?

＊＊＊: (B)

Oliver: Why do you want to listen to it?

＊＊＊: (C)

① 【会話】の(A)に入る最も適切なものを選びなさい。

ア Lecture A　イ Lecture B　ウ Lecture C　エ Lecture D

② 【会話】の(B)，(C)に，それぞれ直前のOliverの質問に対するあなたの答えを英語で入れなさい。(B)は3語以上，(C)は3行以内の英文で書きなさい。

① (　　)

② (B) ＿＿＿＿＿＿＿＿＿＿＿＿＿＿＿＿

(C) ＿＿＿＿＿＿＿＿＿＿＿＿＿＿＿＿

＿＿＿＿＿＿＿＿＿＿＿＿＿＿＿＿

＿＿＿＿＿＿＿＿＿＿＿＿＿＿＿＿

重要 **064** ALT のマイケル(Michael)先生が，英語の授業で次の質問をしました。この質問に答えなさい。(　)にはあなたが選んだ記号 A，B のどちらかを入れ，下線部にはあなたの考えを理由とともに25語以上の英語で書きなさい。英文はいくつでもよいが，まとまった内容の文章にすること。 (富山県)

マイケル先生

【A】 and 【B】 are two *wishes. If you could have one wish, which would you choose? And why would you choose it? Please write about it.

(注) wish　願い

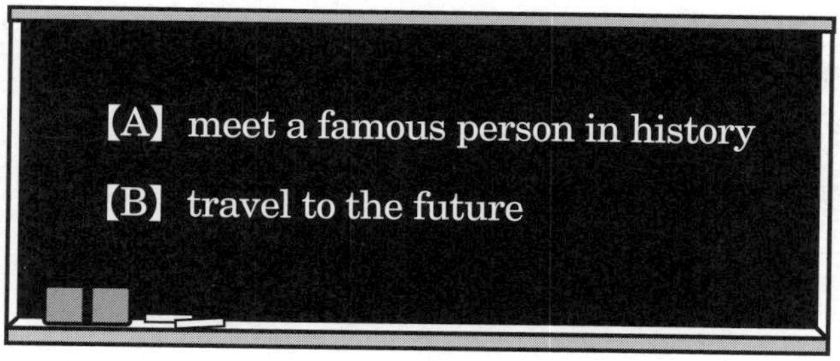

I would choose (　　　). ____

____

____

ガイド　どちらの「願い」を選んだとしても，どんな形を使って書くことが求められているかをよく考えることが大切。

065 あなたは中学校を卒業してから高校に入学するまでにやりたいことについて，ALT の先生に話すことになりました。あなた自身のやりたいことがよく伝わるように，30語程度の英語で答えなさい。 (福井県)

____

____

____

重要 066 カナダからの留学生のナンシー(Nancy)さんが学校から帰ると，ホストファーザー(ホームステイ先のお父さん)が料理をしていました。絵1～4は，そのときの2人の会話の様子を順に示したものです。これを読み，後の問いに答えなさい。 (鳥取県)

絵1

絵2

(注) onion たまねぎ
carrot にんじん

絵3

(注) garbage ゴミ

(注) throw away ～ ～を捨てる
vegetable scraps
野菜の皮や葉および切れはし

絵4

(注) reduce ～を減らす

① 絵1の(1)と絵3の(2)に入る適切な英文を，それぞれ4語以上の1文で書きなさい。

② 次のスピーチは，ナンシーさんがホストファーザーとの会話で印象に残った日本語について述べたものです。これを読み，スピーチの下線部の問いかけに対するあなたの考えを，あとの【条件】に従って書きなさい。

【スピーチ】

> Today, I want to talk about my favorite Japanese word. It is "mottainai." I learned this word when I was cooking with my *host father. We don't have an English word like that, but I think this word is important. For example, a lot of food is *thrown away at *convenience stores, supermarkets and restaurants every day. And we often buy too much food. *Wasting food is really "mottainai" and it is a big problem around the world now. But there are other "mottainai" problems in our daily life. When do you feel "mottainai" and what can you do about the problem?

（注） host father　ホストファーザー（ホームステイ先のお父さん）
thrown away　throw away（～を捨てる）の過去分詞
convenience store　コンビニエンスストア　　wasting　～を無駄にすること

【条件】

［1］ 20語程度の英語で書くこと。

［2］ 主語・動詞を含む文で書くこと。

［3］ 会話やスピーチで述べられている例以外の内容とすること。

① (1) ______________________________

(2) ______________________________

② ______________________________

____

____

ガイド 下線部の問いは，実質的に２つのことを尋ねている。したがって，それぞれを１文にして，20語程度の２文で構成するとよい。

067 あなたは，何をして過ごす時間が好きですか。１つ例を挙げて英語で書きなさい。さらに，その理由を15語以上の英語で書きなさい。

（東京・中央大附高）

I ______________________________. （この英文は語数に含めない）

____

____

重要 068 次の質問を読み，それに対する答えとして Answer A・B のどちらかを選び，□にチェック(☑)を入れなさい。その後，①～④がその答えに関する文章となるように，下線部にそれぞれ7語以上の英語を書きなさい。なお，②～④はそれぞれ，以下の内容を表す文にすること。(①は既に示してある)

（東京・成城学園高）

②：①で示されている理由に関する補足(詳細や具体例など)

③：自分の選んだ Answer(A または B)に関する，もう1つの理由

※①と同じような内容の理由は書かないこと

④：③で示した理由に関する補足(詳細や具体例など)

【Question】 Do you think club activity is important in your school life?

□ Answer A: I think club activity is important in my school life. I have two reasons.

① First, I can learn many things from club activity.

② ________________________________.

③ Second, ________________________________.

④ ________________________________.

For these reasons, I can't think of my school life without club activity.

□ Answer B: I don't think club activity is important in my school life. I have two reasons.

① First, there are other places to improve my skills out of school.

② ________________________________.

③ Second, ________________________________.

④ ________________________________.

For these reasons, I don't think club activity is a necessary part of my school life.

> **ガイド** このタイプの問いへの答え方の基本形が示されている。他のテーマの問いにも同じ文章構成を利用できる。

069 食品ロス(food loss)を減らすためにあなた自身はどんなことができると思いますか。具体例を1つ挙げて30語程度の英語で述べなさい。

（京都・同志社高）

____

____

____

重要 070 ある中学校のあるクラスで，先週の日曜日に最も時間を費やした活動についてアンケートを取り，次のグラフにまとめました。以下の設問に答えなさい。数字は算用数字で書いてかまいません。

（宮城・東北学院高）

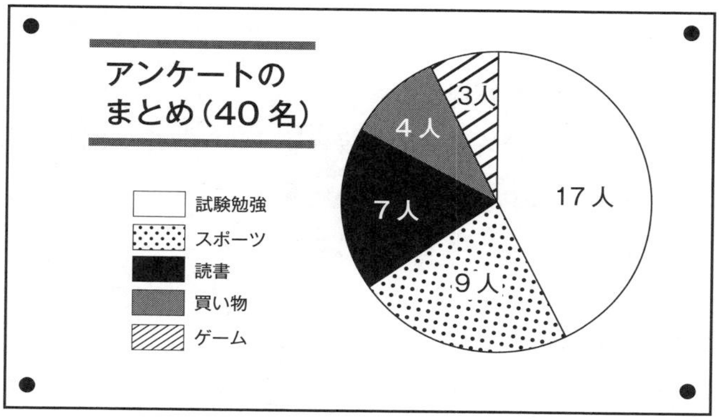

① アンケートのまとめに合うように，次の英文の下線部に 3 語以上の英語を書きなさい。

More than 25 percent of the students ________________________.

② アンケートのまとめから，あなたが感じたこと・考えたことを 2 文以上の英文で書きなさい。

____

____

071 次の質問に対するあなたの答えを，25～35語の英語で述べなさい。なお，（ ）内に語数を記入すること。

（東京・成蹊高）

Who do you respect the most? Why? You can write about a person you have met or a person you have not met.

____

____

____

________________________________ （　　　）語

ガイド 語数制限のある問いでは，たとえば「完成した英文を数えてみたら 1 語足りなかった」といったケースがありうる。その場合，解答欄をはみ出して（矢印などを使って）1 語を加えるような書き方をすると，減点される可能性が高い。下書きをして完成した英文の語数を確認してから，それを解答欄に転記するのがよい。

重要 072 英語の授業で行っている話し合いの中で，ユウト(Yuto)さんとミキ(Miki)さんが自分の意見を述べています。最後の先生の質問に対して，あなた自身の意見を英語で書きなさい。ただし，次の条件のすべてを満たすこと。　　　(島根県)

(1) 1文目はどちらかの名前を選び，どちらの立場に賛成かを明らかにすること。2文目以降の語数は15語以上とする。

(2) 賛成する理由を1つ挙げ，その理由を補足する事柄や具体例とともに書くこと。

(3) 吹き出しの中の語句を使ってもかまわないが，ユウトさんに賛成の場合は，ユウトさんと同じ理由になってはならない。ミキさんに賛成の場合は，Typing messages を書き出しとして省略された部分を答えてもよいし，自分で考えた理由を書いてもかまわない。

These days, we teachers usually use computers and don't have many chances to write *by hand. But you students usually write a lot on your notebooks. Do you think *handwriting is important?

先生

ユウトさん

Writing by hand shows who wrote the message. When we see a *signature on a letter, we can trust that it is a real letter from the writer, not a *fake. So handwriting is important.

ミキさん

I don't think so. *Typing messages ... (省略) ...

Thank you, Yuto and Miki. Maybe there are more good reasons to support their opinions. What do you think?

先生

(注) by hand 手で　handwriting 手書きすること，筆跡　signature サイン
fake にせ物　typing ～をタイプすること(type の ing形)

073 英語の授業で，英語学習の方法について，グループで話し合いました。次のＡ～Ｃは，話し合いの一部を示したものです。Ｃの下線部の質問に対して，あなたは何と答えますか。30語～40語の英語で書きなさい。 （群馬県）

A

Let's talk about ways of learning English. What can we do to improve our English? Do you know any good ways?

B

I sometimes listen to English songs.

How about writing e-mails in English? I think it's good.

Reading English books is really good.

I often talk with our ALT.

C

Thank you for sharing ideas. We have four ideas now, and I think they are all good! Which one would you like to try most to improve your English? And why?

074 あなたは，英語の授業で，ALT（外国語指導助手）にあなたが住んでいる町のお気に入りの場所を紹介することになりました。お気に入りの場所を１つ挙げ，理由や説明を含めて，30語以上の英語で書きなさい。 （和歌山県）

Hello, I'll talk about my favorite place today.

Thank you.

075 次の英文は，真(Makoto)さんの学級で英語のグリーン先生(Mr. Green)が問いかけた内容です。これを読んで，あなた自身の考えとその理由を，15語以上35語以内の英語で書きなさい。(滋賀県)

【グリーン先生の問いかけ】

My American friend who is a photographer will visit Shiga in spring. I want to take her to a nice place in Shiga to take pictures, but I don't know where to go. Could you give me good advice?

重要 076 放課後，英語クラブで裕二と絵美に，留学生のマークが話をしている。会話の流れに合うよう，下線部①・②にそれぞれ30語程度の英語を入れなさい。(福井県)

Yuji: I went to a zoo with my friends yesterday. I saw many animals there. It was very exciting.

Mark: That's good. I like zoos, but I don't think that it is good to keep animals in zoos.

①

Yuji: I see. I understand the idea because animals sometimes look sad.

Emi: Mark, you may be right, but zoos have good points, too.

②

Yuji: Oh, that's true. Going to zoos is fun, but thanks to you, I learned another good point of them.

①

②

ガイド この会話が日本語で行われていたとしても，空所に入る内容が思い浮かばなければ問題は解けない。さまざまなテーマに関して，どんな賛否の意見があるのかを一般常識として知っておこう。

最高水準問題

解答 別冊 p.69

077 英語の授業で，次のテーマについて意見を書くことになりました。あなたなら，田舎と都会のどちらを選び，どのような意見を書きますか。あなたの意見を，下の【条件】に従って英語で書きなさい。 （香川県）

> 将来，あなたが暮らしたい場所は，田舎と都会のどちらか。
> 田舎 the country
> 都会 a city

【条件】

(1) (　　　)内に the country または a city のどちらかを書くこと。

(2) 第 1 文に続けて，4 つの英文を書くこと。

(3) それぞれの文の語数は 5 語以上とする。

(4) 田舎または都会を選んだ理由が伝わるよう，まとまりのある内容で書くこと。

I think living in (　　　　　　　　　　　　) is better.

____

____

____

____

難 **078** Read the following sentences and write your answer in English. （大阪府）

*Suppose you have a goal to *achieve, but you have difficulties to achieve the goal. In such cases, who or what helps you *overcome those difficulties? Write who or what, and after that, from your experience or example, explain why you think so.

（注） suppose 〜を考える　achieve 〜を達成する　overcome 〜を乗り越える

____

____

____

解答の方針

077 よく問われる話題なので，答え方を頭に入れておくとよい。このような頻出テーマに関しては，英文を丸暗記しておくのも試験対策として効果がある。

難 079 あなたは，英語の授業で，“An effective way to learn foreign cultures or customs” というテーマについて陽子と英語で意見交換をしている。次の陽子の発言に対するあなたの答えを，その理由とともに25語以上35語以内の英語で書きなさい。 （熊本県）

【陽子の発言】

> I think visiting other countries even for a few days is an *effective way to learn foreign cultures or *customs. Do you agree with me?

（注） effective 効果的な　　custom 習慣

080 次の質問に対するあなたの答えを，25〜35語の英語で述べなさい。 （大阪桐蔭高）

Today, with smartphones and tablets, some people read e-books instead of paper books. Do you think e-books are better than paper books? And why?

解答の方針

079 Do you agree with me? という問いかけに対しては，まず (Yes,) I agree (with you). または (No,) I don't agree (with you). を使って答えるとよい。

081 Which do you think is better, regular lessons in classrooms or online lessons? Tell us your opinion with two or three reasons. Write in English and use about 50 words. Please write the number of words. (東京・慶應義塾女子高)

082 次の英文を読んで，下線部の質問に対するあなたの考えを，その理由が伝わるように，40語以上50語程度の英語で書きなさい。 (埼玉県)

Making a speech or presentation is effective to *deepen your understanding. When you make a speech or presentation, you may *discover some things that you want to learn more about. To learn more, you will need to do research. For example, you can do this in many ways at school. The school library and the *tablet computers can also help you. <u>How will you use things, such as the library or computers for your research?</u>

(注) deepen ～を深める　discover ～を発見する　tablet タブレット型の

解答の方針

081 複数の理由を述べるときは，first，second などを使って，全体としてまとまりのある文章を書く必要がある。

083 修道高校では，2年生から私服登校が認められます。あなたは，制服(school uniform)と私服(casual clothes)のどちらで登校したいですか。理由を2つ挙げて，40〜50語の英語で意見を述べなさい。 (広島・修道高)

084 Some people think that it would be a good idea for high school students in Japan to learn two foreign languages. Do you agree with this idea? Write 50-60 words in English about it. Give some reasons and examples to support your idea. (京都教育大附高)

難 085 One English word, "wellness" is being used more and more around the world. Write in English about what you think this word means, and what is most important in keeping a good level of wellness. (兵庫・灘高)

解答の方針

083 頻出テーマなので，答えの内容を覚えておくとよい。

難 **086** 次の質問に対するあなたの答えを，40〜60語の英語で述べなさい。 （京都女子高）

Do you want to live a busy life in the future? What are your plans?

087 学校で出される宿題について，「長期休暇には宿題を出さないでほしい」と反対する立場に立って，下の【条件】に従って英文を書きなさい。 （東京・筑波大附駒場高）

【条件】

(1) 第１文に続けて，あなたが宿題に反対する理由を２つ，具体的に述べること。

(2) 40語以上50語以内で書くこと。第１文は語数に含まない。

(3) 使用した語数を(　)内に記入すること。

Teachers shouldn't give us homework during a long vacation. I have two reasons.

(　　　)語

解答の方針

086 問いが２つあるので，どんな構成で文章を組み立てるかを考える。最初の問いへの答えがYesかNoかで，後に続く内容は異なる。a busy lifeとは具体的にどんな生活かをイメージすることが大切。

第 5 回 実力テスト

▶解答→別冊 p.74

時間 30 分　目標 70 点　得点　／100

1 あなたは，アメリカから日本に来たばかりの留学生のサム(Sam)と仲良くなるために今週末の計画を立てている。A・B のどちらかの案を選び，下の【条件】に従って，あなたの考えを英語で書きなさい。　(福岡県)　(30 点)

A　一緒にスポーツを観戦する。

B　一緒に料理をする。

【条件】

[1]　最初の文は，I will choose (　　　). とする。空所には A または B を入れること。

[2]　2つの案について触れながら，あなたの考えを理由とともに書くこと。

[3]　最初の文は語数に含めずに，30語以上の英語で書くこと。

I will choose (　　　).

2 あなたが日本で旅行してみたい場所とその理由を，40語程度の英語で述べなさい。なお，使用した語数を(　)内に記入しなさい。　(大阪星光学院高)　(30 点)

(　　　)語

3 あなたの学校は，国際交流が盛んで，生徒たちが海外経験を積むことを積極的に勧めています。以下は，冬休み前のある先生と生徒の会話です。下線部の質問について，下の【条件】に従って，あなた自身の考えを英語で述べなさい。　（茨城・清真学園高）（40点）

Mr. Smith: Misaki, what are you planning to do this winter?

Misaki: This winter? Well, maybe I'll just do my homework and go to tennis club.

Mr. Smith: Haha, that's fine. But I think you can do more. I hear a lot of students at this school go abroad during vacation.

Misaki: Yes, but I don't know .... Is it a good idea? Do you think students should spend some time abroad?

Mr. Smith: Oh, that's a good question. Let's discuss this topic in our next English class.

【条件】

［1］ 考えに対して，理由を必ず1つ以上含めること。あなた自身の経験に基づいても，客観的な事実を根拠にしてもかまわない。

［2］ 書き出しはYes / Noではなく，I thinkまたはI don't thinkから始めること。

［3］ 30語以上で文章を構成し，(　)内に使用した語数を記入すること。

(　　　)語

□ 編集協力　㈱シー・レップス　渡邉聖子　白石あゆみ

□ 本文デザイン　CONNECT

□ 録音　高速録音㈱

□ ナレーション　Ananda Jacobs　Stuart O　芦澤亜希子

※p.17 都立国際高校の入試問題は2022年に実施されたものです。

シグマベスト

最高水準問題集
中学英作文

著　者　佐藤誠司

発行者　益井英郎

印刷所　株式会社天理時報社

発行所　株式会社文英堂
〒601-8121　京都市南区上鳥羽大物町28
〒162-0832　東京都新宿区岩戸町17
(代表)03-3269-4231

●落丁・乱丁はおとりかえします。

ΣBEST
シグマベスト

最高水準問題集

中学英作文

解答と解説

[付録]
・英作文の勉強の仕方
・暗記用例文100 英語音声つき

文英堂

1 整序英作文問題

001 ① **I found smartphones very useful**
② **The weather is so nice that I want to walk**
③ **Do you know how far it is from Japan to**
④ **I wanted to see was not there**
⑤ **How many books do you read a**
⑥ **made his wife a birthday cake**
⑦ **Would you like to have another piece of cake**
⑧ **the most beautiful temple that I've ever visited**

解説 ①第5文型（SVOC）の文。〈find + O (smartphones) + C (very useful)〉で「O［スマートフォン］がCだ［とても便利だ］とわかる」の意味を表す。

文法 SVOCの形で使う動詞（C＝主に形容詞）
暗記 find+O+C=OがCだとわかる
暗記 keep+O+C=OをCのままに保つ
暗記 leave+O+C=OをCのままに放置する
暗記 make+O+C=OをCにする

②次の形を覚えておくこと。
暗記 **so ～ that ...**「非常に～なので…」
・This curry is **so** hot **that** I **can't** eat it.
（このカレーはとても辛いので私は食べられない）
= This curry is **too** hot **for** me **to eat**.
（このカレーは私が食べるには辛すぎる）

③How far is it from Japan to Korea?（日本から韓国までどのくらいの距離がありますか）という文を間接疑問にすると，下線部（VS）がit isの語順（SV）になる。

文法 間接疑問
疑問文がより大きな文の一部となった形を，間接疑問と言う。
暗記 間接疑問内では**SV**の語順を使う。

(1) Who is that man?（あの男性は誰ですか）
V S
(2) I don't know 〈who that man is〉.
S V
（あの男性が誰なのか私は知らない）
(3) Do you know 〈who that man is〉?
S V
（あの男性が誰なのか知っていますか）
(2)(3)では，(1)の疑問文がより大きな文の一部になっている（〈　〉＝間接疑問）。

④sunfishの後ろにthat[which]（目的格の関係代名詞）が省略された形。(1) The sunfish was not there.（マンボウはそこにはいなかった）＋(2) I wanted to see it [＝the sunfish].（私はそれを見たかった）→(3) The sunfish [(that [which]) I wanted to see] was not there.（私が見たかったマンボウはそこにはいなかった）と考える。

文法 目的格の関係代名詞が省略された形
関係代名詞を含む文は，次のように2つの文を組み合わせて作ることができる。
(1) This is the book.（これが（その）本だ）
(2) I read it [＝the book] yesterday.
（私はそれを昨日読んだ）
→(3) This is the book 〈that I read yesterday〉.
（これが，私が昨日読んだ本だ）
(2)のitを関係代名詞のthat[which]に置き換えてそれを最初に置き（that[which] I read yesterday），(1)のthe book（先行詞）に続けると(3)ができる。(3)の〈　〉内（関係詞節）は，the bookを修飾［詳しく説明］している。thatは，((2)ではitがreadの目的語の働きをしていたので）目的格の関係代名詞である。次の点が重要。
暗記 目的格の関係代名詞は省略することができる。
いくつか例を見てみよう。
・the subject (that) I like best
（私が一番好きな科目）
・the key (that) I was looking for
（私が探していたカギ）
・the watch (that) my father gave me
（父が私にくれた腕時計）
・the woman (that) I met at the party
（私がパーティーで会った女性）
［参考］目的格の関係代名詞は，先行詞が人ならwhom [that]を，先行詞が人以外ならwhich [that]を使うが，しばしば省略される。

⑤返答の文は，たとえばI read three books a

month.（私は1か月に3冊の本を読む）となる。この下線部を How many books で尋ねる形。a は「～につき」の意味。

注意! How many do you read books a month? としないように。How many の後ろには名詞を置くので，books を切り離すことはできない。

⑥第4文型（SVOO）の文。〈make + O_1(his wife) + O_2(a birthday cake)〉で「O_1[妻]に O_2[誕生日ケーキ]を作ってあげる」の意味を表す。

文法 SVO_1O_2の形で使う動詞（O_1＝人，O_2＝物）

(1)〈S＋V＋物＋to＋人〉で言い換えられるもの

- 暗記 give＋O_1＋O_2＝O_1に O_2を与える
- 暗記 lend＋O_1＋O_2＝O_1に O_2を貸す
- 暗記 read＋O_1＋O_2＝O_1に O_2を読んで聞かせる
- 暗記 send＋O_1＋O_2＝O_1に O_2を送る
- 暗記 show＋O_1＋O_2＝O_1に O_2を見せる
- 暗記 teach＋O_1＋O_2＝O_1に O_2を教える
- 暗記 tell＋O_1＋O_2＝O_1に O_2を伝える，話す

(2)〈S＋V＋物＋for＋人〉で言い換えられるもの

- 暗記 buy＋O_1＋O_2＝O_1に O_2を買ってあげる
- 暗記 cook＋O_1＋O_2＝O_1に O_2を料理してあげる
- 暗記 make＋O_1＋O_2＝O_1に O_2を作ってあげる

［参考］「相手を必要とする行為を表す動詞は to，自分一人でできる行為を表す動詞は for で言い換える」と覚えておくとよい。たとえば give には相手が必要だが，make には相手は必要ない。

注意! make は SVOO（第4文型）と SVOC（第5文型）の両方で使う。

・My father sometimes **makes** us dinner.
（父は時々私たちに夕食を作ってくれる）［SVOO］

・The novel **made** her a popular writer.
（その小説は彼女を人気作家にした）［SVOC］

⑦would like は want のていねいな形で，Would you like to *do*? は「あなたは～したいですか（Do you want to *do*?）」の意味。

暗記 **would like** ～「～がほしい」

暗記 **would like to *do***「～したい」

＊ to *do* は不定詞。以下同様。

たとえば「コーヒーを飲みたい」は，次のどちらかで表現できる。

・**I'd[=I would] like** some coffee.

・**I'd like to have** some coffee.

⑧次の形を覚えておくこと。

暗記〈S **is the**＋最上級の形容詞＋A［名詞］**(that) I have ever** ＋過去分詞 **.**〉「S は私が今までに～した最も…な A だ」

・This is **the most scary movie I have ever seen.**
（これは私が今までに見た最も怖い映画だ）

＝ I have **never seen such a scary movie** (as this).（私は今までにこれほど怖い映画を見たことがない）

002 ① **The homework given by my teacher is to write an essay in English**
② **It has been a long time since the Olympic Games were held**
③ **asked the person next to me which train to take**
④ **the workers in the factory want their products to be more popular around the world**
⑤ **There is going to be another cold day**
⑥ **This book gave me some idea of life in**
⑦ **I have not read as many books as Mami**
⑧ **The number of children who like shogi is increasing**

解説 ①次のように，「～すること」の意味の不定詞を is の後ろに置く形がよく使われる。

暗記 S **is to *do*.**「S は～することだ」

・My dream is to be a doctor.
　　S　　V　　C
（私の夢は医者になることだ）

この S が，複雑な形になることがある。この問いでは，S = The homework given by my teacher（私の先生によって与えられた宿題）。下線部の過去分詞句が，前の名詞を修飾している。The homework (which was) given by my teacher の which was が省略された形と考えてもよい（→ 003 -⑥）。

②次の形は重要。

暗記 **It has been X**［時間の長さ］**since ....**「…

以来 **X**(の時間)が過ぎている」

＊ has been の代わりに is も使われる。

・**It has been[It is]** two years **since** we moved here.

(私たちがここに引っ越してから2年になる)

= **Two years have passed since** we moved here.

(私たちがここに引っ越してから2年が過ぎた)

= We moved here **two years ago**.

(私たちは2年前にここに引っ越した)

③ ask(尋ねる)は，次のように使う。

暗記 〈**ask** + O[人] +疑問詞 **...**〉「…を O に尋ねる」

・I **asked him** where he was from.

(私は彼に，どこの出身かと尋ねた)

＊下線部は間接疑問(→ 001 -③)。

この問いのように，O の後ろに〈疑問詞＋ **to *do***〉(～すべきか)の形を置くこともある。which train to take は「どの電車に乗るべきか」という意味。**next to** ～(～の隣に)は前置詞の一種で，the person next to me は「私の隣の人」。

④〈**want** + O + **to *do***〉「O に～してほしい」。

この問いでは，want their products to be more popular が「彼ら[自分たち]の製品がもっと人気になることを望む→自分たちの製品がもっと人気になってほしい」という意味を表す(下線部＝ O)。

文法 〈V+O+to *do*〉の形で使う動詞(O＝主に人)

暗記 advise+O+to *do*＝O に～するよう助言する

暗記 allow+O+to *do*＝O が～するのを許す

暗記 ask+O+to *do*＝O に～するよう頼む

暗記 expect+O+to *do*＝O が～するのを期待する

暗記 get+O+to *do*＝O に～してもらう

暗記 help+O+(to) *do*＝O が～するのを助ける

暗記 tell[order]+O+to *do*＝O に～するよう言う[命じる]

暗記 want[would like]+O+to *do*＝O に～してほしい

⑤次の形が基本形。

暗記 〈**There is[are]**+**X**+場所 **.**〉「～に **X** がある」

この下線部の be 動詞が，複雑な形になることがある。この問いの場合，There is another cold day.(もう1つの寒い日がある)という文をもとにして，下線部の is に be going to(～しそうだ)を加えると，There is going to be .... という形になる。

⑥ give は SVOO の形で使う動詞(→ 001 -⑥)。完成した文の構造は，次のようになる。

・This book gave me some idea of ...

S V O_1 O_2

idea は「理解，知識」の意味。直訳すると「この本は私に…のいくらかの理解を与えた」となる。

⑦次の形が基本形。

暗記 〈**not** + **as** +原級の形容詞・副詞+ **as** ～〉「～ほど…ではない」

・I'm **not as tall as** my father.

(私は父ほど背が高くない)

この文では，〈not ... as many books as Mami〉が「マミほど多くの本を…ない」という意味を表す。

注意! many(多くの)は名詞(books)の前に置いて使う。I have not read books as many as Mami yet. のように並べるのは誤り。

⑧次の形を覚えておくこと。

暗記 **The number of X is increasing.**「X の数が増えている」

この形の X は，しばしば複雑な形になる。この文では，X = children who like shogi(将棋を好む子どもたち)。

[参考] 基本構造は S is increasing.(S が増えている)で，上の 暗記 の下線部が S に当たる。その中心となる語は number(数)だから，S を単数扱いして is increasing を使う(are increasing は誤り)。

003 ① **would like to have something hot to**

② **will be twice as large as the old one**

③ **has been no fruit on this**

④ **is the second time I have been to**

⑤ **The book I need is not in this library**

⑥ **a city visited by many people from foreign contries**

⑦ **how much money I need to study abroad**

⑧ **The first thing you have to do is to clean**

解説 ① would like to *do*「～したい」(→ 001 -⑦)。次の形もよく使われる。

暗記 〈**something** ＋形容詞＋ **to** ***do***〉「～するための(何か)…なもの」

something hot to eat なら,「食べるための(何か)温かいもの, 何か温かい食べ物」という意味になる(to eat は something を修飾する形容詞的用法の不定詞)。

②「～倍」の意味を表す基本的な形は次のとおり。

暗記 **A is X times as ～ as B.**「A は B の X 倍～だ」

・This room is **three times as large as** mine.
(この部屋は私の部屋の 3 倍の広さだ)

・He practices **twice as hard as** you (do).
(彼は君の 2 倍練習している)

＊「2 倍」は twice(または two times)で表す。

この問いでは,「～の 2 倍の広さ」を twice as large as ～で表す。

③ There is no fruit on this tree. (この木には実がついていない)という文の is を, has been(現在完了形)に置き換えた形。There has been no fruit は「(過去から今まで)ずっと実がついていない」という意味になる(→ 002 -⑤)。

④次の形を覚えておくこと。

暗記 〈**This is the**＋序数詞＋**time**＋S＋V[**have** [**has**] (**ever**)＋過去分詞].〉「S が V するのはこれが～回目だ」

序数詞とは,「～番目(の)」の意味を表す first, second, third, fourth, ... のこと。この問いの文の完成形は次のようになる。

・This is the second time I have been to Okinawa.

下線部の have been to ～は「～へ行ったことがある」という意味(経験を表す現在完了形)。直訳すると「これは私が沖縄へ行ったことがある 2 番目の回だ」となる。

⑤ be 動詞には, 次のような使い方がある。

暗記 〈S **is**[**are**] ＋場所 **.**〉「S は～にある[存在している]」

この問いでは,「S = The book (that) I need」,「場所 = in this library」である。

⑥現在分詞・過去分詞で始まる句が, 前の名詞(や代名詞)を修飾する形がある。

文法 名詞を後ろから修飾する分詞句

暗記 〈X＋過去分詞句〉「～され(てい)る[された]X」

暗記 〈X＋現在分詞句〉「～している[する]X」

(a) This is a book **written** in easy English.
(これは易しい英語で書かれている本だ)

＊ a book (which is) written ... の( )内が省略された形と考えてもよい。

(b) The man **sitting** on the bench is my father.
(ベンチに座っている男性は私の父だ)

＊ the man (who is) sitting ... の( )内が省略された形と考えてもよい。

この問いは(a)と同様で, a city visited by ～が「～によって訪問される都市」という意味を表す。

[参考] (a)のように過去分詞句が前の名詞を修飾する形では, 常に〈that [which]＋be 動詞〉を補って考えることができる。一方(b)のように現在分詞句が前の名詞を修飾する形では,「現在分詞＝who [which]＋一般動詞の現在形」という関係になる場合がある。

・She is a first-year student belonging [＝who belongs] to the tennis club.
(彼女はテニス部に所属する 1 年生だ)

＊ belong to ～(～に所属する)は状態動詞で進行形にできないから(→ 009 -⑥), ... student (who is) belonging ... と考えることはできない。

⑦ How much money do I need to study abroad? (私は留学するためにどのくらいのお金を必要としますか)という疑問文を間接疑問にすると, do I need が SV の語順(I need)になる(→ 001 -③)。下線部は「留学するために」(目的を表す副詞的用法の不定詞)。need to *do*「～する必要がある」ではない。また, ... how much I need money to study abroad のように much と money を切り離すのは誤り(→ 001 -⑤)。

⑧ S **is to** ***do***. (S は～することだ)の S が複雑化した形(→ 002 -①)。完成した文は次の構造になる。

・The first thing you have to do (S) is (V) to clean .... (C)

S は「あなたがしなければならない最初のこと」。thing の後ろに目的格の関係代名詞(that [which])が省略された形(→ 001 -④)。

004 ① **Who is the girl crying over there**
② **Forty divided by eight is**
③ **The dog should be taken care of by someone**
④ **so heavy that we need four people to move it**
⑤ **the windows open in order to keep the air**
⑥ **known as an expensive fish caught in**
⑦ **spoke loud enough for all the students to hear**

解説 ①現在分詞句(crying over there)が前の名詞(the girl)を修飾する形(→ 003 -⑥)。

Q&A

Q Who is the crying girl over there? と並べるのは間違いですか？

A この文の場合は完全に間違いとは言えませんが，基本的には次のルールを覚えてください。

暗記 〈名詞＋分詞句〉の形から，分詞だけを名詞の前に出すことはできない。

○ The man sitting on the bench is my father.

× The sitting man on the bench is my father.

(ベンチに座っている男性は私の父だ)

［参考］ 1語の分詞は，an increasing population(増えている人口)のように分詞の前に置く。ただし，〈現在分詞＋人〉の形は実際にはあまり使われない。たとえば「ジョギングしている女性」は a jogging woman ではなく a woman who is jogging と表現するのが普通。

② Forty divided by eight is five. は「8によって割られた40は5である」の意味。下線部(過去分詞句)が前の名詞(forty)を修飾している。

［参考］「8 × 5 ＝40」は，Eight multiplied by five is forty.（5によって掛けられた8は40だ）または Eight times five is forty.（8倍の5は40だ）と表現する。

③ be と by があるので，受動態で表現する。

文法 能動態と受動態

「〜される」という意味を表す動詞の形(**be** 動詞＋過去分詞)を受動態と言い，そうでない形を能動態と言う。受動態を使った文には，対応する能動態の文がある。次の点が重要。

暗記 受動態のS(主語)は，能動態ではO(目的語)の働きをする。

(a) Everyone likes Betty.《能動態》
S V O
(みんながベティを好きだ)

(b) Betty **is liked** by everyone.《受動態》
S V
(ベティはみんなに(よって)好かれている)

＊(b)のSである Betty は，(a)ではOの働きをしている。

③では，take care of 〜(〜の世話をする)を1つの動詞として考える。

(a) Someone should take care of the dog.
S V O
(誰かがその犬の世話をしなければならない)

(b) The dog **should be taken care of** by someone.
S V
(その犬は誰かに(よって)世話をされなければならない)

(b)(受動態の文)は，be taken care of(世話をされる)＋by someone(誰かによって)という形になる。2つの前置詞(of と by)が連続する形になるが，どちらも必要な語だから省くことはできない。このような形はよく問われる。特に次の2つが頻出。

暗記 be spoken to by 〜「〜に話しかけられる」

暗記 be laughed at by 〜「〜に笑われる」

・A stranger spoke to me.
(知らない人が私に話しかけた)

→ I **was spoken to by** a stranger.
(私は知らない人に(よって)話しかけられた)

・His friends laughed at him.
(友人たちは彼を笑った)

→ He **was laughed at by** his friends.
(彼は友人たちに(よって)笑われた)

④ so 〜 that ...(非常に〜なので…)の形を利用する(→ 001 -②)。This sofa is so heavy that ....(このソファはとても重いので…)という形を作り，その後に we need four people to move it(私たちはそれを運ぶために4人を必要とする)と続ける。下線部は目的(「〜するために」の意味)を表す副詞的用法の不定詞。

⑤選択肢に order があるので，次の形を使う。

暗記 **in order to *do***「〜する(目的の)ために」

不定詞にはさまざまな使い方があるので，「目的」の意味をはっきりと表したいときはこの形(または **so as to *do***)を使う。leave the windows open は，〈leave + O + C［形容詞］〉（O を C のままに放置する）の形（→ 001 -①）。次の形も重要。

暗記 **〈keep + O + ～ing〉「O を～しているままに保つ」**

・Don't **keep** your friend **waiting** outside.
（友だちを外で待たせたままにしてはいけない）

この問いでは，keep the air circulating が「空気を循環しているままに保つ」という意味を表す（circulate「循環する」）。

⑥次の 3 つの前置詞の使い分けを覚えておこう。

暗記 **be known to** ～「～(人)に知られている」

暗記 **be known for** ～「～(の理由)で知られている」

暗記 **be known as** ～「～として知られている」

この問いでは，is known as an expensive fish で「高価な魚として知られている」という意味を表す（as は「～として」の意味の前置詞）。この fish の後ろに，(which is) caught in clean rivers（きれいな川で捕られる）という過去分詞句を続ける。

⑦次の基本形をセットで覚えておくこと。

暗記 **〈形容詞・副詞＋ enough (for X) to *do*〉「(X が)～できるほど(十分に)…」**

暗記 **〈too ＋形容詞・副詞＋ (for X) to *do*〉「(X が)～するには…すぎる」**

・This room is **large enough for us to have** a party.（この部屋は私たちがパーティーを開けるくらいの広さがある）

・This room is **too small for us to have** a party.（この部屋は私たちがパーティーを開くには狭すぎる）

注意！ **enough は形容詞・副詞の後に置く。**
上の例で，This room is enough large .... と並べる誤りがよく見られるので注意しよう。

この問いの場合，speak loud enough for all the students to hear で「生徒全員が聞こえるほどの大声で話す」という意味を表す。

［参考］「大声で話す」は speak loudly が普通の言い方だが，speak louder（もっと大声で話す），speak loud enough to *do*（～できるくらいの大声で話す）などの形のときは，しばしば loudly の代わりに loud を使う。

005 ① **have been looking for the book which**
② **Do you think your father can use**
③ **it will show you what**
④ **tell him to call you**
⑤ **What will the weather be like**
⑥ **is the camera my father gave me**
⑦ **Do you know who that person is**
⑧ **is an animal shaped like a star**

解説 ① look for（～を探す）を現在完了進行形で使う（→ 009 - ⑥）。the book which I borrowed は「私が借りた本」。

全訳
マサキ：借りた本を探しているんだ。君は見たかい？
リリー：いいえ。探すのを手伝うわ。

② Do you think (that)（～だと思いますか）の形を使う。

全訳
ヨシエ：あなたのお父さんはこのコンピューターを使えると思う？
デイビッド：うん。父さんはそれを使ってよくメールを書いているよ。

③ it は前の文中の this list（このリスト）を指す。直訳は「それは君が何を入れるべきかを君に示すだろう」。

全訳
A：この救急セットの中に何を入れればいいか知ってる？
B：このリストを見て。君が何を入れればいいかがそれに書いてあると思うよ。

［参考］ what you should put は「あなたが何を入れるべきか」(what＝疑問代名詞)，「あなたが入れるべきもの」(what＝関係代名詞) の 2 つの解釈が可能。

④電話の会話。〈tell + O + to *do*〉（O に～するよう言う）の形を利用する（→ 002 -④）。call you back は「あなたに後で(折り返し)電話する」。

全訳
A：もしもし。トムをお願いできますか。
B：ごめんなさい。今外出中なの。後であなたに電話するよう言うわ。

⑤次の形は重要。

暗記 **What is S like?**「Sはどのようなものですか」
この形のlikeは「～のような」の意味の前置詞で，次のように使う。

・**What is** your teacher **like**?
（君の先生はどんな人？）

＊What does you teacher like?（君の先生は何が好きですか）と混同しないように。

・**What's** the weather **like**? = How is the weather?
((今の)天気はどんな様子ですか)

この問いの場合，上の文のisをwill beに置き換えた疑問文を作ればよい。

Q&A

Q What will be the weather like tomorrow? と並べるのは間違いですか？

A はい。次のルールを覚えてください。

暗記 S+V+ ... のVが2語以上から成る場合，
・否定文はVの最初の語の後ろにnotを加えて作る。
・疑問文はVの最初の語をSと入れ換えて作る。
次の例で考えてみましょう。

(a) He has finished his homework.
S: He / V: has finished
（彼は宿題を終えた）

→(b) He hasn't finished his homework.
（彼は(まだ)宿題を終えていない）

→(c) **Has** he finished his homework?
（彼は宿題を(もう)終えましたか）

(a)では，V=has finishedです。これを否定文にするときは，Vの最初の語(has)の後ろにnotを加えて，(b)のようにします。同様に疑問文は，hasをS(He)の前に出して作ります。

この問いの場合は，V=will beです。したがって疑問文を作るときは，Vの最初の語であるwillをS(the weather)の前に出し，What will the weather be like? と並べるのが正しい形です。

全訳
A：明日の天気はどうなるでしょうか。
B：晴れるでしょう。

⑥This is the camera (which) my father gave me .... という形。下線部の関係詞節が，前の名詞(the camera)を修飾している。このwhichはgaveの目的語の働きをする(目的格の)関係代名詞だから，省略することができる(→ 001 -④)。

全訳
A：君はすてきなカメラを持っているね。
B：ありがとう。これは誕生日に父からもらったカメラだよ。

⑦Who is that person?（あの人は誰ですか）という疑問文をDo you knowの後ろに置くと，S(that person) + V(is)の語順(間接疑問)になる。

Q&A

Q Who is that person? のS(主語)を，Whoと考えることはできませんか？

A できません。日本語で考えても，「あの人は誰ですか」の主語は「あの人」ですね。次の例も参照してください。

(a) Beijing is the capital of China.
（北京は中国の首都だ）

(b) The capital of China is Beijing.
（中国の首都は北京だ）

(c) What is the capital of China?
（中国の首都はどこですか）

それぞれ，下線部がSです。したがって，(c)を間接疑問にすると次のようになります。

(d) Do you know what the capital of China is?
S: the capital of China / V: is
（中国の首都がどこか知っていますか）

全訳
A：あの男の人には以前に会ったことがない。あの人が誰だか知っている？
B：彼は私たちの新しい先生だと思う。
A：ああ，きっとそうだ[君が正しいに違いない]！

⑧**A shaped like B**は「**B**の形をした**A**」という意味。慣用表現として覚えておくとよい。

全訳
A：答えを推測できます[当てられます]か。それは星に似た形の動物です。それは海中にいます。それは何でしょう。
B：それはヒトデです！
A：ええ，正解です。英語ではそれをstarfishと呼びます。

006
① **How are you going to spend this weekend**
② **was kind enough to show me the way**
③ **how long she has been in Japan**
④ **book I need is not in this library**
⑤ **want to leave Japan without visiting Kyoto**
⑥ **is known to all the people living in this town**
⑦ **have never read such an interesting book**
⑧ **which the teacher asked us was too difficult**

解説 ①howは「どのようにして」。be going to(～する予定[つもり]だ)の後ろに，spend this weekend(この週末を過ごす)を置く。

全訳
A：この週末はどうやって過ごすつもり？
B：姉さん[妹]と一緒に買い物に行く計画を立てているの。

②S was kind enough to *do*. で「Sは～するほど(十分に)親切だった」という意味を表す。enoughをkind(形容詞)の後ろに置くのがポイント(→004-⑦)。

全訳
A：どうやって私の家を見つけたの？
B：ある女性が親切にも道を教えてくれたんだ。

③たとえばShe has been in Japan for five years.(彼女は5年間(ずっと)日本にいる)の下線部をHow long(どのくらいの期間)で尋ねる疑問文は，How long has she been in Japan? となる。これをDo you knowの後ろに間接疑問として置くときは，下線部(VS)がSVの語順になる(→001-③)。

全訳
A：彼女は日本語を話すのが上手です。彼女にはたくさんの日本人の友人がいます。
B：彼女はどのくらい日本にいるか知っていますか。

④S is not in this library. (Sはこの図書館(の中)にない)のSに当たるのが，The book (which) I need(私が必要としている本)。

全訳
A：君はなぜもう1つの図書館へ行くの？
B：私が必要な本がこの図書館にないの。

⑤前置詞の後ろに動詞を置くときは，動名詞(～ing)を使う。次のような形を覚えておこう。

暗記 **by ～ing**「～することによって」
暗記 **without ～ing**「～しないで」
暗記 **be good at ～ing**「～するのが上手だ」
暗記 **be interested in ～ing**「～することに興味がある」

この問いでは，without visiting Kyotoで「京都を訪ねないで」という意味を表す。

全訳
A：君はもう1週間日本に滞在したそうだね。それはなぜなの？
B：京都へ行かずに日本を去りたくなかったからだよ。

⑥be known to ～「～(人)に知られている」(→004-⑥)，all the people living[＝who live] in this town「この町に住む人々」(→003-⑥)

全訳
A：あの男性は誰ですか。
B：あなたも知っていると思いますよ。彼はこの町に住むすべての人たちに知られています。

⑦次の形を覚えておくとよい。

暗記 **〈I have never seen[heard, read] such a[an]＋**形容詞**＋X**[名詞]**.〉**「私はこんなに～なXを今までに見た[聞いた，読んだ]ことがない」

such(この[その]ような，これ[それ]ほど)の後ろは，〈a[an]＋(形容詞＋)名詞〉の語順になる。次の言い換えも覚えておこう。

・I have never read such an interesting book. (私はこんなに面白い本を今までに読んだことがない)
＝This is the most interesting book (that) I have ever read.
(これは私が今までに読んだ最も面白い本だ)

(→ 001 -⑧)

全訳

A：この本は本当に素晴らしい。君はこれを読んだの？

B：うん。そんなに面白い本は今までに読んだことがないよ。

⑧ The teacher asked us the question.（先生は私たちにその質問をした）→ the question (which) the teacher asked us（先生が私たちにした質問）と考える。

全訳

A：先生が私たちに尋ねた質問は，難しすぎたわ。

B：誰もそれに答えることはできないよ。

007 ① **Which museum do you want to visit**

② **there are many pictures drawn by famous cartoonists**

③ **energy problems that we have to solve**

④ **it takes only 5 minutes to walk from**

解説 ①会話の状況から考えて，サトルは「どちらのミュージアムへ行きたいか」と尋ねている。不要な語は how。

［参考］ museum は，日本語の「博物館」「美術館」の両方の意味で使う。後者の意味を明らかにしたいときは，art museum と言う。

② many pictures (which were) drawn by ～で「～によって描かれた多くの絵」という意味を表す。過去分詞(drawn)で始まる句が前の名詞を修飾する形。不要な語は taken。draw a picture で「(線で)絵を描く」という意味を表す。

［参考］ 絵の具を使って絵を描く場合は，paint a picture と言う。

③あおい科学博物館のポスターには２つの特別企画が書かれている。solve a problem（問題を解決する）という表現を思い出して，energy problems that we have to solve（私たちが解決しなければならないエネルギー問題）という形を作る（that は関係代名詞で，下線部が前の名詞を修飾している）。不要な語句は the amazing ocean。

④次の形は重要。

暗記 **〈It takes (X［人］) + 時間 + to *do*.〉**「(X が)～するのに…(の時間が)かかる」

・**It took (me) two hours to do** my homework.

（私は宿題をするのに２時間かかった）

この問いでは，〈It takes + 時間 + to walk ....〉で「歩くのに～(の時間)がかかる」という意味を表す。ポスターによればあおい美術館はあおい駅から歩いて５分だから，不要な語句は only 20 minutes。

全訳

サトル：ポスターを見てください。ぼくたちは電車であおい駅へ行き，それからミュージアムの１つまで歩いて行きます。どちらのミュージアムを訪ねたいですか。アイシャ，君はあおい美術館が好きですよね。

アイシャ：ええ，この美術館には有名な漫画家が描いたたくさんの絵がありますから。

フェイロン：なるほど。実は，ぼくの考えは違います。ぼくは科学博物館に興味があります。

サトル：なぜですか。

フェイロン：ぼくたちが解決しなければならないエネルギー問題について多くのことを学べるからです。

アイシャ：でも，私たちは美術館でも多くのことを学ぶことができます。たとえば，あおい町の歴史とか…。ああ，それに，あおい駅から美術館までは歩いて５分しかかかりません。

サトル：うーん…。決めるのはとても難しいですね。

008〉
① **not as cold as it was last week**
② **The cat which has blue eyes always looks**
③ **asked my teacher which dictionary to buy**
④ **walk around the lake took me two hours**
⑤ **is this small fruit called in English**
⑥ **how hard he has prepared for the exam**
⑦ **your room as quickly as you can**
⑧ **spent all the money that he had**
⑨ **twice as many CDs as I do**
⑩ **you to meet the man who joined**

解説 ①完成した文は「先週ほど寒くない」という意味。not as ～ as ... で「…ほど～ない」という意味を表す(→ 002〉-⑦)。

Q&A

Q ... as it was last week の下線部がよくわかりません。

A 次の例で考えてみましょう。

(a) Tom is **as tall as** Ken (is).
（トムはケンと同じくらいの背の高さだ）

2つ目のasは接続詞なので，後ろには〈S＋V〉の形を置くことができます。この文では前のisに合わせてas Ken is. という形にしますが，このisは省くことができます。前の動詞が一般動詞なら，do[does, did]を使います。

(b) Tom plays the guitar **as well as** Ken (does).
（トムはケンと同じくらい上手にギターを弾く）

では，次の文はどうでしょうか。

(c) It is **as cold** today **as** (it was) yesterday.
（今日は昨日と同じくらい寒い）

これは，asの後ろにS(it)＋V(was)を置いた形です。この文では今日(の寒さ)と昨日(の寒さ)を比べているので，it wasを省略してもかまいません。同じことは，比較級のthanの後ろの形についても言えます。

(d) I'm richer (now) than (I was) ten years ago.
（私は(今では)10年前よりも金持ちだ）

(e) I have more money than (I did) ten years ago.
（私は10年前よりも多くのお金を持っている）

［参考］たとえば(a)で，Tom is as tall as Ken is tall. と言うのは誤り。同様に(c)でも，It is as cold today as it was cold yesterday. とは言えない。

②完成した文は，「青い目を持つそのネコは，いつも寂しそうに見える」という意味。S looks lonely.（Sは寂しそうに見える）のSを，the cat which has blue eyes（青い目を持つそのネコ）という形にする。下線部の関係詞節が，前の名詞(the cat)を修飾している。

③完成した文は，「私はどの[どちらの]辞書を買うべきかと先生に尋ねた」という意味。which dictionary to buyは〈疑問詞＋**to** ***do***〉の形で，「どの[どちらの]辞書を買うべきか」という意味を表す。

④完成した文は，「その湖を歩いて回るのに私は2時間かかった」という意味。S(To walk around the lake) + V(took) + O(me) + O(two hours). という構造で，「湖のまわりを歩くことは，私に(とって)2時間を必要とした」という意味になる。Sの位置にItを置き，to walk ... を後ろへ回すと次のようになる(この形の方がよく使われる)(→ 007〉-④)。

・It took me two hours to walk around the lake.

⑤完成した文は，「この小さな果物は英語で何と呼ばれますか」という意味。次のように考える。

(a) People call this small fruit X in English.
　　S　V　O　C
（人々はこの小さな果物を英語でXと呼ぶ）

〈**call** + O + C〉は「OをCと呼ぶ」の意味。このOを主語にして受動態の文を作ると，次のようになる。

(b) This small fruit **is called** X in English.
　　S　V
（この小さな果物は英語でXと呼ばれる）

次に，このXをWhatで尋ねる疑問文を作ると，次のようになる。

(c) What **is** this small fruit **called** in English?
V S
(この小さな果物は英語で何と呼ばれますか)
(c)を What is called this small fruit in English? とするのは誤り。(b)のVは is called だから，疑問文を作るときはその最初の語(is)をSの前に出す(→ 005 -⑤)。

⑥完成した文は，「彼がどれほど熱心に試験の準備をしたか知っていますか」という意味。How hard has he prepared for the exam? (彼はどのくらい熱心に試験の準備をしましたか)という文を間接疑問にして，know の後ろに置いた形。下線部が SV の語順(he has prepared)になる。

⑦完成した文は，「あなたの友人たちがまもなく来ます。あなたの部屋をできるだけ素早くきれいにしなさい」という意味。次の形を覚えておくこと。

暗記 〈**as**＋形容詞・副詞＋**as** S **can**〉「できるだけ～」
・I ran **as fast as I could**.
(私はできるだけ速く走った)
＊下線部は as fast as possible とも言う。

⑧完成した文は，「トムは持っていた金をすべて使ってしまったので，何も買うことができなかった」という意味。spent(～を費やした)の後ろに，all the money **that** he had(彼が持っていたすべての金)を置く。that は関係代名詞で，下線部が前の the money を修飾している。この that は目的格の関係代名詞だから，省略することもできる。

⑨完成した文は，「メアリーはクラシック音楽を聞くのが大好きだ。彼女は私の2倍のCDを持っている」という意味。形を確認しよう。
・She has **twice as many CDs as** I (do).
下線部が「2倍の数のCD」という意味を表す(→ 003 -②)。many は名詞(CDs)の前に置くので，She has CDs as many as I do. と並べないように(→ 002 -⑦)。最後の do は省略してもよい(→ 008 -①)。

⑩完成した文は，「私はあなたに，先週私たちのプロジェクトチームに加わった男性に会ってもらいたい。彼はビジネスにおいて豊富な経験を持っている」という意味。〈**want** ＋ O ＋ **to** ***do***〉(Oに～してもらいたい)の形を利用する(→ 002 -④)。the man **who** joined ～は「～に加わった男性」で，下線部の関係詞節が前の the man を修飾している。

009 ① **not to play with you but to take the examination**
② **A lot of interesting classes make my school life enjoyable**
③ **how many times you were told to**
④ **afraid that I don't know what to**
⑤ **cried because of the earthquake that happened this**
⑥ **long have you been learning swimming from**
⑦ **the second tallest tower that I have ever**
⑧ **will cook the fish my father caught this morning**

解説 ①次の形が重要。

暗記 **not A but B = B, not A**「**A**でなく**B**」
この形では，「but ＝しかし」とは訳さない。
・She is **not** a nurse **but** a doctor.
＝ She is a doctor, **not** a nurse.
(彼女は看護師ではなく医師です)
この問いの文で確認してみよう。
・I came here **not** to play with you **but**
A
to take the examination.
B
AとBはどちらも「～するために」の意味を表す不定詞だから，「私はここに来た」＋「Aをするためではなく B をするために」という意味になる。

② make を使った第5文型(SVOC)の文。〈make ＋ O ＋ C〉で「OをCにする」という意味を表す(→ 001 -①)。
・A lot of interesting classes make
S V
my school life enjoyable.
O C
この文を直訳すると，「多くの興味深い授業が，私の学校生活を楽しくする」となる。無生物主語構文の一種である。

文法 無生物主語(構文)

英語では，無生物を主語にして「物[ことがら]が(人に対して)～する」のような意味を表すことがある。このような形を無生物主語構文と言う。いくつか例を見てみよう。

・This song **made** the singer famous.
（この歌がその歌手を有名にした[その歌手はこの歌によって有名になった]）

・The Internet **enables** us to communicate easily.（インターネットは私たちが簡単にコミュニケーションをとることを可能にする[インターネットのおかげで私たちは簡単にコミュニケーションをとることができる]）

＊enable O to *do*「O が～することを可能にする」

・What **brought** you here?
（何があなたをここへ連れて来たのですか[あなたはなぜここへ来たのですか]）

・Ten minutes' walk **took** us to the beach.
（10分の歩行が私たちをビーチへ連れて行った[私たちは10分歩いてビーチに着いた]）

このような定型表現で使う動詞は数が限られているので，文法・作文問題でしばしば問われる。

③不要な語は did。remember(～を覚えている)の後ろに間接疑問を置いた文で，もとの疑問文は次の形。

・How many times were you told to do your homework?
（あなたは宿題をするよう何回言われましたか）

肯定文に直すと，たとえば次のようになる。

(a) You **were told to do** your homework three times.
（あなたは宿題をするよう 3 回言われた）

この文は，次の文をもとにしている。

(b) I **told** you **to do** your homework three times.
　　S　V　O
（私はあなたに宿題をするよう 3 回言った）

＊〈tell ＋ O ＋ to *do*〉「O に～するように言う」

(b)の O に当たる you を主語にして受動態の文を作ると，(a)になる。これを一般的な形で表すと，次のようになる。

暗記 〈S ＋ V ＋ O ＋ **to** ***do***〉「S は O に～するよう[することを]…する」
→〈O ＋受動態[**be** 動詞＋過去分詞]＋ **to** ***do***〉「O は～するよう[することを]…される」

この形でよく使われる動詞は，tell の他，ask(頼む)，allow(許す)，advise(助言する)，force(強制する)，expect(期待する)など。

・I **was asked to make** a speech.
（私はスピーチをするよう頼まれた）

・We **are** not **allowed to use** this room.
（私たちはこの部屋を使うことを許されていない）

④ I don't know what to do は「私は何をすべきかを知らない[わからない]」。**I'm afraid (that) ....** は「残念ながら[申し訳ないが]…」の意味。不要な語は of。

文法 前置詞と接続詞の使い分け

暗記 前置詞の後ろには名詞(のかたまり)を置く。接続詞の後ろには SV を含む形を置く。

(a) I'm **afraid of** making mistakes.
　　　　　　　　名詞句
（私はミスをすることが怖い）

(b) I'm **afraid that** I might make mistakes.
　　　　　　　　S　V
（私はミスをするかもしれないことが怖い）

(a)の of(前置詞)の後ろには，名詞の働きをするもの(動名詞を使った句)を置く。(b)の that(接続詞)の後ろには，SV を含む形を置く。

④では，I'm afraid that I don't know .... のように SV の形を使うので，この that を of で置き換えることはできない。

⑤不要な語は for。「今朝の地震で」を，because of 〈the earthquake **that** happened this morning〉(今朝起きた地震のために)と表現する。〈　〉は全体として名詞のかたまりになっている(that は主格の関係代名詞)。次の例を参照。

(a) I was absent from school **because of** my cold.
　　前置詞　名詞(句)
（私は風邪のために学校を休んだ）

(b) I was absent from school **because** I had a cold.
　　接続詞　S　V
（私は風邪をひいていたので学校を休んだ）

(a)の because of(～の(理由の)ために)は前置詞の一種だから，後ろには名詞(句)を置く。一方，(b)の because(…なので)は接続詞だから，後ろには SV の形を置く。この問いの場合，... because of the earthquake happened this morning と並べることはできない(前置詞の because of の後ろに下線部の SV が続くことになるから)。

⑥たとえば I **have been learning** swimming 〈for six months〉. (私は6か月間(ずっと)水泳を習っている)という文の〈 〉を，How long(どのくらい長く)で尋ねる疑問文を考える。下線部は現在完了進行形で，不要な語は learned。この文の V は3語(have been learning)だから，疑問文を作るときはその最初の語(have)を S の前に置いて，How long have you been learning swimming? とする(→ 005 －⑤)。

文法 現在完了形と現在完了進行形

現在完了形は「過去から現在に至るまでの時間」を意識した時制である。次の4つの意味と形を覚えておこう。

■完了・結果(現在完了形)

(a) I **have caught** a cold.
(私は風邪をひいた(今も治っていない))

■経験(現在完了形)

(b) I **have** never **seen** a French movie.
(私はフランス映画を一度も見たことがない)

■状態の継続(現在完了形)

(c) I **have known** him for ten years.
(私は10年間[10年前から]ずっと彼を知っている)

■動作の継続(現在完了進行形)

(d) I **have been learning** the piano for ten years.
(私は10年間ずっとピアノを習っている)

(c)と(d)の違いを理解するには，動詞が次の2種類に分類されることを知っておく必要がある。

(1)動作動詞＝行為や出来事を表す(例：walk，die)
(2)状態動詞＝状態を表す(例：have，know)

(1)型の動詞は，「(今)～している」の意味を現在進行形で表す。一方(2)型の動詞には，進行形にできないという特徴がある。

(e) I **am having** lunch. (私は昼食を食べている)
(f) I **have** [×am having] a sister.
(私には姉[妹]がいる)

(e)の have は「～を食べる」の意味の動作動詞で，「(今)食べている」は現在進行形で表す。一方(f)の have(～を持っている)は状態動詞であり，進行形にできない。区別の目安としては，「～しつつある[～している最中だ]」と言える動詞は動作動詞，言えない動詞は状態動詞である。(c)の know は「知りつつある」とは言えないから状態動詞。(d)の learn は「学びつつある」と言えるから動作動詞。そこで，(c)と(d)を改めて見てみよう。

(c) I **have known** him for ten years.
　現在完了形
(私は10年前からずっと彼を知っている)

(d) I **have been learning** the piano for ten years.
　現在完了進行形
(私は10年間ずっとピアノを習っている)

(d)のように，過去から現在まで継続している動作[行為・出来事]を表すには，現在完了進行形(have [has]＋been＋現在分詞)を使う。次のように考えるとよい。

(1)現在完了形(**have [has]**＋過去分詞)
(2)進行形(**be動詞**＋現在分詞)
→(1)と(2)を組み合わせると，□の2つが合体して **be** 動詞の過去分詞(**been**)に変化する。

[参考] (c)の know は状態動詞だから進行形にできない。したがって，現在完了進行形(have been knowing)にもできない。

⑦次の形を覚えておくこと。

暗記 〈**the** ＋序数詞＋最上級の形容詞＋ **X**[名詞]〉
「(上から数えて)～番目に…な **X**」

「序数詞」とは，「～番目(の)」を表す second，third，fourth などのこと。この問いの「2番目に高い塔」は，the second tallest tower で表す。不要な語は taller。

[参考] 「1番目に[最も]～な」は最上級だけで表す(「一番高い塔」は the first tallest tower ではなく the tallest tower)。

⑧全部の語(句)を使えば，次の文を作ることができる。

・My sister will cook the fish caught by my father this morning.

これは正しい文で，下線部(過去分詞句)が前の the fish を修飾する形になる。しかし「不要な語(句)が1つ含まれている」という条件を満たすには，次のように並べる必要がある。

・My sister will cook the fish my father caught this morning.

この文の下線部は関係詞節であり，my father の前に which [that] (目的格の関係代名詞)を補って考えることができる。不要な語は by。

010 ① **my mother asked me to come home as soon**
② **I couldn't answer the questions asked by the American lady**
③ **was so wet that we couldn't sit on it**
④ **French students that I met were impressed with the beauty**
⑤ **Nothing is as important as having good friends in**
⑥ **We have known each other for five years**
⑦ **Many people were injured in the accident**
⑧ **It will be my first trip abroad**
⑨ **These photos remind me of my childhood**

解説 ①〈**ask** ＋ O ＋ **to** ***do***〉「O に～するよう頼む」，**as soon as** ～「～するとすぐに」(接続詞)。不要な語は please。

② the questions (which was) asked by the American lady は「そのアメリカ人女性によって尋ねられた質問」。下線部が前の名詞を修飾している。不要な語は was。

③ **so** ～ **that ...**(非常に～なので…)の形を利用する。不要な語は too。次のような言い換えができることも知っておこう(→ 001 -②)。

・The grass was **so wet that we couldn't sit on it**.
＝The grass was **too wet for us to sit on**.
(草は私たちが(上に)座るにはぬれすぎていた)
＊too を使った文では，on の後ろに it は不要。

④不要な語は them。The French students **(that)** I met で「私が会ったフランス人の学生たち」という意味を表す(下線部が前の名詞を修飾している)。that(目的格の関係代名詞)は省略してもよい。be impressed with [by] ～は「～に(よって)感銘を受ける」という意味。

⑤不要な語は anything。次の形は重要。

暗記 〈**Nothing is as** ＋(原級の)形容詞＋ **as** ～.〉「～ほど…なものはない」
次のような言い換えも覚えておこう。

・**Nothing is as important as** friendship.
(友情ほど大切なものはない)
＝**Nothing is more important than** friendship.
(友情よりも大切なものはない)
＝Friendship is **more important than anything else**.
(友情は他の何よりも大切だ)
＝Friendship is **the most important** (thing).
(友情は最も大切(なもの)だ)

⑥完成した文の意味は，「私たちは5年間ずっとお互いを知っている[私たちはお互いに知り合ってから5年になる]」。不要な語は with。

注意！ **each other**(お互い)は代名詞の働きをする。
・We know each other.
　S　V　O
(私たちはお互いに知り合いです)
＊each other は know の目的語の働きをしている。
・We talked with each other.
　S　V
(私たちはお互い(と)話し合った)
＊たとえば「彼と話す」は talk with him。同様に「お互いと話す」は talk with each other。この with を入れ忘れないように。

⑦完成した文の意味は，「多くの人々がその事故でけがをした」。不要な語は have。injure は「(人)を負傷させる」という意味の動詞で，「(人が)負傷する，けがをする」は **be injured**(負傷させられる)という受動態で表す。

⑧完成した文の意味は，「それは私の初めての外国旅行になるだろう」。不要な語は to。trip abroad は「外国への旅行」の意味。abroad は副詞なので前に to をつけない(→ 015 -②， 030 -②)。

⑨不要な語は remember。次の形を覚えておくこと。

暗記 S **remind(s)** O **of** ～「S[物]は O[人]に～を思い出させる」
(a) These photos **remind** me **of** my childhood. (これらの写真は私に子どものころを思い出させる)

(b)I **remember** my childhood when I see these photos.（これらの写真を見ると私は子どものころを思い出す）

(a)は無生物主語構文の一種で，(b)のように言い換えることができる（→ 009 -②）。

011
① **All you have to do is wear this uniform and walk with them**
② **parents never go to Hokkaido without staying at the hotel**
③ **played basketball for the first time in three years**
④ **Have you found the book I asked you to look for**
⑤ **Deciding when to upgrade our smartphones is harder than**
⑥ **clever he is by counting the number of riddles that**
⑦ **about learning is that no one can take it away**

解説 ①S is to *do*.（Sは～することだ）の形の一種。次の2つをセットで覚えておこう。

暗記 **All** S **have[has] to do is (to)** ***do***.「Sは～しさえすればよい」

暗記 **All** S **can do is (to)** ***do***.「Sは～するしかない」

・All you have to do is (to) wait here.
　S　V　C
（あなたはここで待つだけでよい）

＊直訳は「あなたがしなければならないすべてのことは，ここで待つことだ」。Allの後ろにthat(目的格の関係代名詞)が省略された形。isの後ろのtoは省略できる。

・All we could do was (to) wait there.
　S　V　C
（私たちはそこで待つしかなかった）

＊直訳は「私たちにすることができたすべてのことは，そこで待つことだった」。上の文と同様の形。

この問いは，次の形になっている。

・All you have to do is (to) wear this uniform ....
　S　V　C

なお，この文は次のようにも表現できる。

・You **only have to wear** this uniform ....

＊**only have[have only] to** ***do***「～しさえすればよい」

②次の形を覚えておくこと。

暗記 **never[can't]** V **without ～ing**「～せずにVすることは決してない[できない]，Vすれば必ず～する」

・My aunt **never** comes to my house **without giving** me something.（おばは私に何かをくれずに私の家に来ることは決してない[おばが私の家に来るときはいつでも私に何かをくれる]）

＊My aunt always gives me something when she comes to my house. と言い換えることができる。

③次の形を覚えておくこと。

暗記 **for the first time in** ～「～ぶりに」

・It snowed this morning **for the first time in** three years.
（けさ3年ぶりに雪が降った）

④完成した文の形を確認しよう。

・Have you found the book (which) I asked you to look for?

下線部(関係詞節)が前の名詞を修飾している。which(目的格の関係代名詞)が省略された形で，I asked you to look for the book.（私はその本を探すよう君に頼んだ）という文をもとにして考える。

⑤動名詞(動詞の原形＋ing)は「～すること」の意味を表し，SやOなどの働きをする。

・**Playing** this game is fun.
　S　V　C
（このゲームをするの[プレーすること]は楽しい）

この問いの場合も，Deciding(～を決めること)で始まる動名詞句をSの位置に置けばよい。

・**Deciding** when to upgrade our smartphones
　S
is harder than we imagine.
V　C

Sのwhen to *do*は「いつ～すべきか」の意味。upgradeは「等級(grade)を上げる」の意味で，この文では「(スマートフォンをより高性能な機種に)買い替える」という意味で使っている。

⑥「数えて」をby countingという形で表すのがポイント(countingは動名詞)。by ～ingは「～することによって」の意味(→ 006 -⑤)。the number of riddles that he can solveは「彼が解くことのできるなぞなぞの数」。thatは目的格の関係代名詞で，下線部が前のriddles(なぞなぞ)を修飾している。

⑦S is C(SはCだ)のCの位置に，that(接続詞)で始まる名詞節を置いた形。

暗記 S **is that ....**「Sは…ということだ」

・The problem is that we don't have enough time.
　S: The problem　V: is　C: that we don't have enough time
(問題は私たちに十分な時間がないということだ)

＊thatは「…ということ」という意味の名詞節を作る接続詞。I think that ....(私は…だと思う)のthatと同じ。

この問いの文の構造も確認しておこう。

・The beautiful thing about learning is that no one can take it away.
　S(学びに関して素晴らしいこと): The beautiful thing about learning　V: is　C(誰もそれを奪えないということ): that no one can take it away

文法 句と節

２語以上でまとまった意味を表す形には，次の２種類がある。

句＝SVの形を含まない意味のかたまり
節＝SVの形を含む意味のかたまり

句や節は，名詞・形容詞・副詞のどれかの働きをする。

・The book on the desk is mine.
　形容詞句: on the desk
(机の上の本は私のです)

＊下線部はSVを含まないから句であり，前の名詞(The book)を修飾する形容詞の働きをしている。

・I went to the U.S. when I was a child.
　副詞節: when I was a child
(子どものとき私はアメリカへ行った)

＊下線部はS(I)＋V(was)を含むから節であり，前の動詞(went)を修飾する副詞の働きをしている。

Q&A

Q take it awayは，take away itとはならないのですか？

A はい。この点を理解するには，次のような文法知識が必要です。

まず，英語の動詞は，「後ろにO(目的語)を置くかどうか」によって次の２種類に分類されます。

(1)自動詞＝後ろにOを置かない動詞
(2)他動詞＝後ろにOを置く動詞

・A boy is walking (in the park).
　S: A boy　V: is walking
(男の子が(公園の中で)歩いている)

＊後ろにOがないので，walk(歩く)は自動詞。in the parkは(省いても文が成り立つので)Oではなく修飾語。一般に前置詞で始まる句は修飾語であり，Oにはなれない。

・I have a puppy.(私は子犬を飼っている)
　S: I　V: have　O: a puppy

＊後ろにOがあるので，have(～を持っている)は他動詞。

［参考］１つの動詞が自動詞・他動詞の両方の用法を持つこともよくある。たとえばwalk a dog(犬を散歩させる)のwalkは他動詞。５文型との対応で言えば，第１文型(SV)・第２文型(SVC)で使う動詞は自動詞，第３文型(SVO)・第４文型(SVOO)・第５文型(SVOC)で使う動詞は他動詞。

次に，２語以上がまとまって１つの動詞の意味を表すものを，句動詞[群動詞]と言います。たとえばlook for(～を探す)，take care of(～の世話をする)など。句動詞にも，自動詞と他動詞があります。

・I get up at six.(私は６時に起きます)
　S: I　V: get up

＊get up(起きる)は自動詞の働きをする句動詞。

・I looked for the shop.(私はその店を探した)
　S: I　V: looked for　O: the shop

＊look for(～を探す)は他動詞の働きをする句動詞。

句動詞には，〈動詞＋前置詞〉または〈動詞＋副詞〉の形のものがたくさんあります。たとえばget upのupは副詞，look forのforは前置詞です。

この問いで使われているtake awayは，「～を持ち去る，奪い去る」という意味の他動詞の働きをする句動詞で，awayは副詞です。このタイプの句動詞は，次のように使います。

暗記 〈動詞＋副詞〉の形の句動詞が他動詞の働きをするとき，代名詞のOは副詞の前に置く。

これは少し複雑なルールなので，いくつかの例で説明します。

(a) I looked for the shop[it].
　S: I　V: looked for　O: the shop[it]
(私はその店[それ]を探した)

＊for(前置詞)は名詞・代名詞の前に置くので，looked the store for，looked it forとは

言わない。

(b) We gave up the plan.
 S V O
=We gave the plan up.
(私たちはその計画をあきらめた)

＊give up(～をあきらめる)の up は副詞。名詞の目的語(the plan)は，up の前後どちらに置いてもよい。

(c) We gave it up. [×We gave up it.]
(私たちはそれをあきらめた)

＊give up の目的語が代名詞(it)のときは，副詞(up)の前に置かねばならない。

この問いの take away(～を奪い去る)の away も副詞なので，「それを奪い去る」は take it away と言います。(c)と同様に，take away it は誤りです。

ここで当然，「前置詞と副詞はどのように区別するのか？」という疑問が起こるでしょう。目安としては，「**away**，**back**，**down**，**out**，**up** などは副詞」と覚えてください。たとえば call back (後でまた[折り返し]電話する)の back は副詞です。したがって，give up と同様に，「あなたに後で電話します」は I'll call you back. と言います(つまり，代名詞の目的格である you を副詞の back の前に置きます)。これを I'll call back you. と言うことはできません。

［参考］ in，off，on，over は前置詞または副詞として使う。たとえば get on the bus は「バスの上に乗る」という意味だから，on は前置詞。したがって「それに乗る」は get on it と言う。一方 put on a shirt(シャツを着る)の場合，「シャツの上に」という意味ではないから on は前置詞でなく副詞。したがって「それを着る」は put it on と言う。

012 ① **No one understands what to do about**
② **sitting next to me ran away as soon**
③ **not be able to walk as fast as before**
④ **on their way of looking at the things**
⑤ **technology has made our lives more convenient in**

解説 ①完成した文の意味は，「その問題について何をすべきかを理解している人は誰もいない」。不要な語は doesn't。No one understands で「誰も理解していない」という否定の意味になるので，doesn't は必要ない。

［参考］ No one doesn't understand のように否定語(no と doesn't)を２つ並べて使うことはない。

②完成した文の意味は，「私の隣に座っていたそのお年寄りは，電車が渋谷駅で止まるとすぐに走り去った」。The old man (who was) sitting next to me の下線部が前の名詞を修飾する形。この who was は省略できるが，who だけを省くことはできないから，不要な語は was。as soon as は「…するとすぐに」の意味の接続詞。

③ will の後ろには not be able to(～できない)を続ける。walk as fast as before は「以前と同じくらい速く歩く」。前に not があるので，「以前ほど速く歩けない」という意味になる。

全訳
クマは冬の間ずっと，約６か月間眠る。そんなに長い間あまり動かないのに，春になって(巣から)出てくるとすぐに，苦もなくあちこちを歩き回ったり走り回ったりできる。しかし，人間にはそんなことはできない。患者が寝たきりで全く動かない場合，１週間かそこらで以前ほど速く歩けなくなる。いつか科学者たちは，長い間床についていた後で特別な世話を必要とする人々を助けるために，クマの驚異的な体についてより多くのことを解明するかもしれない。

語句
even though ～「～だけれど」
walk[run] around「歩き[走り]回る」
without any trouble「何も苦労しないで」
soon after ～「～のすぐ後で」 patient「患者」
～ or so「～かそこら」
find out ～「～を(調べて)発見する，解明する」
amazing「驚異的な，見事な」 care「世話」

④次の形を覚えておこう。

暗記 **depend on** ～「～に左右される，～しだいだ」

暗記 **A's way of ～ing**「A が～する方法」

完成した文は次のとおりで，不要な語は how。

・It depends on 〈their way of looking at the things they have〉.

〈 〉の部分は，It depends on X.(それは X しだいだ[X によって決まる])という形の X に当たる。下線部は前の the things を修飾する関係詞節で，which（目的格の関係代名詞）が省略されている。they は前の文の people を指す。

全訳

2010年にワールドカップが初めてアフリカに来た［で開催された］とき，ヨーロッパのある写真家がアフリカへ行った。彼女はそこで10か国を回り，地元のサッカーチームで働く人々と話した。サッカーのコーチの1人は，人々はサッカーが本当に大好きで，サッカーは人々を団結させると言った。フィールドとボールとゴールしか必要ないので，誰でもこのスポーツをすることができる。子どもたちはゴミでサッカーボールを作り，それで遊ぶ。あまりお金がないときでも，人々は幸せに暮らすことができる。それは自分が持っているものの見方によって決まる。

語句

photographer「写真家」　coach「コーチ，監督」
bring ～ together「～を団結させる」
field「（サッカーの）フィールド，競技場，野原」
garbage「ゴミ」

⑤完成した文は次のとおり。

Information technology has made our lives more convenient in many ways.
（Information technology = S，has made = V，our lives = O，more convenient = C）

〈make + O + C〉の形で「O を C にする」という意味を表す。in many ways は「多くの点で」。直訳すると「情報技術は多くの点で私たちの生活をより便利にした」となる。不要な語は been。

全訳

コンピューターやインターネットがない生活を想像できるだろうか。この50年ほどの間に私たちはこの技術を開発し，それが私たちの生活を大きく変えた。コンピューターを使うことによって，人々は机を離れることなく情報を探したり，メッセージを送ったり，話したりすることさえもできる。これは学校にも職場にも当てはまる。情報技術によって，私たちの生活は多くの点でより便利になった。今日では学生たちは教室の外で学ぶことができるし，人々は自宅で仕事をすることができる。

語句

imagine「～を想像する」　develop「～を開発する」
technology「科学技術」　message「メッセージ」
outside「～の外で」

013（下線の語を補う）

① **What do you think is the easiest to cook**
② **aren't very different from those of softball**
③ **The more famous you become**
④ **Let me know what made you angry**
⑤ **of you to buy the books for me**
⑥ **What are you looking forward to doing after the exam is**
⑦ **We were surprised at how large the country's population was**
⑧ **We might not be able to find one［another］ for a while from here**

解説 ①次の点がポイント。

暗記 疑問詞を含む文を間接疑問として **do you think** の後ろに置くときは，疑問詞を文頭に出す。

次の2つの文を比較してみよう。

(a) Do you know who he is?
（彼は誰なのかを知っていますか）

＊Who is he?（彼は誰ですか）という疑問文を間接疑問にして，know の後ろに置いたもの。この文では，Yes か No か（知っているかどうか）を尋ねている。

(b) **Who do you think** he is?
（彼は誰だと思いますか）

＊(a)と同じように Do you think +〈who he is〉? と考えるが，この文で尋ねているのは「彼は誰か」ということだから，質問の中心となる who を前に出す。

この問いは，(b)と同様に考える。

・What is the easiest to cook from now?
（What = S，is = V，the easiest to cook = C）
（何が今から一番簡単に作れますか）

この文を間接疑問にして Do you think の後ろに置くと，次のようになる。

・Do you think 〈what is the easiest to

cook from now〉?

＊もとの疑問文では what が S なので，〈 〉内の語順は変化しない。

この文から，質問の中心となる what を前に出すと，正解の文が完成する。

②日本文は，I think the rules of baseball aren't very different from the rules of softball. と表現できる（be different from ～「～とは異なる」）。この文の下線部を，同じ名詞のくり返しを避けるために those で置き換えた形（→ 016 -①）。

③次の形は重要。

暗記 **〈The ＋比較級＋ S_1 ＋ V_1, the ＋比較級＋ S_2 ＋ V_2.〉**「S_1 が V_1 すればするほど，それだけいっそう S_2 は V_2 する」

・**The harder** you practice, **the better** you can play.

（you = S_1, practice = V_1, you = S_2, can play = V_2）

（熱心に練習すればするほど，あなたは上手にプレーできる）

2つの〈the ＋比較級〉の後ろに SV の形を置くのがポイント。この問いでは，You become famous.（あなたは有名になる）という文の famous を the more famous に変え，その後ろに you become を続けて，「あなたが有名になればなるほど」という意味を表す。

④ let は使役動詞で，**Let me *do*.**（私に～させて（ください））という形でよく使う。

・**Let me try** this puzzle.

（このパズルを私にやらせて）

この問いの **Let me know** ～は，「～を私に知らせて［教えて］（ください）」の意味。その後ろに，次の文を間接疑問として置く。

・What made you angry?

（What = S, made = V, you = O, angry = C）

（何があなたを怒らせたのか［あなたはなぜ怒ったのか］）

＊〈make ＋ O ＋ C〉（O を C にする）の形を使った無生物主語構文（→ 009 -②）。

文法 原形不定詞と組み合わせて使う動詞

原形不定詞とは，to のない（動詞の原形だけの）不定詞のこと。主に次の2つの形で使う。

⑴使役動詞など

暗記 let O *do* ＝ O に～させておく，O が～するのを許す

暗記 make O *do* ＝ O に（むりやり）～させる

暗記 have O *do* ＝ O に～してもらう［させる］

暗記 help O (to) *do* ＝ O が～するのを助ける

⑵知覚動詞

暗記 see O *do* ＝ O が～するのが見える

暗記 hear O *do* ＝ O が～するのが聞こえる

・What **made you change** your mind?

（何があなたを心変わりさせたのですか［あなたはなぜ気が変わったのですか］）

・I'll **have someone copy** this paper.

（誰かにこの書類をコピーしてもらいます）

・I'll **help you (to) wash** the dishes.

（あなたが皿を洗うのを手伝いましょう）

＊to は入れても入れなくてもよい。

・I **heard someone call(ing)** my name.

（誰かが私の名前を呼ぶ［呼んでいる］のが聞こえた）

＊原形不定詞の代わりに現在分詞（calling）を使うと，「O が～しているのが聞こえる」という意味になる。

・I **saw some boys play(ing)** soccer.

（何人かの男の子がサッカーをする［している］のが見えた）

＊この文も同様。play なら「（プレー）する」，playing なら「（プレー）している」という意味。

⑤ It と不定詞を組み合わせた文として，次の2つの形を覚えておこう。

暗記 **〈It is ＋形容詞＋ for X to *do*.〉**「～することは X にとって…だ」

暗記 **〈It is ＋人の性格を表す形容詞＋ of X to *do*.〉**「～するとは X は…（な人）だ」

・**It is difficult for me 〈to solve** this problem〉.

（この問題を解くことは私にとって難しい）

＊〈To solve this problem〉 is difficult for me. という文をもとにして，〈 〉を後ろへ回して，その位置に It（形式主語）を置いた形。「It は私にとって難しい」＋「It とはこの問題を解くことだ」のように考える。

・**It is kind of you to help** me.

＝ You are kind to help me.（私を手伝ってくれるとは（あなたは）親切だ）

＊この形の文では，〈of ＋人〉を使う。この形で使う主な形容詞は，kind［nice］（親切な），foolish（愚かな），wise（賢明な），clever［smart］（利口な），careless（不注意な）など。

この問いの nice は kind（親切な）の意味で，It

was nice of you to *do*. で「～するとはあなたは親切だった」という意味を表す。

⑥次の形はよく問われる。

暗記 **look forward to ～ing**「～することを楽しみにしている」

・I'm **looking forward to** seeing you again.
(あなたにまた会うのを楽しみにしています)

＊この形の to は前置詞だから，後ろには動名詞(seeing)を置く。不定詞(to see)と混同しないように。

上の文の下線部を尋ねる疑問文は，What are you looking forward to doing?(あなたは何をするのが楽しみですか)となる。この問いではその形を利用する。

⑦ be surprised at ～(～に驚く)の後ろに，次の感嘆文を置いた形。

・How large the country's population is!
　　C　　　　　　S　　　　　　　V
(その国の人口は何と多いことか！)

＊is は前の were (surprised) との時制の一致で was になる。間接疑問と同じ理屈で SV の語順になるが，感嘆文自体が SV なので語順は変わらない。

Q&A

Q 上の疑問文で，How many や How much ではなく How large を使うのはなぜですか？

A 名詞の中には，それ自体が数量の意味を含むものがあります。たとえば，**number**(数)，**amount**(量)，**population**(人口)，**price**(値段)，**income**(収入)などです。これらの名詞の数量の大小は，**large**・**small** や **high**・**low** で表します。

・a large[small] number(多い[少ない]数)
・a high[low] price(高い[安い]値段)

したがって，「多い人口」は a large population と言い，many[much] population とは言いません。だから人口について「どのくらい多いか」を尋ねるときは，How large を使います。

⑧「私たちはガソリンスタンドを見つけられないかもしれない」は，We might not be able to find a gas station. と表現できる。しかし最初の文にも gas station が出てくるので，同じ言葉のくり返しを避けるために，下線部を one で置き換える。another gas station(もう１つのガソリンスタンド)の意味で another を使ってもよい。one の使い方を確認しておこう。

・My bicycle was broken, so I want to buy one.
(自転車が壊れたので，１台買いたい)

＊one = a bicycle。one の代わりに it を使うことはできない(「私の持っている(壊れた)自転車を買う」ことになるから)。「新しい自転車を１台買いたい」なら，... to buy a new one. と言う。

014 (⑥・⑦は下線の語を補う)

① **I bought the day before yesterday is different from hers**
② **She has not finished doing the homework yet**
③ **is no other mountain so beautiful as Mt. Fuji**
④ **The door must not be left open**
⑤ **was such a beautiful morning that they went for**
⑥ **Things like this happen when you don't charge your battery**
⑦ **How did you know you were lied to**

解説 ① **be different from** ～(～とは異なる)という表現を利用して，A is different from B. (A は B とは異なる)という形を作る。A は The bag (which) I bought the day before yesterday (私が一昨日買ったかばん)，B は hers(＝her bag)。

暗記 **the day before yesterday**「一昨日」

暗記 **the day after tomorrow**「あさって」

② finish の後ろは動名詞を置いて，「～し終える」の意味を表す。finish doing the homework は「宿題をし終える」。「まだ～していない」は，現在完了形の文の最後に yet を置いて表す。

③次の形はセットで覚えておこう。

暗記 **No other X is as[so] ～ as Y.**「他の

どのXもYほど～ではない」

暗記 **〈No other X is ＋比較級＋ than Y.〉**「他のどのXもYより～ではない」

暗記 **〈Y is ＋ 比較級 ＋ than any other X.〉**「Yは他のどのXよりも～だ」

(a) **No other** mountain in Japan is **as[so] high as** Mt. Fuji.
（日本の他のどの山も富士山ほど高くない）

(b) **No other** mountain in Japan is **higher than** Mt. Fuji.
（日本の他のどの山も富士山より高くない）

(c) Mt. Fuji is **higher than any other** mountain in Japan.
（富士山は日本の他のどの山よりも高い）

(d) Mt. Fuji is **the highest** mountain in Japan.
（富士山は日本で一番高い山だ）

＊これら4つの文は，(ほぼ)同じ意味を表す。(a)～(c)では，otherの後ろに単数形の名詞(mountain)を置く。

この問いでは(a)の形を利用して，次の文を作る。

・There is no other mountain (which is) so beautiful as Mt. Fuji in the world.
（世界中で富士山ほど美しい他の山はない）

＊下線部が前の名詞を修飾する形。

④ leave the door open(ドアを開けたままにしておく)というVOCの形を受動態にして，the door is left open(ドアが開いたままにされる)という形を作り，このisをmust beで置き換える。「～してはいけません」なのでmust not beとなる。

⑤次の形を覚えておこう。

暗記 **〈such a[an]＋形容詞＋X[名詞]＋that ...〉**「とても～なXなので…」

この問いでは，It was such a beautiful morning that ....(とても美しい朝だったので…)となる。aの位置に注意。

［参考］この形では，suchをsoで置き換えることはできない。soを使って言い換えれば，The morning was so beautiful that .... となる。

⑥「充電できるときにしておかないと」は，when you don't charge your battery when you canと表現できる(同じ言葉のくり返しを避けるために，canの後ろには下線部が省略されている)。残る語はhappen，things，thisだが，this things happenとは言えない(thisの後ろには単数形の名詞を置くので，この形ならthis thing happensとなるはず)。そこでlike(～のような)を補って，things like this happen(このようなことが起こる)という形にする。

⑦「どうしてわかったのですか」は，How did you knowと表現できる。残る語はlied，were，youだが，knowの後ろにthatを補ってHow did you know that you were lied?とするのは誤り。下線部を能動態で表現すると，that someone lied youではなくthat someone lied to you(誰かがあなたにうそをついた)。したがって「あなたは(誰かに)うそをつかれた」は，you were lied to (by someone)となるので，toを補うのが正しい。

015 ①(1) **grew up in a house surrounded by**
(2) **looked forward to hearing the birds**
②(1) **go abroad to teach the people**
(2) **to help young children with reading**
③(1) **other species that need it**
(2) **leave flowers as they are**

解説 ①(1) grow upは「(人が)育つ」。a house (which was) surrounded by woodsは「森に囲まれた家」(下線部が前の名詞を修飾する形)。この前の文のthe environment surrounding usは，the environment which surrounds us(私たちを取り囲む環境)の意味。

(2) look forward to ～ing「～するのを楽しみにする」(→ 013 -⑥)

全訳

レイチェル・カーソンは自然科学作家として知られている。彼女の著書『沈黙の春』は，汚染の危険性と，それが私たちを取り巻く環境に与える影響を私たちに教えてくれる。彼女はペンシルベニア州西部の森に囲まれた家で育った。毎朝彼女は窓の外の鳥の声を聞くのを楽しみにしていた。登校中に，彼女はしばしばまるで友だちのように鳥に話しかけた。彼女は自然界への驚異の念を育んだ。著作の中で彼女は，子どもたちに地球の声を聞くよう教えている。

語句

danger「危険(性)」 pollution「汚染，公害」
surround「～を取り囲む」 western「西部の」
develop「～を発達させる」
a sense of wonder「驚異の念，驚きの感覚」

②(1) go abroad(外国へ行く) + to teach the people(人々に教えるために)と並べる。次の点が重要。

暗記 副詞の前には前置詞をつけない。

よく問われる形は，**go there**(そこへ行く)，**get there**(そこに着く)，**go abroad**(外国へ行く)，**go home**(家へ帰る)，**on one's way home**(家へ帰る途中で)など。there, abroad, homeは副詞であり，たとえばabroadは「外国へ[に，で]」の意味。したがってgo(行く) + abroad(外国へ)と言えばよく，go to abroadは誤り。これに関連して，次の点も覚えておこう。

暗記 **this, last, next** などを使った「時を表す副詞句」の前には前置詞や**the**をつけない。

・I got up early **this morning**.
(けさは早く起きた)
＊「朝に」はin the morningだが，この文ではin this morningとはしない。
・I played tennis **last Sunday**.
(先週の日曜日にテニスをした)
＊「日曜日に」はon Sundayだが，on[the] last Sundayとはしない。
・We have an English test **next week**.
(私たちは来週英語のテストがある)

[参考] 過去や未来のある時点から見て「その翌週」という意味を表すときはthe next weekと言う。同様に「その前の日曜日に」はthe last Sunday。

(2) help young children to readingと並べないように。「小さな子どもたちが読むのを助ける」なら，help young children to readとなる(help + O + (to) *do*「Oが～するのを助ける」)。この問いではwithがあるので，次の形を使う。

暗記 **help O with ～**「O[人]の～を手伝う」

・I'll **help** you **with** the dishes.
((あなたが)皿を洗うのを手伝いましょう)

この問いでは，to **help** young children **with** reading and math(小さな子どもたちの読書や算数(の勉強)を手助けするために)という形を作る。

全訳

ボランティア活動に興味はありますか。ボランティア活動をすることは，新しい場所を見たり，新しい人に出会ったりする素晴らしい方法です。またボランティアたちは，多くの子どもや大人が，生活を通して役立つ情報を学ぶ手助けをします。世界中にボランティアの教師がいます。彼らはさまざまな方法で活動しています。あるボランティアは海外に行き，数か月から数年間，現地の人たちに教えます。自分の国にとどまるボランティアもいます。その人たちは週に1～2時間だけ学校に行き，小さな子どもの読書や算数の手助けをすることもあります。また，外国から移住してきた人たちに，その国の言葉，たとえばフランス語，スペイン語，英語などを教えることもあります。

③(1) 後ろにwill dieがあるので，並べ替えた語句はSの働きをする名詞のかたまりになるはず。そこで，other species that need it(それを必要とする他の種)と並べる。thatは関係代名詞で，下線部が前の名詞を修飾する形。itはコンマの前のone speciesを指す(speciesは単数形も複数形も同じ形)。

(2) 次の形を覚えておくこと。

暗記 **leave O as it is[they are]**「Oをそのままにしておく」

・**Leave** my desk **as it is**.
(私の机を(触らずに)そのままにしておきなさい)
＊it = my desk。asは「～のとおりに」の意味。

この問いでは，leave flowers as they areで「(散歩中に)花を(摘まずに)そのままにしておく」という意味を表す(they = flowers)。

全訳

すべての動植物は死ぬが，ある種の植物や動物がすべて死ぬとその種は絶滅する。これはその種が永遠に失われることを意味する。ある種が死ぬと，それを必要とする他の種も死ぬかもしれない。人々は地球上のすべての植物や動物を保護する必要がある。もしそうしなければ，将来多くの種が絶滅するだろう。私たちは皆，ささいな方法で動植物を守ることができる。散歩するときは，常に花を(摘まずに)そのままにしておくべきだ。そうすれば将来，その種《たね》からさらに多くの植物が育つだろう。庭や公園では，動物が食べ物や住みかとして必要とする植物を育てることができる。これらすべてが，大切な生物種を守るのに役立つだろう。

語句

species「(生物)種」 forever「永久に」
seed「(植物の)種《たね》」

016 ① **from that of the everyday office worker**
② **get about five hours of sleep a**
③ **have to get used to sleeping**
④ **to keep their food from going away**

解説 ① A is different from B.(AはBと異なる)という形を作る。Aはan astronaut's average day(宇宙飛行士の平均的な1日)。したがってBをthe office worker's average dayとすればよいが，それだとAとBの両方に下線部の言葉が入ることになる。そこで，同じ言葉のくり返しを避けるために，Bをthat of the office workerとし，これにeveryday(普通の)を加える。このthatはthe average dayの意味の代名詞。

暗記 同じ名詞のくり返しを避けるために，**that [those] of** ～という形を使うことがある。

・The population of Japan is larger than **that of** Britain.
(日本の人口はイギリスの人口より多い)

＊that = the population。このようにthat ofの形は，2つのものを比べる文でよく使われる。

・The ears of a rabbit are longer than **those of** a cat.
(ウサギの耳はネコの耳よりも長い)

＊those = the ears。複数形の名詞の代わりにはthoseを使う。

② They getの後ろにabout five hours of sleep(約5時間の睡眠)を置き，a night(1晩につき)を続ける。〈**a [an]** ＋名詞〉で「～につき」の意味を表すことができる。

・She goes to the gym twice **a week**.
(彼女は週に2回スポーツジムに通っている)

③次の表現は重要。

暗記 **get used to ～ing**「～することに慣れる」

暗記 **be used to ～ing**「～することに慣れている」

このtoは前置詞なので，後ろに動詞を置くときは動名詞にする。

・I'm not **used to speaking** in front of people.
(私は人前で話すことに慣れていない)

この問いでは，have to(～しなければならない)＋get used to sleeping(眠ることに慣れる)という形を作る。

④次の表現は重要。

暗記 **keep O from ～ing**「Oが～するのを防ぐ」

この問いでは，**keep** their food **from** going awayと並べて，「食べ物がどこかへ行ってしまうのを防ぐ」という意味にする。この文では「食事中に食べ物をこぼしてしまうと，それが機械に入り込んで故障の原因になるかもしれないので，こぼさないよう注意しなければならない」という内容を説明している。

keepと同様に，**stop**(～を止める)や**prevent**(～を防ぐ，妨げる)も**from**と結びつけて使う。

・They tried to **stop** the fire **from** spreading.
(彼らは火が広がるのを止めようとした)

・The storm **prevented [kept]** us **from** going out. (その嵐は私たちが外出するのを妨げた[その嵐のせいで私たちは外出できなかった])

語句・構文

この文章はリーディングの素材としてもレベルが高いので，語句や構文を確認しておこう。

◆Have you ever **wondered what it would be like to look out** the window of a spaceship and see the Earth below? (宇宙船の窓から眼下の地球を見るのはどんな感じだろうか，と思ったことがあるだろうか)

・wonderは「～だろうかと思う」の意味で，後ろには疑問詞やif(…かどうか)を置く。

(例)I **wonder if** it will be sunny tomorrow.
(明日は晴れるだろうか)

・この文では，wonderedの後ろにwhatで始まる間接疑問の形が置かれている。もとの疑問文は，What would it be like to look out ...?。この文は次のように考えることができる。

(1) What is X like? は「Xはどのようなもの

か」の意味(→ 005 -⑤)。

(2)このXの位置に，後ろの不定詞を指すit(形式主語)を置くと，次の形になる。

What is it like to *do*?

(～することはどのようなものか)

(3) to *do* の部分に「(実際はできないだろうが)もし～したら」という仮定の意味が含まれる場合は，is を would be で置き換えることができる。

この文の場合，「もしあなたが宇宙船の窓から外を見れば」は実現する可能性が低い仮定だから，仮定法過去の would を使っている。次の文(Can you ...?)中の would も同様。

◆ To begin with, a day in the life of an astronaut might include **as many as** 15 sunrises **as** the space station goes around the Earth. (まず第一に宇宙飛行士の生活の１日は，宇宙ステーションが地球を回る間に現れる15回もの日の出を含む)

・**as many as** ～「～もの数の」。このように原級の形容詞を使って，数量などの大きさを強調することができる。

(例) I spent **as much as** twenty thousand yen during the trip.
(私は旅行中に２万円も使った)

・３つ目の as は「…しながら，…するとき」の意味の接続詞。

◆ ..., they need to **make sure** they get enough fresh oxygen **instead of** breathing in their own exhaled carbon dioxide. (彼らは自分の吐く二酸化炭素を吸い込む代わりに，新鮮な酸素を確実に十分に取り込む必要がある)

・**make sure (that) ...**「…(ということ)を確かめる，確実に…する」

(例) **Make sure (that)** all the windows are locked.
(全部の窓にカギがかかっていることを確かめなさい[必ず全部の窓にカギをかけなさい])

・**instead of ～ing**「～する代わりに」

(例) We went shopping **instead of going** to the movies. (私たちは映画を見に行く代わりに買い物に行った)

◆ The zero-gravity environment can **cause** people **to lose** muscle and bone ... (無重力環境では(人は)筋肉と骨が衰えることがありうる)

・**cause O to *do***「Oが～する原因となる」

直訳は「無重力環境は，人々が筋肉と骨を失う原因となりうる」。

◆ They tie themselves into an exercise bike 〈**so** they **can** work out and keep their bodies feeling strong〉. (彼らは運動用バイクに体をくくりつけて体を鍛え，体が丈夫な感覚を保っている)

暗記 **so (that) S can[will]** ～「Sが～できる[する]ように」

・I got up early **so (that)** I **could see** the sunrise.
(私は日の出を見られるよう早起きした)

＊話し言葉では，that はしばしば省略される。

＝ I got up early to see the sunrise.
(私は日の出を見るために早起きした)

上の文では，〈　〉の部分が「(自分が)トレーニングをして…できるように」という意味を表している。

全訳

宇宙船の窓から眼下の地球を見るのはどんな感じだろうか，と思ったことがあるだろうか。無重力環境がどのようなものか想像できるだろうか。もしあなたが国際宇宙ステーションにいる宇宙飛行士だとしたら，これが１日のスケジュールの一部かもしれない。宇宙飛行士の平均的な１日が普通のサラリーマンの１日とは大違いであることは明らかだ。

まず第一に宇宙飛行士の生活の１日は，宇宙ステーションが地球を回る間に現れる15回もの日の出を含む。そのため，宇宙飛行士は時間の感覚を失うことがよくある。しかし彼らはそれでもなお規則正しい予定に従い，１晩に約５時間の睡眠をとる。扇風機の隣で休むのが一番よい。宇宙では人間が吐く熱い空気が上昇しないので，自分の吐く二酸化炭素を吸い込む代わりに，新鮮な酸素を確実に十分に取り込む必要がある。また彼らは，騒がしい環境で眠ることに慣れなければならない――宇宙ステーション内部の音は，常に電源が入っている掃除機のようだと言う人もいるのだから。目覚めた後，宇宙飛行士は１日３食のうちの１食目をとる。食べ物がどこかへ行ってしまうとステーションの機械に損傷を与えるかもしれないので，そうならないよう注意する必要がある。そのため，飲む際にはストローを使う。

無重力環境では筋肉と骨が衰えることがありうるので，宇宙飛行士は多くの運動をする必要がある。

彼らは運動用バイクに体をくくりつけて体を鍛え，体が丈夫な感覚を保っている。

語句

spaceship「宇宙船」 below「下に」
astronaut「宇宙飛行士」
the International Space Station「国際宇宙ステーション」
average「平均的な」
be light years different from ～「～とは大違いである」（直訳は「～と数光年異なる（light year＝光年）」。違いの程度の差を強調した言い方）
office worker「事務職員，会社員」
to begin with「まず初めに」 include「～を含む」
sunrise「日の出，朝日」 sense「感覚」
regular「定期的な，規則正しい」 rest「休む」
next to ～「～の隣で」 fan「扇風機」
breathe out ～「（呼吸により）～を吐き出す」
oxygen「酸素」 breathe in ～「～を吸い込む」
straw「ストロー」 muscle「筋肉」 bone「骨」
get exercise「運動する」
tie O into ～「O を～の中に結びつける，固定する」
work out「トレーニングをする」

第 1 回　実力テスト

1
① **The apple pie I ate yesterday was made by my brother**
② **This map will help you to find the place for the party**
③ **I was spoken to by a stranger at**
④ **It was careless of you to leave the door open**
⑤ **A ship carrying more than five hundred passengers is missing**
⑥ **The red coat costs three times as much as the brown**
⑦ **You had better eat in a hurry, or you'll miss**
⑧ **Cathy has lost the ring her mother bought for her**

解説 ①the apple pie (which) I ate yesterday＝私が昨日食べたパイ。下線部が前の名詞を修飾する形。which（目的格の関係代名詞）は省略できる（→001-④）。
②〈**help** + O + **(to)** ***do***〉「O が～するのを助ける」（→002-④）
③A stranger spoke to me.（見知らぬ人が私に話しかけた）の me を主語にした受動態の文は，I was **spoken to by** a stranger. となる（→004-③）。
④〈**It is** ＋人の性格を表す形容詞＋ **of X to** ***do***.〉「～するとは X は…（な人）だ」（→013-⑤），leave O C「O を C のままに（放置）しておく」
⑤S is missing.（S は行方不明だ）の S に当たるのは，A ship (which is) **carrying** more than five hundred passengers（500人を超える乗客を運んでいる船）。下線部が前の名詞を修飾する形。
⑥〈S **cost(s)** ＋金額〉「S には～の費用がかかる」。「3 倍（の額）」は **three times as much as**

で表す(→003-②)。

⑦〈**had better** ＋動詞の原形〉「～する方がよい」，**in a hurry**「急いで」，**or**「さもなければ」（しばしば命令文の後ろで使う。この文ではコンマの前が命令文に近い意味を表している）

⑧ the ring (which) her mother bought for her(母親が彼女のために買った指輪)。①と同様に，下線部が前の名詞を修飾している。

2
① **too busy with farm jobs to take Walt to school**
② **was the most embarrassing thing that could happen**
③ **It was about a boy who never grows up**
④ **was so good that he asked for a picture**
⑤ **Their parents were not happy at all when they saw**

解説 ①〈**too** ＋形容詞・副詞＋ **to *do***〉(…するには～すぎる，～すぎて…できない)の形を利用する。**be busy with** ～は「～で忙しい」，take O to ～は「O を～へ連れて行く」。

② that を主格の関係代名詞として使う。the most embarrassing thing that could happen to a boy は「男の子(の身)に起こりうる最も恥ずかしいこと」。下線部が前の名詞を修飾している。

③ It was about a boy(それ[＝ Peter Pan という劇]は，男の子について(の劇)だった)という形を作り，それに who never grows up(決して成長しない)を続ける。who は前の a boy を先行詞とする主格の関係代名詞。

④ **so ～ that ...**(非常に～なので…)の形を利用する。**ask for** ～は「～を求める」。

⑤ **not (～) at all**(全く～ではない)の形を利用する。Their parents were not happy at all で「彼らの両親は全くうれしくなかった」の意味。Their parents were not at all happy とも言う。

全訳

1901年12月5日に，ウォルター・エリアス・ディズニーはシカゴのノース・トリップ通りにある2階建ての小さな家の2階の寝室で生まれた。

両親と兄たちは農作業でとても忙しく，ウォルトを学校へ連れて行くことはできなかった。そのため，7歳近くになるまで彼は学校に通い始めていなかった。そのころまでに，5歳の妹のルースも学校に行く準備ができていた。ウォルトは，妹と一緒に学校に通い始めることは「男の子に起こりうる一番恥ずかしいことだった」と語った。

ウォルトはいつも，人を楽しませ，人に楽しい時間を過ごしてもらいたいと考えていた。あるとき，ピーターパンを上演するために俳優の一団が町に来た。それは決して大人にならない少年の話だった。ウォルトはその劇が大好きで，学校の公演でピーターを演じた。兄のロイは，ワイヤーを使ってウォルトを空中に持ち上げた。観客には，まるで彼が空を飛んでいるように見えた。

鉛筆を握れるようになるのとほとんど同時に，ウォルトは何時間も絵を描いて過ごした。彼はみんなに自分は芸術家だと言った。彼には本当に才能があった。隣人のドク・シャーウッドは，ウォルトがとても上手だと思ったので，自分の馬の絵を描いてくれと頼んだ。ドク・シャーウッドと彼の妻は，その絵をほめた。そのためウォルトはとても誇らしい気持ちになった。

ある日，彼は黒いタールの入った樽《たる》を見つけた。彼とルースは大きな棒をタールに浸して，自分たちの白い家の側面じゅうに絵を描いた。その芸術作品を見た両親は，全く喜ばなかった。タールは取り除けなかったのだ！

語句

upstairs「上の階の」 two-story「2階建ての」
cottage「小さな家，別荘」 avenue「(大)通り」
almost「ほとんど(～近く)」
be ready for ～「～の準備ができている」
embarrassing「ばつが悪い，恥ずかしい」
entertain「～を楽しませる」
have a good time「楽しい時を過ごす」
actor「俳優」 perform「～を演じる」
grow up「成長する」 play「劇」
performance「公演」 wire「ワイヤー，針金」
lift「～を持ち上げる」 audience「観客，聴衆」
look like ～「～のように見える」 hold「～を握る」
spend O ～ing「～して O[時]を過ごす」
draw「(線で絵)を描く」 talent「才能」
neighbor「隣人」 praise「～をほめる」
proud「誇らしい」 discover「～を発見する」
barrel「樽」 dip「～を浸す」 stick「棒」
artwork「芸術作品」 remove「～を取り除く」

2 和文英訳問題

017 ① **How long has she lived [been living] there?**

② **This bag is the heaviest of the three (bags).**

③ **The students (who were) waiting for the bus looked sleepy.**

④ **He was not only sleepy but (also) hungry.**

⑤ **I don't know when the temple was built.**

⑥ **I am interested in collecting dolls.**

⑦ **Ken had to get up early to take the first train.**

⑧ **I have known him for three years.**

⑨ **I want someone to talk to [with].**

解説 ①たとえば「彼は３年間そこに住んでいる」は，He has lived there for three years. のように現在完了形を使って表現する。この下線部を How long（どのくらい長い間）で尋ねる疑問文を作る。has lived の代わりに has been living（現在完了進行形）を使ってもよい。

Q&A

Q 「彼は３年間そこに住んでいる」を He is living there for three years. と表現するのは誤りですか？

A is living を使うのは誤りです。現在進行形は，「今（この瞬間）」に焦点を当てて，「今は，過去に始まって未来に終わる行為や出来事が進行している最中だ」という意味を表します。一方，for three years は「３年の間ずっと」という意味です。つまり，現在進行形は時の流れの中の「今」という１点を指すのに対して，**for**（～の間）は幅のある期間を指します。だから意味の面で相性が悪く，この２つを組み合わせて使うことはできません。

Q&A

Q has lived と has been living はどう違うのですか？

A → 009 -⑥の説明を確認しましょう。

・状態動詞は，現在完了形で「状態の継続」を表す。

・動作動詞は，現在完了進行形で「動作の継続」を表す。

live は（「住みつつある」とは言えないから）一般には状態動詞であり，進行形にしません。しかし状態動詞の中には，一時的な状態を強調したいときは進行形を使うものがあります。live や wear（身に着けている）はそのグループの動詞です。たとえば「彼は大阪に住んでいる」は，次のように表現できます。

(a) He **lives** in Osaka.

(b) He **is living** in Osaka now.

(a)が普通の表現。(b)は「彼は今（一時的に）大阪に住んでいる」という意味（だから now を加えるのが普通）です。

(c) She **is wearing** a red dress.

（彼女は赤いドレスを着ている）

(c)は「着ている最中だ」ではなく，「今（一時的に）身に着けている」という意味です。

［参考］「一時的な状態」であっても進行形にしない状態動詞もあります。たとえば have（～を持っている）や belong to ～（～に所属している）などです。

以上の知識をもとにして，次の２つの文を比べてみましょう。

(d) He **has lived** there for three years.

(e) He **has been living** there for three years.

live は状態動詞だから，普通は進行形にしません。したがって「彼は３年間そこに住んでいる」は，(d)で表すのが普通です。しかし「彼は３年間そこに住んでいる（が将来は引っ越すかもしれない）」のように，「一時的に住んでいる」という意味を強調したいときは，(e)の現在完了進行形を使うこともできます。

②次の形を覚えておくこと。

暗記 〈S **is the** ＋最上級の形容詞＋ **of** ～.〉「S は～のうちで最も…だ」

of の後ろには複数の人や物を置く。「３つ（のかばん）のうちで」は of the three (bags)。

注意！ heavy，happy，busy など y で終わる語は，y を i に変えて比較級・最上級を作る。たとえば「より忙しい」は busier，「一番忙しい」は busiest。

③「バスを待っている生徒たち」は，the students (who were) waiting for the bus。一般に，〈関係代名詞＋ **be** 動詞〉は省略することが多い。who were を省くと，waiting 以下の分詞句が前の the students を修飾する形になる。「眠そうだ[眠そうに見える]」は look sleepy。

文法 SVC の形で使う動詞（C＝主に形容詞）

暗記 become [get, turn]＋C＝C になる

暗記 feel＋C＝C に感じられる

暗記 keep [stay]＋C＝C のままである

暗記 look＋C＝(外見が) C に見える

暗記 seem [appear]＋C＝C に思われる

暗記 sound＋C＝C に聞こえる［思われる］

④次の形を覚えておくこと。

暗記 **not only A but (also) B**「**A** だけでなく **B** も」

・She speaks **not only** English **but (also)** Chinese.

＝ She speaks Chinese **as well as** English.

（彼女は英語だけでなく中国語も話す）

⑤「その寺はいつ建てられましたか」は，When was the temple built?。これを間接疑問にして know の後ろに置くと，下線部の VS が SV の語順になる（→ 001 -③）。

⑥ **be interested in ～ing**「～することに興味がある」（→ 006 -⑤）。前置詞(in)の後ろに動詞を置くときは，ing を加えて動名詞にする点に注意。

⑦「⑴ Ken は早起きしなければならなかった」＋「⑵始発電車に乗るために」という語順にする。⑴は，have to（～しなければならない）の過去形(had to)を使う。⑵は目的を表す（副詞的用法の）不定詞を使う。

注意！「電車に乗る」は，「乗り込む」という動作を表すときは get on the train を使う。一方，「（交通機関として）電車［バス，タクシー］を利用する」は，**take the train [bus, taxi]** で表す。

⑧「彼を3年前から今までずっと知っている」と考えて，状態の継続を表す現在完了形(have known)を使う。know は進行形にできない状態動詞だから，have been knowing とは言わない（→①）。

［参考］ I came to know him three years ago.（3年前に彼と知り合った）とも表現できる（come to *do*「～するようになる」）。

⑨ talk to [with] someone（誰かと話す）→ someone to talk to [with]（話すための誰か）と考える。下線部は前の someone を修飾する形容詞的用法の不定詞。live in a house（家に住む）→ a house to live in（住むための家）などと同様。

［参考］「話し相手がいればいいのに（実際はいないのが残念だ）」と言いたいときは，I wish I had someone to talk to [with]. を使う。

018 ① **Can [Could] you lend me your dictionary?**

② **My father told me to stop using social media.**

③ **Riko has just finished brushing her teeth.**

④ **I have [have caught] a cold, so I can't go out with you today.**

⑤ **I can't play the guitar as well as she does [can].**

⑥ **He looked tired the day before yesterday.**

⑦ **My father has been looking for his glasses for 30 minutes.**

⑧ **If I were you, I wouldn't buy her that flower [those flowers].**

⑨ **Learning how to cook is one of the most important things in life.**

⑩ **I hope to see [(that) I can see] you again when you come back to Japan.**

解説 ①〈**lend** ＋ O_1 ＋ O_2〉「O_1［人］に O_2［物］を貸す」（→ 001 -⑥）。次の形も重要。

暗記 **Can [Could] you (please) ～?**「～してもらえますか」

Can you ～？は「(あなたは今)～することができますか」の意味で，Can you help me?(私を手伝ってもらえますか)のように使う。could を使う方がていねいな言い方。

［参考］（状況によっては）Will [Would, Won't] you ～？も使えるが，相手に何かを頼むときは Can [Could] you ～ (, please)? の形を使うと覚えておけばよい。

なお，この問いの日本文の意味は，Can [May] I use [borrow] your dictionary?(あなたの辞書を使って[借りて]もいいですか)とも表現できる。

②〈**tell ＋ O ＋ to *do***〉「O に～するよう言う[命じる]」(→002-④)。「使うのをやめる」は stop using。stop (～をやめる) の後ろには～ing 形(動名詞)を置く。stop to use だと「使うために立ち止まる」という別の意味になるので誤り。

文法 「～することを…する」の表現

次の３つのパターンがある。

(1)〈V＋～ing〉の形を使う動詞：**enjoy** (～を楽しむ)，**finish** (～を終える)，**practice** (～を練習する)，**stop** (～をやめる，止める) など

・I've already **finished having** [×to have] lunch.

(もう昼食を食べ終えました)

(2)〈V＋to *do*〉の形を使う動詞：**decide** (～を決心する)，**hope** (～を希望する)，**plan** (～を計画する)，**want [would like]** (～を欲する) など

・I **hope to enter** [×entering] the high school.

(私はその高校に入れればいいと思う)

(3)〈V＋～ing〉〈V＋to *do*〉の両方の形を使える動詞：**begin [start]** (～を始める)，**like** (～を好む)，**love** (～を愛する) など

・It **began raining [to rain]** in the afternoon.

(午後に雨が降り出した)

③「ちょうど～したところだ」は，〈**have [has] just** ＋過去分詞〉(現在完了形)で表す。「歯磨きを終わらせる」は，**finish brushing** one's teeth「歯を磨くことを終える」と表現する。finish は後ろに動名詞を置く動詞だから，finish to brush ... は誤り。

④「(私は)風邪をひいてしまった」は，次の２つの文のどちらかで表現できる。

(1) **I have a cold.**

(2) **I've [I have] caught a cold.**

(1)の **have a cold** は「風邪をひいている」という状態を表す。「私は今風邪をひいている状態だ」ということ。(2)の **catch a cold** は「風邪をひく」という出来事を表す。catch を現在完了形 (have caught) にすることで，「過去に風邪をひいて，今もまだ治っていない」という意味を表すことができる。「…なので」は，so または because を使って表す。

文法 「…なので」(理由)の表し方

たとえば「私は風邪をひいているので外出できない」という内容は，次の形で表現できる。

(1) I have a cold, **so** I can't go out.

(2) I can't go out **because** I have a cold.

下線部(「風邪をひいている」)の位置の違いに注意。

(1)の **so** は「だから」の意味で，日本語の順番に英語を並べればよい。(2)の **because** は「なぜなら…だから」の意味で，「私は外出できない＋なぜなら風邪をひいているから」ということ。

注意！ コンマの有無を使い分けよう。

次のように覚えておこう。

暗記 場所や時を表す副詞句・副詞節を文の最初に置くときは，その後ろにコンマを入れる。

・On my way home from school, I found a homeless cat. (学校からの帰り道で，私は野良ネコ[家のないネコ]を見つけた)

＊下線部(副詞句)の後ろにはコンマを入れる。これを後ろに置くときは，コンマを入れない。

・I found a homeless cat on my way home from school.

because (…なので)，**when** (…するとき)，**if** (もし…なら)，**before** (…する前に)，**after** (…した後で)，**though** (…だけれど) などの接続詞は，(SV を含む) 副詞節を作る。その節が文の最初にあるときは，後ろにコンマを入れる。

(1) **When** I was six, I lived in Osaka.

(2) I lived in Osaka **when** I was six.

(私は６歳のとき大阪に住んでいた)

＊(1)ではコンマを入れる。(2)ではコンマを入れないのが普通。

［参考］「…なので」の意味は as を使っても表せるが，as にはいろいろな意味があるので，because や so を使う方がよい。

Q&A

Q (2)は，I caught a cold. ではいけませんか？

A はい。この文は「私は(過去のある時点で)風邪

をひいた」という意味なので，今風邪をひいているかどうかはわかりません。また，過去形の動詞を使う場合は，たとえば，I caught a cold last week.（先週風邪をひいた）のように，「いつの時点の出来事か」を言い添えるのが普通です。したがって，I caught a cold. だけでは不完全な文に感じられます。

⑤〈**not** ＋ **as** ＋原級の形容詞・副詞＋ **as** 〜〉（〜ほど…ではない）の形を使う（→ 002 -⑦）。正解例の文を見てみよう。

・I can't play the guitar **as well as** she does[can].

not と as well as 〜を組み合わせて「〜ほど上手に…ではない」という意味を表す。as の後ろの she does は，she plays the guitar の下線部を（同じ言葉のくり返しを避けるために）does で置き換えたもの（she can は，she can play the guitar の下線部を省略したもの）。2つ目の as（や比較級に続く than）は接続詞だから，後ろには SV の形を置く。このときの V は，**be** 動詞，助動詞，**do** などを使う。

・My brother is taller than I am.
（兄［弟］は私よりも背が高い）

＊この文の am や，上の文の最後の does は，省略することもできる。ただし，... as she. や ... than I. のように主格の代名詞を文末に置く形は堅苦しく響くので避ける方がよい。

［参考］ くだけた表現では，... as her., than me. のように（as や than を前置詞とみなして）目的格の代名詞を続けることも多い。なお，as や than の後ろに名詞を続ける場合は，... as my brother., ... than Tom. のように V を省いてよい。

⑥「（外見が）〜に見える」は，〈**look** ＋ **C**［形容詞］〉で表す（→ 017 -③）。「おととい」は the day before yesterday。（yesterday と同様に）副詞の働きをするので，on the day before yesterday とは言わない（→ 015 -②）。

Q&A

Q The day before yesterday, he looked tired. とも言えますか？

A 可能ですが，全く同じ意味ではありません。基本的には，次のように覚えてください。

暗記 場所や時を表す副詞（句・節）は，原則として文末に置く。

次の２つの文を比べてみましょう。

(1) I went to see a movie yesterday.
（私は昨日映画を見に行った）

(2) Yesterday(,) I went to see a movie.
（昨日（は）私は映画を見に行った）

(1)が普通の語順です。(2)は，たとえば「ふだんの日曜日は家にいるが，昨日（の日曜日）は映画を見に行った」のような状況で使います。また，「昨日私が何をしたかと言えば，映画を見に行ったのです」のように，movie を強調したいような状況でも（movie を最後に置く）(2)を使います。

なお，場所と時を表す副詞（句）の両方を文末に置くときは，〈場所＋時〉の順に並べるのが基本です。

・I bought a novel at the bookstore yesterday.
　　　　　　　　　　場所　　　　　時
（昨日本屋で小説を買った）

⑦ look for 〜（〜を探す）は動作動詞なので，現在完了進行形（has been looking for）で「（今までずっと）〜し続けている」の意味を表す（→ 009 -⑥）。

⑧ **if I were you**（もし私があなたなら）という形を使う。これは一種の決まり文句なので，この形で覚えておくこと。

文法 仮定法過去

現在または未来のことを過去形で表現することがある。これを仮定法過去と言い，次のどちらかの意味を表す。

(1)現在の事実とは反対のことを仮定する。

(2)未来に起こる可能性が低いことを仮定する。

if を使った仮定法過去の文の基本形と意味は，次のとおり。

暗記 If S_1＋V_1［過去形］，S_2＋V_2［would＋動詞の原形］．

(1)もし（今）S_1がV_1なら，S_2はV_2なのに（実際はそうではないのが残念だ）

(2)（起こる可能性は低いが）もしS_1がV_1することがあれば，S_2はV_2だろう

＊V_2は，would の代わりに could や might を使うこともある。

(1)と(2)の例を１つずつ見てみよう。

・If she **were**[**was**] my classmate, we **could have** lunch together.（もし彼女が私のクラスメイトなら，一緒にお弁当を食べられるのに）

＊仮定法過去の be 動詞は，主語が何であっても **were** を使う（話し言葉では，主語が I や３人称単数のときは was を使うことも多い）。コンマの後ろ（主節）では，would，could などを使う。この

文は「実際には彼女は(今)私のクラスメイトではないから，一緒にお弁当を食べられないのが残念だ」という気持ちを表している。

・What **would** you **do** if you **got** a million yen?（もし100万円を手に入れたら，あなたは何をしますか）

＊if 節を後ろに置いた形。「あなたが100万円を手に入れる可能性は低いけれど，もし仮に手に入れたら」という未来の仮定を表している。

⑧で if I were you(もし私があなたなら)という形((1)の意味の仮定法過去)を使うのは，実際には「私＝あなた」ではないから。現在のことを語るのに過去形を使うのは，「もし私があなた<u>だったら</u>」という日本語の感覚に近いと考えてもよい。

⑨まず，次の形を確認しておこう。

暗記 **〈one of the**(＋形容詞)**X**[複数形の名詞]〉「(～な)**X** のうちの１つ[１人]」

・She is **one of the most popular** <u>**singers**</u> in Japan.
（彼女は日本で最も人気の高い歌手の１人です）

＊意味から考えて，singers(複数形)を使う点に注意。これを singer と書く誤りが非常に多く見られる。

この問いの場合，「S は人生において最も重要なことの１つです」は，S is one of the most important things in life. と表現できる。この S の位置に，Learning how to cook(料理のしかたを学ぶこと)という名詞のかたまりを置く(Learning は動名詞)。不定詞を使えば，次のようにも表現できる。

・It is one of the most important things in life **to learn** how to cook.

＊形式主語の It が後ろの不定詞を指す形。

⑩「～することを希望する」は，**hope to *do***(または **want[would like] to *do***)で表す。「あなたに再び会う」は see you again。「会う」を意味する動詞には meet と see があるが，meet は初対面のときに，see は２回目以降に会うときに使うことが多い。この問いでは，「あなたが日本へ戻ってくるときに」を **when** you <u>**come**</u> back[return] to Japan で表す点もポイント。この come を will come とするのは誤り。

文法 時・条件を表す節中の現在形

暗記 時や条件を表す接続詞の後ろでは，未来のことも現在形で表す。**will** は使わない。

具体的に言うと，**when**(…するとき)，**before**(…する前に)，**after**(…した後に)，**until**(…するまで)，**if**(もし…なら)などの後ろでは，まだ起きていないことを表す際にも現在形を使う。

・Let's go home **before** it <u>**gets**</u>[×will get] dark.
（暗くなる前に家に帰ろう）

・I won't go out **if** it <u>**rains**</u>[×will rain] tomorrow.
（もし明日雨が降ったら，外出しません）

019〉
① **If I were in your place, I would tell her what she should do.**
② **Did anyone help you (to) choose this dress?**
③ **This newspaper says (that) it will[is going to] rain (very) hard in Kyoto.**
④ **Do you know what this animal is called in English?**
⑤ **You had better be careful in crossing the[a] road.**

解説 ①「もし私があなたの立場なら」は if I am in your place とも表現できるが，were を使うよう指示されているので，if I **were** in your place と仮定法過去で表現する(「もし私があなたなら」と言い換えて if I were you を使ってもよい)。これに対応させて，後半(主節)は I **would tell** her ...(彼女に…を伝えるだろう)の形にする(→ 018〉-⑧)。「何をすべきか」は what to do(または what she should do)。

Q&A

Q 次の２つはどう違うのですか？
(1) if I <u>am</u> in your place
(2) if I <u>were</u> in your place

A (1)のような(普通の)形を，仮定法と対比させて直説法と言います。if の後ろに直説法を置くと，「五分五分の可能性」を表します。これに対して仮定法は「ゼロの(または低い)可能性」を表します。したがって，(1)(2)は次の意味に解釈できます。

(1)私は(この先)あなたの立場になることがあるかもしれない。もしそうなれば(未来に向けての仮定＝

五分五分の可能性)

(2)(a)私は今あなたの立場にはないが，もしそうであるなら(現在の事実とは反対の仮定＝ゼロの可能性)

(b)私が(この先)あなたの立場になる可能性は低いが，もしそうなれば(未来に向けての仮定＝低い可能性)

このことから考えて，if I were you(もし私があなたなら)をif I am youと直説法で表現することはできません。直説法は五分五分の可能性を表しますが，「私が今あなたである」可能性はゼロだし，「私が将来あなたになる」可能性もないからです。

②〈**help＋O＋(to) *do***〉(Oが～するのを手伝う)の形を使うのがポイント。

・X **helped me (to) choose** this dress.
(Xは私がこのドレスを選ぶのを手伝った)

この文をもとにして，Did anyone help you ...?(誰かがあなたを手伝いましたか)という疑問文を作る。

③次の形を覚えておこう。

暗記 **The newspaper says (that) .... ＝ According to the newspaper, ...**「新聞によれば…」

この問いでは，This newspaper says (that) ....(この新聞は…と言っている)という形にする。「大雨になる」は，it will rain (very) hard(雨が(とても)激しく降るだろう)と表現できる。

④**What is S called?**「Sは何と呼ばれますか」What is called S?としないよう注意(→008-⑤)。

⑤hadに着目して，**had better**(～する方がよい)を使う。助動詞なので，後ろにtoをつけないように。inは，後ろに動名詞を置いて「～するとき」の意味で使う。

[参考] in ～ing(～するとき)は改まった表現。「道路を横断する際は」は，when you cross the road(またはwhen crossing the road)と表現するのが普通。

Q&A

Q「道路を横断する際は」を次のように表現した場合，意味に違いはありますか？

(1)in crossing the road
(2)in crossing a road
(3)in crossing road
(4)in crossing roads
(5)in crossing the roads

A まず，(3)は文法的に誤りです。次の点を常に意識してください。

文法 可算名詞は，原則として無冠詞単数形では使えない。

英語の名詞には，可算名詞(C)・不可算名詞(U)の2つの種類があります(C＝countable noun，U＝uncountable noun)。Cは一定の形を持つ名詞で，「1つ，2つ」と数えたり，複数形にしたりすることができます。Uは一定の形を持たず，数えられないので複数形にもできません。road(道路)はCだから，無冠詞単数形(aやtheのつかない単数形)では使えません。

(1)～(5)の例で言うと，(3)以外は文法的に正しい形ですが，次のような違いがあります。

(1)(あなたも知っている)その道路を渡る際には
(2)(普通の1本の)道路を渡る際には
(4)(どんな道路であれ)道路というものを渡る際には
(5)(あなたも知っている)それらの(何本かの)道路を渡る際には

(1)(5)のように，**the**は「相手がすでに知っているもの」を表すのが基本です。(2)(4)は近い意味ですが，(4)だと「複数の道路を同時に渡る際に」という意味にも感じられるので，(2)を使うのがベターです。

020 ① **Please tell me why the girl is crying.**
② **It is important for you to have a dream when you are young.**
③ **Before I answer your question, please tell me why you want to know the answer.**
④ **What made you join the party?**

解説 ①「私に～を教えてください」は，Please tell me ～.で表現する(**tell＋O_1＋O_2**「O_1にO_2を伝える，話す」)(→001-⑥)。「その少女はなぜ泣いているのですか」はWhy is the girl crying?。これを間接疑問にして，meの後ろに置く。

注意!「教える＝**teach**」ではない。

teachは，勉強などを教える場合に使う。相手に何かの情報を伝える(たとえば道を教える)ときは

tell を使う。

②形式主語の It が後ろの不定詞を指す形を使う(→ 013 -⑤)。この問いでは，It is **important** for you to *do*. で「～することはあなたにとって大切だ」という意味になる。この形でよく使われるその他の形容詞は，**impossible**(不可能だ)，**necessary**(必要だ)，**natural**(当然だ)など。

③後半は①と同様の形を使う。前半は，before の使い方がポイント。before や after は，接続詞としても前置詞としても使う。

・Where shall we go **after** we have lunch.
(after＝接続詞，we＝S，have＝V，lunch＝O)

・Where shall we go **after** having lunch.
(after＝前置詞，having lunch＝(動)名詞句)

(昼食をとった後でどこへ行きましょうか)

この問いでは「私が君の質問に答える前に」と考えて，before を接続詞として使い，before I answer your question と表現する。

注意！ before を befor と書かないように。このミスはよく見られる。また，until を untill と書くミスも多い。

④無生物主語構文の典型的な形の1つ(→ 009 -②)。

暗記 〈**What makes you** ＋原形不定詞？〉「何があなたを～させるのか→あなたはなぜ～するのか」この問いでは，「何があなたをそのパーティーに参加させたのか」と表現する。

021 ① **I've [I have] had it since I was eight (years old).**
② **Cats are the animal(s) that I like (the) best.**
③ **Does your father often take you to a pet shop?**

解説 ①「過去から今までずっと～している」という意味は，現在完了形で表す。have(～を持っている)は状態動詞だから，have had で「状態の継続」の意味を表すことができる(→ 009 -⑥)。

②「関係代名詞を用いて」という指示があるので，「一番好きな動物」は the animal(s) that I like (the) best と表現する。that(目的格の関係代名詞)は，話し言葉では省略するのが普通。

［参考］ which も使えるが，that よりも改まった響きになる。また，関係代名詞を使わなくてもよければ，Cats are my favorite animal(s). とも表現できる(favorite「一番好きな」)。

Q&A

Q 主語を cats(複数形)にするのはなぜですか？ また，the animal(s) の s はあってもなくてもよいのですか？

A cat や animal は可算名詞だから，無冠詞単数形では使えません(→ 019 -⑤)。たとえば「ネコはかわいい動物だ」は，次のように英訳できます。

(1) **Cats are cute animals.**
(2) Cats are a cute animal.
(3) A cat is a cute animal.
(4) The cat is a cute animal.

この中では，(1)が最も普通の言い方です。(1)(S＝無冠詞の複数名詞)は「いろんな種類のネコがいるが，どのネコもかわいい動物だ」という意味。S is [are] C. の形では，S が複数形なら C も複数形にするのが普通です。ただし，ネコを1種類の動物と考えれば，(2)のように言うこともできます。(3)(S＝a [an]＋単数名詞)は，典型的な1匹のネコをイメージした言い方。(4)(S＝the＋単数名詞)はネコを他の動物と区別する響きを持ち，辞書の定義や図鑑の説明などでよく使われます(その(特定の1匹の)ネコという意味ではありません)。

②の場合，「私はどんなネコでも好きだ」と言いたいわけだから，(1)の形を応用して Cats are the animals .... と表現するのが自然です。(2)の形に準じて，(ネコを1種類の動物とみなして) Cats are the animal .... としてもかまいません。

なお，次の2つの文の違いも考えてみましょう。

(a) Cats are the animals I like the best.
(ネコは私が一番好きな動物です)

(b) Cats are animals I like very much.
(ネコは私が大好きな動物です)

(a)では，「私が一番好きな動物は1種類だけだ」と考えて，animals の前に the をつけます。このように，「1つに特定できるもの」の前には **the** をつけます。最上級の形容詞や only などの前に the をつけるのも同じ理由です。一方(b)の animals の前に the がついていないのは，「私が大好きな動物」はネコ以外にもおり，ネコはそのうちの1つだ，と言いたいからです(Cats are one of the animals I like very much. とも言います)。(b)の animals の前に the をつけると，「私が大好きな動物はネコだけだ」と言っていることになります。

「私は X が好きだ」と言いたいとき，I like

X. の X[＝like の目的語]の形も確認しておきましょう。

(1) I like a cat. (私はある(あなたは知らない特定の1匹の)ネコが好きだ)

(2) I like the cat. (私はその(あなたも知っている例の)ネコが好きだ)

(3) **I like cats.**
(私はネコという動物が(全部)好きだ)

(4) I like the cats. (私は(あなたも知っているその[例の])ネコたちが好きだ)

したがって「私はネコ好きです」と言いたいときは，(3)(無冠詞複数形)を使うのが適切です。一方，後ろに不可算名詞を置くときは，無冠詞単数形にします。

(5) **I like listening to music.**
(私は音楽を聞くのが好きです)

この文でも，music の前に the をつけると「(あなたも知っている)その音楽を聞くのが好きだ」という意味になります。(3)と(5)を，「～が好きだ」の意味の基本例文として覚えておきましょう。

③「O を～(場所)に連れて行く」は，〈take O to ＋場所〉で表す。「よく」は often(しばしば)で表す。Does you father often take you ...? という語順になる点に注意。また，pet shop は可算名詞だから，無冠詞単数形では使えない。

文法 頻度を表す副詞の位置

頻度を表す副詞とは，**sometimes**(時々)，**often**(しばしば)，**usually**(たいてい)，**never**(一度も～ない)など。これらの副詞は，普通一般動詞[＝**be** 動詞以外の動詞]の前に置く。

・I **sometimes** go to the library.
(私は時々図書館へ行きます)

[参考] 正確に言うと，「V＝1語の一般動詞」のときはその前に置く。「V=be 動詞」のときは be 動詞の後ろに，V が2語以上から成るときは最初の語の後ろに置く。

・I have never been to Hokkaido.
(私は北海道へは一度も行ったことがない)

文法 a[an]と the の選択，名詞の単複の選択

名詞を使う際には，これらを常に意識するようにしよう。これらの使い分けは慣れないと難しいので，できるだけ詳しく説明する。

③の「あなたをペットショップへ連れて行く」は，次の3通りに英訳できる。

(1) take you to a pet shop
(2) take you to the pet shop
(3) take you to pet shops

(1)の下線部は「ペットショップ(という種類の1軒の店)へ」，(2)は「(自分も相手もどの店のことかを知っている)例のペットショップへ」。(3)は「(どの店であれ)ペットショップ(という種類の店)へ」ということ。この会話の場合，たとえば「2人の生活空間の中にペットショップが1軒しかなく，マサオもその店の存在を知っている」という状況なら(2)を使う。(3)は「一度に2軒以上のペットショップへ連れて行く」ようにも響くので，(3)よりは(1)を使う方がよい。

全訳

マサオ：やあ，アイコ。君の筆箱はすてきだね。色が気に入ったよ。

アイコ：ありがとう，マサオ。これはとても古いの。①私は8歳からずっとそれを持っているのよ。兄さんが私の誕生日にくれたの。次の年にはバッグをくれたわ。これがそのバッグよ。

マサオ：それもすてきだね。描いてあるネコの絵がいいね。

アイコ：私はネコが好きよ。今度の日曜日は私の16歳の誕生日で，父さんが本物のネコを買ってくれることになっているわ。②ネコは私が一番好きな動物なの。ずっと前からネコがほしかったから，待ちきれないわ！

マサオ：よかったね。③あなたのお父さんはよくあなたをペットショップに連れて行ってくれるの？

アイコ：もちろん。私は父さんが大好きよ。父さんのような先生になりたいとも思うわ。

022 ① **It took them twenty years to build it.**
② **I had it repaired at that shop[store].**

解説 ①〈**It takes** (**X**[人]) ＋時間＋ **to** ***do***.〉「(X が)～するのに…(の時間が)かかる」(→ 007 -④)

A の発言は「何と見事な城だろう！ それを建てた人々は熱心に働いたに違いない！」という意味(**must have** ＋過去分詞「～したに違いない」)。

②次の形は語順を間違いやすいので注意。

暗記 〈**have** ＋ O ＋過去分詞〉「O[自分の持ち物など]を～してもらう」

・I **have my hair cut** at that barbershop.
=I get haircuts at that barbershop.
(私はあの理髪店で髪を切ってもらいます)

＊上の文の cut は過去分詞。

注意! 整序作文問題でこの形が問われたとき，下線部を have cut my hair と並べないこと。その語順(現在完了形)だと，自分で自分の髪を切ったという意味になる。

この問いでは，A の「昨日腕時計を壊したんじゃないの？」という発言に対して，I had it repaired (それを修理してもらった)と返答する。

［参考］「O を～される」の意味でも使う(例：I had my bicycle stolen.「自転車を盗まれた」)が，「O を～してもらう」の意味で使うことの方が多い。

023 ① **How far is it from**
② **Can[Could] you help me with[do]**
③ **Why don't you take[have] a[some]**
④ **about twice as tall[high] as**

解説 ①日本語と B の返答から，東京と京都の間の距離を尋ねているとわかる。したがって，次の形を使う。

暗記 **How far is it from A to B?**「A から B までの距離はどのくらいですか」

全訳
A：東京から京都までどれくらいだっけ。
B：ええと，たぶん300キロくらい？ よくわからない。インターネットで調べる方がいいよ。

②**help O with** ～「O[人]の～を手伝う」(→ 015 –②)。help me with tomorrow's homework の代わりに help me (to) do tomorrow's homework を使ってもよい。なお，「～してくれませんか」と相手に頼みごとをするときは，**Can [Could] you (please)** ～**?** を使う(→ 018 –①)。

注意! 所有格を 2 つ並べて使うことはできない。help me with my homework は正しいが，help me with my tomorrow's homework は誤り(2 つの所有格が並んでいるから)。ただし，my father's car(私の父の車)のような形は可能(my father's を 1 つの所有格と考える)。

全訳
A：明日の宿題，手伝ってくれないかな。答えがわからないんだ。
B：いいよ。どの問題？
A：ありがとう。第 2 問をお願い。

③次の 2 つの形をセットで覚えておこう。この問いでは 1 つ目の形を使う。

暗記 **Why don't you** ～**?**「～してはどうですか」
暗記 **Why don't we** ～**?**「(一緒に)～するのはどうですか」

・**Why don't you** see a doctor?
(お医者さんにみてもらったらどう？)
＊直訳は「あなたはなぜ医者にみてもらわないのか」。相手に助言や提案をする際に使われる会話表現。
・**Why don't we** go for a drive?
= **How about** going for a drive?
(ドライブに行かない？)

「休む」は，**take a[some] rest** で表す。これは主にアメリカ英語で，イギリス英語では take の代わりに have を使う。take[have] a bath (入浴する)なども同様。

全訳
A：どうしたの？ 具合が悪そうよ。
B：今日はひどく頭が痛いんだ。
A：少し休んだらどう。今日はとてもたくさん勉強したでしょう。

④**A is twice as** ～ **as B.**「A は B の 2 倍～だ」(→ 003 -②)

全訳
A：向こうのあの高い塔は何？
B：知らないの？ 東京スカイツリーだよ。高さは634メートルだ。東京タワーの倍くらいあるんだよ。

語句
look on the Intenet「インターネットで検索する」
have a headache「頭が痛い」

024 ① **I got a phone call from an old friend who (had) moved to a distant town.**

② **We've been friends since we were (small[little]) children, so we talked a lot about our memories.**

③ **I wonder how many young people know what to do for their future.**

④ **The story (that) my grandfather told me last night moved me to tears.**

⑤ **My mother eagerly went shopping in the afternoon, but (she) came home without buying anything after all.**

⑥ **It is said that most Japanese do not express their opinions clearly, but I don't think so.**

⑦ **"That hat is nice[That's a nice hat], isn't it? Who gave it to you?" "My aunt in Nagoya did."**

解説 ①「～から電話をもらう」は，get a phone [telephone] call from ～と表現できる。完成した文で，いくつかのポイントを確認しよう。

・I got a phone call from an old friend who (had) moved to a distant town.

下線部の関係詞節が前の名詞を修飾している。had moved は過去完了形。

文法 過去完了形 (had＋過去分詞)

現在完了形が「現在に至るまでの時間」を意識した時制であるのに対して，過去完了形は次のような場合に使う。

(1)過去のある時点まで(に)完了［経験・継続］していたことを表す。

(2)過去のある時点から見てさらに過去に起きたことを表す。

・When he called me, I **had** already **finished** my work.（彼が電話してきたとき，私はもう仕事を終えていた）

＊(1)の例。過去の(彼が電話してきた)時点より前に仕事を終えていたということ。

・Yesterday I lost the watch (that) my father **(had) bought** for me.（昨日私は父が買ってくれた腕時計をなくした）

＊(2)の例。過去の(腕時計をなくした)時点よりさらに過去の時点で「父が腕時計を買ってくれた」ということ。文脈上で時間の前後関係がはっきりしていれば，過去完了形の代わりに過去形(bought)を使ってもよい。

(1)では，友だちが「引っ越した」のは，電話をくれた時点から見てさらに過去だから，過去完了形(had moved)を使うのが基本だが，(2)の例文と同様に過去形(moved)で代用することもできる。

「なつかしい友だち」は，an old friend(旧友)と表現できる。「ここから遠く離れた町」は，a town (that is) far from here とも表現できるが，a distant town(遠くの町)でよい(「ここから」は言わなくてもわかる)。

Q&A

Q a friend who moved ... の代わりに，my friend who moved ... も使えますか？

A 間違いではありませんが，避けるべきです。my friend だと，「私の友人」が1人しかいないように感じられます。ただし，my friend と言えば誰のことかが相手にわかる状況なら，my friend を使ってもかまいません。

「昨日友人と買い物に行った」

→○ I went shopping with a friend yesterday.

△ I went shopping with my friend yesterday.

「友人の1人と買い物に行った」という意味なら，○の文を使います。a friend of mine, one of my friends とも言えますが，a friend で十分です。△の文は「あなたも知っている例の私の友人と買い物に行った」という状況なら使えます。

②「ぼくたちは幼なじみだ」は，(1) we've [we have] been friends (2) since we were (small[little]) children(ぼくたちは(小さな)子どものころからずっと友だちだ)と表現する。下線部(1)は we've known each other(ぼくたちはお互いをずっと知っている)，(2)は since childhood(子どものころ以来)でもよい。また，全体を we are childhood friends とも表現できる(下線部＝幼なじみ)。「思い出話に花が咲い

た」は，talked a lot[very much] about our memories（ぼくたちの思い出についてたくさん話した）と表現すればよい。

③**〈I wonder ＋疑問詞節〉「～だろうかと思う」**（→ 016 -語句・構文）。疑問詞節は wonder の目的語の働きをするので，間接疑問（SV の語順）になる。「自分の将来のために何をすべきか」は，what to do[what they should do] for their future。

④ **move O to tears**「O[人]を感動させて泣かせる」。主語を the story (that) my grandfather told me（祖父が私にした話）として，その後ろにこの形を続ける。**tell O a story**（O[人]に話をする[語る]）はこの形で覚えておくこと。受動態を使えば，次のようにも表現できる。

・I was moved to tears when I heard a story from my grandfather[a story my grandfather told me].（祖父からある話を聞いたとき，私は感動して涙を流した）

［参考］ when I heard の代わりに to hear を使うことはできない。感情の原因を表す不定詞は，感情を表す形容詞（happy, sad, surprised など）とセットで使う。

⑤ **go shopping**「買い物に行く」，**without ～ing**「～しないで」，after all「結局（のところ）」。「いそいそと」は eagerly（熱心に）などを使って表す。後半は，... but (she) ended up returning without buying anything. とも言える（**end up ～ing**「結局～する（はめになる）」）。

⑥次の表現を覚えておこう。

・**It is said (that) ....**「…と言われている」
・**I (don't) think so.**「私はそう思う[思わない]」

「日本人のほとんど」は，次のどちらかで表現できる。

(1) **most** Japanese（ほとんどの日本人）
(2) **most of the** Japanese people（日本人のほとんど）

(1)の most（ほとんどの）は形容詞で，後ろには複数形の名詞を置く（Japanese「日本人」は複数形も同じ形）。(2)の most of ～は「～の（うちの）大部分」の意味。次の点に注意。

・(1)の most の前に the をつけないこと。
・(2)は of の後ろに the（や所有格）が必要。

「自分の意見をはっきりと述べる」は，express one's opinions clearly と表現する（express「～を言い表す」）。ここでは自分の意見は 1 つだけではないから，opinions（複数形）を使う。

⑦「～ですね」と念を押したいときは，次のような付加疑問（文）を使う。

・It's a nice day, **isn't it?**（いい天気ですね）
・You look happy, **don't you?**（君はうれしそうだね）

「すてきな」は，nice[good]（よい），cool（かっこいい），pretty（きれいな）などで表す。What a nice hat!（感嘆文）を使ってもよい。

「誰にもらったの？」は，Who gave it to you?（誰があなたにそれをくれたのか）と表現できる。Who did you get it from?（あなたはそれを誰から手に入れたのか）でもよい。

「名古屋のおばさんがくれたんだ」は，My aunt (living) in Nagoya did.。did は前に出てきた言葉（gave it to me）のくり返しを避けるために使う。

025 ① **I fell asleep perhaps because I was very tired from after-school club activities.**

② **No one talks to me or turns on a noisy TV.**

解説 ①「私は眠ってしまった」は，I fell asleep. と表現する（**fall asleep**「眠り込む」）。「放課後の部活でくたくたに疲れていたのか」は理由を表しているので，because を使って表現する。正解例の **perhaps because ...** は「もしかしたら…なので」の意味。perhaps の代わりに **maybe**（たぶん），**probably**（おそらく）なども使う。「～で疲れている」は **be tired from ～**。「くたくたに疲れて」は very[really, so, dead] tired。**exhausted**（疲れ切って）という形容詞もある。「放課後の部活」は after-school club activities。**so ～ that ...**（とても～なので…）の形を使って，次のように表現してもよい。

・I must have been **so** tired from the club activities after school **that** I fell asleep.

＊**〈must have ＋過去分詞〉**「～したに違いない」

②「誰も私に話しかけたりうるさいテレビをつけた

りしない」と表現すればよい。「テレビをつける［消す］」は **turn on[off]** the TV[television]。日本語に忠実に訳せば，次のようになる。

・There is no one who talks to me or ....

＊下線部が前の no one を修飾する形。

「～に話しかける」は，**talk[speak] to[with]** ～。「うるさい」は，noisy（騒がしい）の他，loud（音が大きい），annoying（うっとうしい）なども使える。

注意！「**A** も **B** も～ない」は，〈**not＋A or B**〉で表す。

・I don't like soccer **or**［×and］baseball.
（私はサッカーも野球も好きではない）

＊and だと「サッカーと野球の両方を好きなわけではない」（どちらか一方なら好きだ）という意味に解釈される。

026
① **Mike wouldn't make mistakes if he worked more slowly.**
② (1) **I went to that (art) museum (that) you told me about the other day.**
(2) **It was interesting because there were a lot of picture books collected from around the world. I couldn't look at all of them in a[one] day.**

解説 ①日本語から考えて，仮定法過去を使うのが適切（→ 018 -⑧）。正解例で確認しよう。

・Mike **wouldn't make** mistakes（マイクはミスをしないだろう）＋ if he **worked** more slowly（もし彼がもっとゆっくり仕事をすれば）

if 節中では動詞の過去形（worked）を，主節中では〈would ＋動詞の原形〉を使う。

「間違える，ミスをする」は make a mistake。この文の場合，ミスは1つだけとは限らないから，複数形の mistakes を使う。

②(1)まず「私は例の美術館へ行った」と言った後で，「美術館」を詳しく説明する関係詞節を続ける。関係詞節は，次の文をもとに考える。

・You told me about it the other day.
（君は先日それ［美術館］について私に話した）

＊**tell O about** ～「～について O［人］に話す」

この文の it を関係代名詞（that）に置き換えて，先行詞（that (art) museum）の後ろに置く。it は前置詞（about）の目的語の働きをしているから，that は目的格の関係代名詞。したがって省略してもよい。

(2)「その絵本展はおもしろかった」という意味だから，It was interesting と表現する。「たくさんあって」は，and で2つの文を結びつけるよりも，「たくさんあったのでおもしろかった」と考えて，because を使うとよい。「世界中から集まったたくさんの絵本」は，a lot of[many] picture books (that were) **collected** from around[all over] the world（世界中から集められた多くの絵本）と表現する（本が自分から集まるわけではない）。「1日じゃ」は in a[one] day（in「～の時間をかけて」）。「全部見て回る」は，look at all of them（それらの全部を見る）でよい（them は絵本のこと）。

027
① **When she sees a bee, she tries to catch it and put it into her mouth.**
② **The sight[scene] is so scary that when I see a bee, I ask her not to touch it.**
③ **Though she doesn't want to attack a bee, it thinks it has got attacked**
④ **The best way to protect her may be to learn more about bees**

解説 ①「彼女はハチを見ると」は，when she see a bee（彼女がハチを見るとき）と表現する。「見る」を意味する主な動詞には，次の3つがある。

・**see**「（意識しなくても自然に）見える」
・**watch**「（動いているものを）じっと見る」
・**look at**「特定のものに（意識的に）目を向ける」

この問いでは「ハチの姿が目に入ると」という状況だから，see を使うのが適切。

「捕まえて口に入れようとする」は，try to catch it and put it into her mouse(それを捕まえ，そしてそれを口に入れようとする)と表現する(catch や put は他動詞だから)(→ 011 -⑦)。主語が she(３人称単数)で現在形だから，try を tries に変える点に注意。

② **so 〜 that ...**(とても〜なので…)の形を利用するとよい。scary は「(ものが)怖い」の意味で，a scary movie(怖い映画)のように使う。この形容詞を知らない場合は，次のようにも表現できる。

・I'm **so** afraid[scared] of the sight **that** ...
(私はその光景をとても恐れているので…)

次の形にも注意。

暗記 〈**ask[tell] + O + not to *do***〉「O[人]に〜しないよう頼む[言う]」

「私がハチを見つけたときはハチを触らないように」は，when I find it not to touch a bee(私が(一匹の)ハチを見つけたとき＋ハチを触らないように)と表現する。下線部をそれぞれ bees，them としてもよい。

③ Though she doesn't want to attack a bee は「彼女はハチを攻撃したいとは思っていないが」。it thinks it has **got attacked** は「それ[ハチ]は自分が攻撃されたと思う」。〈**get ＋過去分詞**〉は「〜される」の意味で使う。married(結婚して)，injured(けがをして)などの過去分詞がもとになった形容詞は，get と結びついて「〜する」の意味を表す。

・He **got injured** in the accident.
(彼はその事故で負傷した)

また，〈**get** ＋ C[形容詞]〉は「〜になる(**become** ＋ C)」の意味を表す。

・I **got sick** on the bus.
(私はバスに乗っていて気分が悪くなった)

④ S **is to *do*.**(S は〜することだ)の形をもとにして考える(→ 002 -①)。

・The best way to protect her (S) may be (V) to learn .... (C)

この形で，「S は…を学ぶことかもしれない」という意味になる。the best way to *do* は「〜するための最善の方法」(下線部は前の名詞を修飾する形容詞的用法の不定詞)。

028 ① **I had enough time, but I didn't start writing it.**

② **A teacher who gave me a lot of advice said[told me] that my report was not as good as Kouji's.**

③ **I changed my way of thinking.**

解説 ① I had enough time(私は十分な時間を持っていた)＋ but I didn't start writing[to write] it.(しかし私はそれ[大事なレポート]を書き始めなかった)という文を作る。

② S said that ....(S が…と言った)という形の文を作る。S は a teacher who gave me a lot of advice(私に多くの助言を与えたある先生)。advice は不可算名詞なので，many advices とは言えない。that 節は，〈**not** ＋ **as** ＋原級の形容詞＋ **as** 〜〉(〜ほど…ではない)の形を使う(→ 002 -⑦)。

なお，この問いでは日本文の途中から下線が引かれている。このような問いでも，普通は(大文字で文を始めて最後にピリオドを入れる)完全な形の英文で答えてかまわない。

③「A の考え方」は A's way of thinking で表す(→ 012 -④)。また，the way SV で「S が V する方法」の意味を表すこともできる。たとえば「彼女の話し方」は the way she speaks，「私たちの先生の英語の教え方」は the way our teacher teaches English と言う。

029 ① **She's reading the book (that) you advised her to read last week.**

② **He's[He has] been studying without having anything since morning.**

③ **If we had more time to practice, we could play better.**

④ **I don't have as much homework as (I did) last week**

解説 ①「勧める」は「読むように勧める」ということだから，〈**advise** + O + **to** ***do***〉(O に〜するよう助言する)の形を利用する(→002-④)。

②「朝から(今まで)ずっと勉強し続けている」という意味だから，動作の継続を表す現在完了進行形(**has been studying**)を使う。「飲まず食わずで」は，eat と drink を使わなくても，**without having anything**(何も飲み食いしないで)と表現できる。「朝から」は **since (this) morning**。「今日の朝から」という意味を明確にしたい状況でない限り，this は省いてよい。

③「実際には練習時間が足りない」と言おうとしているので，仮定法過去を使って表現する。主語は前の文にそろえて we を使う。「練習時間」は practice time でもよい。「うまくなれる」は，could play better(もっと上手にプレーできる)と表現できる。

④日本語は「宿題は」だが，I を主語にして書くのが適切。次の点を頭に入れておこう。

暗記 英作文では，人間を主語にして書くと自然な英文になることが多い。

「彼女の歌は上手だ」

→×Her song is good.

○She is a good singer.

＊×の文は「彼女が作った歌はいい歌だ」と誤解される。日本語の主語は「彼女の歌」だが，「彼女は上手に歌う人だ」と表現するのがベター。

この問いも，I を主語にして，I don't have as much homework as (I did) last week.「私は先週ほど多くの宿題を持っていない」と表現できる。下線部は「〜と同じ量の宿題」ということ。homework は不可算名詞だから，many homeworks とは言えない。I did は省略してもよい(→008-①)。

第 2 回 実力テスト

1 ① **Could you tell me why you didn't come to school yesterday?**

② **This elephant has been one of the most popular animals in this zoo since it opened.**

③ **He asked me to take care of his dog while he was traveling.**

④ **This question was so difficult that some students couldn't answer it.**

⑤ **Doing something for the future is much better than doing nothing.**

解説 ①「〜してもらえますか」は，**Could [Can] you** 〜？で表すとよい(→018-①)。「教える」は teach でなく **tell** を使う(→020-①)。why 以下は間接疑問で，SV(you didn't come)の語順になる。

②「開園以来(ずっと)〜だ」は，状態の継続を表す現在完了形(**has been**)で表す。「一番人気のある動物の 1 つ」は，one of the most popular animals。下線部の s を入れ忘れないこと(→018-⑨)。... animals since this zoo opened. でもよい。

③「…している間」は，接続詞の **while** を使って表す。「彼が旅行している間」は while he was traveling または while he was on a[the] trip。前置詞の **during**(〜の間)を使って，during his trip とも表現できる。「犬の世話を彼は私に頼んだ」は，〈**ask** + O + **to** ***do***〉(O に〜するよう頼む)の形を利用する。「〜の世話をする」は **take care of** 〜。

④ **so 〜 that ...**(とても〜なので…)の形を利用する。次のようにも表現できる。

・This question was **too difficult for some students to answer.**(この問題は，何人かの生徒にとって答えるには難しすぎた)

［参考］「問題」は question または problem，answer a question（問題［質問］に答える），solve a problem（問題を解く）というフレーズを覚えておくこと。

⑤ A is much better than B.（A は B よりずっとよい）という形を作る。

暗記 〈**much** ＋比較級＋ **than** ～〉「～よりもずっと［はるかに］…」

A と B はそれぞれ動名詞を使って，**doing** something for the［your］ future（将来のために何かをすること），**doing** nothing（何もしないこと）と表現する。

2 ① **when a long vacation comes, I always think about which country to go to next.**

② **It is very hard to learn so much, but I'm looking forward to studying to be a cabin attendant.**

解説 ①「S が来ると」は，when を使って when S comes（S が来るとき）と表現する。「今度は」は直訳すると this time だが，この文では next（次は）を使うのが適切。「どの国へ行こうか」は，which country to go to（どの国へ行くべきか）で表せる。which country I would like to go to（（自分が）どの国へ行きたいか）でもよい。これを think about（～について考える）の後ろに置く。

②前半は，形式主語の It を使って表現できる。「楽しみです」は，**look forward to ～ing**（～するのを楽しみにしている）を使って表現する（→ 013 −⑥）。「～になるために」は，to be［become］～と表現できる（目的を表す副詞的用法の不定詞）。

3 ① 例 (1) **Are you interested in Japanese culture?**

(2) **There are a lot of places to visit in Japan.**

(3) **Could you show me (some of) the pictures you took in Australia?**

② 例 (1) **It's famous for Mt. Hikari.**

(2) **If you climb it in (the) spring, you can see many beautiful flowers.**

(3) **Near that［the］ mountain, there is the most popular restaurant in (the) town.**

解説 ①(1)「あなたは日本の文化（Japanese culture）に興味がありますか」という文を作る（be interested in ～「～に興味がある」）。

(2)「日本には訪れるための多くの場所（a lot of［many］ places to visit）がある」という文を作る。Our country has many spots to visit.（私たちの国は訪れるための多くの場所を持っている）などでもよい。

(3)正解例の文は，たとえば次のような状況で使うと考えられる。

あなた：Did you take (any) pictures in Australia?
（オーストラリアで写真を撮りましたか）

ALT　：Yes, I did.（はい）

あなた：Do you have them with you now?
（その写真を今持っていますか）

＊with you は「手元に，携行して」の意味。

ALT　：Yes, I do.（はい）

あなた：Could you show me some of them?（そのうちの何枚かを私に見せてもらえますか）

この them を the pictures you took in Australia に置き換えれば，正解例の文になる。

Could you show me the pictures you took in Australia? なら，「その（あなたが今持っている）写真を全部見せてもらえますか」という意味になる。

［参考］ Can you ～？も使えるが，相手が目上の人なら Could you ～？の方がていねいな言い方。

これに関連して，次の例も見ておこう。

(a) I read a book yesterday. It was interesting.（私は昨日（1 冊の）本を読んだ。それは面白かった）

(b) The book I read yesterday was interesting.
（昨日私が読んだその本は面白かった）

(a)は，「私は昨日本を読んだ」という事実を初めて話題に出す場合に使う。一方(b)は，その事実を相手がすでに知っている状況で使う。(b)を(a)の意味で使うことはできない。

②(1) **be famous [well known, well-known] for ～**「～で有名だ[よく知られている]」。It has a famous mountain called Mt. Hikari.（それ[あおぞら町]はひかり山と呼ばれる有名な山を持っている）などでもよい。

注意！ 文章を完成する問題では，前の文とのつながりを考えること。
この問いの場合，日本語は「あおぞら町は…」だが，前の文に Aozora Town がすでに出てきているので，主語は It にするのがよい。

(2) 前半は，If you climb it in (the) spring（もし春にそれ[ひかり山]に登れば）と表現する。下線部の the は入れても入れなくてもよい。

注意！ 季節や方角を表す名詞を大文字で始めないこと。
たとえば「夏に」を in Summer，「東に」を in the East と書く誤りが時に見られる。季節や方角を表す名詞は，固有名詞（人や物の具体的な名前を表す名詞）ではないから，下線部は小文字で書くのが正しい。

次のように表現してもよい。

・You will find a lot of lovely flowers if [when] you go up Mt. Hikari in (the) spring.（春にひかり山に登れば[登るとき]，多くの美しい花を見つけるだろう）

［参考］ if は「（あなたがひかり山に登るかどうかはわからないが）もし登れば」の意味。when は「あなたは春にひかり山に登る」という前提で使う。

Q&A

Q 正解例では主語が you になっています。we も使えますか？

A you の方がベター。「一般の人々」は **you** で表すのが普通です。

・**You** [People] can get almost anything at a 100-yen shop.
（100円ショップでほとんど何でも買えます）

この文の you は「一般の人々」を表します。we は基本的に「（他の人々とは違って）私たちは…」という響きを持っています。たとえば「日本には100円ショップという便利な店がある。だから（外国とは違って）私たち（日本人）は…」と言いたいときは we を使うのが適切です。一方，100円ショップの一般的な便利さを説明したいときは，you を使うのがベターです。

この問いの場合はさらに，「あおぞら町に来てほしい」という気持ちで紹介文を書くなら，相手の行動を想定して you を使う方がよいでしょう。If we climb Mt. Hikari .... と書くと，「（他の人のことは知らないが）町の住人である私たちが登れば…」という客観的な説明に響きます。

比較のために次の例も見ておきます。

・**We** should save energy.
（私たちはエネルギーを節約すべきだ）

この文の場合は，we を使う方が「あなたも私も」という親しみをこめた言い方になります。

(3) 正解例は「その山の近くには，町で最も人気の高いレストランがある」という意味。次の 2 つの文と比べてみよう。

(a) The restaurant near the mountain is the most popular in the town.

(b) A restaurant near the mountain is the most popular in the town.

(a)は，たとえば「町にはいくつかのレストランがあります」という文に続けて言うのに適している。この原稿の場合，花の話題からいきなり The restaurant .... と話題を変えると，聞き手は「どのレストランのことなのか？」と感じるので，(a)はよくない。(b)は基本的に正解例の文と同じ意味だが，正解例の方がベター。There is .... と聞くと，相手は「ああ，『どこかに何かがある』という説明がこれから始まるのだな」という心の準備ができる。There is .... の形にはそのような働きがある。

4 Many students (often) enjoy talking louder than usual when they are with their friends on a train or bus. You[We] should be careful about public manners to avoid trouble with other passengers.

解説 日本語を直訳しようとするとうまくいかない。最初の文については，正解例では次のように表現している。

Many students (often) enjoy ⑴talking louder than usual（多くの学生は(しばしば)ふだんより大声で話すのを楽しむ）+ when they are with their friends ⑵on a train or bus.（彼らが電車やバスで友人と一緒にいるとき）

⑴は talk loud(大声で話す)の loud を比較級にして，後ろに than usual(ふだんより)を加えた形。

［参考］「大声で話す」は talk loudly が普通の言い方だが，比較級のときは talk more loudly よりも talk louder を使うことが多い。talk in a louder voice でもよい。

⑵は，on a train or on a bus の下線部を省略した形。「電車[バス]に乗って」は，アメリカ英語では on を使う(イギリス英語では in)。

２つ目の文は，⑶You[We] should be careful about[of] public manners（公共のマナーに気をつけるべきだ）+⑷to avoid trouble with other passengers.（他の乗客たちとのトラブルを避けるために）。⑶では，you を使えば「人々は(みんな)」，we を使えば「私たち学生は」という響きになる。自分が学生なら we を使えばよい。

⑷は，avoid(～を避ける)という動詞を知らなければ，**so that** you **will not** be in[get into] trouble with other passengers(他の乗客とトラブルにならないように)などとも表現できる(**so (that)** S **can[will]** ～「Sが～できる[する]ように)」(→016-語句・構文))。下線部は，bother(～に迷惑をかける)や disturb(～のじゃまをする)を使ってもよい。

［参考］fight with ～(～とけんかをする)も使えなくはないが，大きなトラブルのように響く。

3 状況に応じて会話を完成する問題

030 ［A］ 例① **(but) can I help you**
② **I know the way to the station**
［B］ 例① **am cleaning my desk**
② **today is my last day here**

解説 ［A］ ① Can I help you? の直訳は「私はあなたを助けることができますか[助けてもいいですか]」。Shall[Should] I help you?（あなたを助けましょうか）とも表現できる。また，Can I do anything for you[Is there anything I can do for you]?（私があなたのために何かできますか[できることは何かありますか]）なども使える。

② I know the way there. とも言える。下線部は「そこへ行く道筋」の意味。it's a long way from here(ここからは遠い道のりです)，you might get lost on the way there[to the station](あなたはそこ[駅]へ行く途中で道に迷うかもしれません)などを入れることもできる。

文法 名詞＋場所・時を表す副詞

the way there(そこへ行く道)は，there(副詞)が前の名詞 (the way) を修飾する形になっている。副詞の前に前置詞は不要だから，the way to there は誤り(→015-②)。このように，〈名詞＋場所・時を表す副詞〉という形がある。

- on my way **home**（家へ帰る途中で）
- my first trip **abroad**（私の初めての海外旅行）
- young people **today**（今日の若者たち）
- the meeting **tomorrow**（明日の会合）

全訳 （正解例を入れて完成した会話）

A：すみません①(が)，お助けしましょうか。
B：ああ，ええ，お願いします。あさひ駅を探しているところです。その駅を知っていますか。
A：ええ，②その駅へ行く道を知っています。駅までお連れしましょう。
B：ありがとう。あなたはとても親切ですね！

注意！ 英文の一部を答える形式であり，最後の「?」は下線の外側にある。したがって，Can I help you? と書くと減点されるおそれがある。

［B］ ②の正解例の today is my last day here

も，副詞のhereが前の名詞(句)を修飾する形。today is the last day for me(今日は私にとって最終日です)，this is my last time to use it[this is the last time for me to use it, this is the last time (that) I will use it](これが私がそれ[机]を使う最後の時です)とも表現できる。

全訳 (正解例を入れて完成した会話)
A：何をしているの？
B：①机の掃除をしているの。
A：なぜ？
B：②今日はここでの私の最後の日だから。明日日本へ帰国するの。
A：ええ，本当に？ とても悲しいけれど，また会えるといいね。

031〉例① It's January 15[fifteenth].
② It's nice.

解説 ①「あなたの誕生日はいつですか」という質問。正解例は「それ[私の誕生日]は1月15日です」。I was born on January 15. (私は1月15日に生まれました)でもよい。

注意！ 日付を数字ではなく英単語で書くよう求められている場合は，序数詞(「～番目」を表す語)を使う。
・May **third** (5月3日)
・September **twenty-second** (9月22日)

②「この歌をどう思う？」という質問。正解例は「いいね」。niceの代わりにvery[pretty] good, cool, greatなども使える。I really like it.(それを実に気に入っている)などと答えてもよい。

032〉例① How many (fish) did you catch?
② I'm afraid that's my seat.

解説 ①(4)で「いい質問だね」と答えているので，(3)には疑問文が入る。I caugh ten. という返答から考えて，捕れた[釣れた]魚の数を尋ねる疑問文を作る。Did you catch many fish? (魚はたくさん釣れた？)などでもよい。**fish**は特殊な名詞で，数を数える場合には複数形もfishを使う。「1匹の魚」はone fish，「2匹の魚」はtwo fish[×fishes]。

全訳 (正解例を入れて完成した会話)
(1)どこへ行ってきたの？
(2)湖へ釣りに行ったんだ。
(3)何匹(の魚を)釣ったの？
(4)いい質問だね。10匹釣れたよ。

②男性が座る座席を間違えている状況。正解例の**I'm afraid ....**は，「すみません[残念です]が…」と言いにくいことを相手に伝えるときの決まり文句。This is my ticket. Could you check yours? (これが私の切符です。あなたの(切符)を確かめてもらえますか)などを入れてもよい。

全訳 (正解例を入れて完成した会話)
(1)すみません。
(2)はい？
(3)そこは私の席だと思います。
(4)ちょっと待って…。ああ，すみません。

033〉① part in ② are interested
③ on, stage

解説 チラシの日本語を見ながら考える。
① take **part in** ～「～に参加する」
② **be interested in** ～「～に興味がある」
③ walk **on** the **stage**「ステージ上を歩く」

全訳 (正解例を入れて完成した会話)
A：見て！ 高校生にファッションコンテストへ①参加してほしいそうよ。
B：どうすれば参加できるの？
A：デザインを送る必要があるわ。ファッションに②興味のある生徒を歓迎するそうよ。
B：君はデザインについて何かアイデアがあるの？
A：ええ，おばあちゃんの着物からアイデアを思いついたわ。
B：それはすごくいいね！
A：もし5月の一次審査に通ったら，8月の最終審査で③ステージの上を歩けるわ。
B：いいね！

034〉例 ④ **Which one is the best**
⑧ **I enjoyed listening to the CD, too**
⑪ **Let's go together next time**

解説 全訳を参照。④は文の最後に「?」があるので，疑問文を入れる必要がある。正解例以外の応答の例は，④ Can you tell me which book to read(?)（どの本を読めばいいか教えてくれる？），⑧ I liked it very much.（それ[その本]がとても気に入ったわ），

全訳 （正解例を入れて完成した会話）
①こんにちは，友子，ここで会えてうれしいわ。手伝ってくれる？ モーツァルトについての本がほしいの。
②もちろんよ。どこにあるか知っているわ。行きましょう。
③ありがとう。
④まあ，モーツァルトの本がこんなにたくさんあるわ。どの本が一番いい？
⑤この本はどう？ 特典 CD もついているわ。
⑥面白そうね！ これを買うわ。
（翌日）
⑦こんにちは，ウェンディ。昨日買った本は楽しんだ？
⑧ええ。CD を聞くのも楽しんだわ。
⑨あなたはモーツァルトを聞くの？
⑩ええ，それによくクラシックのコンサートに行くわ。
⑪すごいわ。今度一緒に行きましょう。

035〉例 **I'm looking for ABC Hotel, but I don't know where I am on this map. Could you tell me how to get there, please?**
（24語）

解説 女性が自分の行きたい ABC ホテルを探している状況。Could you tell me the way to ABC Hotel?（ABC ホテルへ行く道を教えてもらえますか）などと尋ねるのがシンプルだが，「25 語程度」という条件があるのでもっと長い発言を考える必要がある。正解例は「私は ABC ホテルを探していますが，この地図上で自分がどこにいるかわかりません。ABC ホテルにはどのようにして行けばよいか教えてもらえますか」という意味。

【別解】I'm a tourist from Japan and I don't know about this town. Could you please tell me how I can get to ABC Hotel?（私は日本からの旅行者で，この町について知りません。ABC ホテルへはどのようにして行けるか教えてもらえますか）(24語)

036〉例 ① **What does she like (about Japanese culture)?**
② **I want her to have some Japanese food. Let's have the party at my house. I'll make *takoyaki* for her.**

解説 ①マイクが「彼女は日本のマンガが好きだ」と答えているので，果歩は彼女の好きなものを尋ねたと考えられる。
②果歩の立場になって，何ができるかを考えて答える。「彼女のために何をしたいか」という質問に対する答えを最初に書き，それに関連する内容を 2 文以上で続ければよい。

全訳 （正解例を入れて完成した会話）
果歩：新しい交換留学生が，来月私たちのクラスに来る予定よ。
マイク：知っているよ！ 名前はアリスだね。とてもわくわくしてるよ。
果歩：彼女について何か知っている？
マイク：うん，少しね。英語の先生から彼女のことを聞いた。日本文化に興味があるそうだ。
果歩：彼女は(日本文化について)何が好きなの？
マイク：日本のマンガが好きだって。だから彼女は日本語を勉強しているんだ。
果歩：まあ，本当？ じゃあ，彼女のために歓迎会を開きましょう。
マイク：それがいいね。果歩，君はパーティーで彼女のために何をしたいの？
果歩：私は彼女に何か日本の料理を食べてもらいたいわ。私の家でパーティーを開きましょう。彼女にたこ焼きを作ってあげます。

037 例① **Let's make the plan together. Do you have any ideas?**（10語）

② **I'd like to go to the beach. It's getting hotter and hotter in summer. You'll want to swim in the sea.**（21語）

解説 ①第1文はLet's ～.（～しましょう）を使う。第2文の「何か」は，any で表す。

②最後のティムの発言から考えて，ビーチと山のどちらかを選び，その理由を説明する内容を入れる。

Q&A

Q ①で ideas を複数形にするのはなぜですか？

A 次のように覚えておきましょう。

暗記 **可算名詞を使って疑問文や否定文を作る場合，「1つしかないもの」は単数形で，「2つ以上ありうるもの」は複数形で表す。**

「あなたには何か考えがありますか」という質問の場合，相手の考え［アイデア］は1つだけとは限りません。だから複数形の ideas を使います。次の例も参照してください。

・Do you have any questions［hobbies］?
（何か質問［趣味］はありますか）
＊相手には2つ以上の質問［趣味］がありうる。

・My town doesn't have (any) supermarkets.
（私の町にはスーパーマーケットが（1軒も）ない）
＊1つの町が2軒以上のスーパーマーケットを持つことがありうる。

・Our school doesn't have a library.
（私たちの学校には図書室がない）
＊学校の図書室は普通1つだけなので単数形を使う。

全訳 （正解例を入れて完成した会話）

あなた：やあ，ティム。今度の夏に君とぼくは，ぼくの家族と一緒に旅行に行くよね？ ①その計画を一緒に作ろう。君は何か考えがあるかい？

ティム：うん。今は，ビーチへ行くか，山へ行くかの2つのアイデアがあるんだ。ぼくにはどちらもよさそうだけれど，決められない。ビーチと山のどちらの場所がいいだろう。いい方の場所を決めて，そこで何を楽しめるかをぼくに教えてよ。

あなた：わかった。②ぼくはビーチへ行きたいな。夏はどんどん暑くなっているから，海で泳ぐのは最高だろう。

ティム：なるほど。そちらの方がいい理由がわかったよ。わくわくするな。

038 例① **I can exercise while I'm listening to them**

② **happened (to you)**

解説 ①ハナが「（あなたは）2つのことを一緒にできるということ（を意味しているの）ね」と答えている。この「2つのこと」のうち，1つはオーディオブックを聞くこと，もう1つは，ティムの最初の発言から，運動することだと考えられる。正解例は，「それら［オーディオブック］を聞いている間に運動することができる」という意味。接続詞の **while**（…する間に）は，しばしば進行形とともに使う。I can listen to (audio) books and (get) exercise at the same time（私は（オーディオ）ブックを聞くのと運動するのを同時にできる）などでもよい。

全訳 （正解例を入れて完成した会話）

ハナ：空いた時間には何をするのが好き？

ティム：そうだね，ぼくは運動するのが好きだ。（スポーツ）ジムに通うのが好きだよ。それと，読書を楽しむことも時々あるね。

ハナ：私も時間のあるときは読書を楽しむわ。

ティム：でも近ごろは，読む代わりに本を聞くことが多いね。オーディオブックを聞くんだ。

ハナ：まあ，そうなの？

ティム：うん，ぼくはオーディオブックを聞くのが好きだよ。

ハナ：なぜ？

ティム：それらを聞きながら運動することができるからだよ。

ハナ：つまり，2つのことを一緒にできるということね。

ティム：そのとおり。これは「マルチタスキング」と呼ばれている。ぼくはマルチタスキングが大好きだ。

②会話の状況から考えてケンジは，ジョンとアヤの間で言い争い（argument）があった理由を尋ねている。正解例は最もシンプルな答え方で，What happened (to you)? は「（君に）何が起きたのか」の意味。その他，What was wrong (with you)?（（君は）どこが悪かったのか），What was the problem?（何が問題だったのか），

What caused the trouble?（何がそのトラブルを引き起こしたのか）などでもよい。

全訳　（正解例を入れて完成した会話）

ケンジ：やあ，ジョン。元気かい？

ジョン：やあ，ケンジ。ぼくは昨日アヤと一緒に映画に行ったんだ。

ケンジ：楽しそうだね。映画はどうだった？　楽しかったかい？

ジョン：あんまり。彼女と言い合いになったんだ。

ケンジ：それは残念だ。何が起きたの？

ジョン：あのね，映画は問題なかったんだけど，主役のボブ・デップがあまりかっこよくないとぼくが言ったんだ。でも彼女は彼の大ファンだったんだ。

ケンジ：おや，君は彼女がファンだと知らなかったの？ 彼女はいつも友だちと彼のことを話しているよ。

ジョン：しまった，それは知らなかったよ。

039 例 ① **We must[have to] remember to wear a mask**

② **we should keep the windows open**

③ **We should wash our hands (carefully) with soap**

④ **the gym doesn't have enough space for all the students**

⑤ **we should[must] not believe everything on the Internet**

解説 ①直後の先生の発言中の take it off（それを外す）に着目する。it が指すものを考えると，この空所には「マスクをつけておかねばならない」という内容が入るはず。**remember to *do***（～することを覚えておく，忘れずに～する），**wear a mask**（マスクを身に着ける）を使って文を作る。

②直前の先生の質問は，「どのようにすればいつも新鮮な空気を保てるか」ということ。keep the windows open（窓を開けたままにしておく）という形を使う（**keep**＋O＋C「OをCのままに保つ」）。the windows は教室の窓のこと（教室の窓は１つだけではないから複数形にする）。

③「食べる前に何をすべきか」という質問と，soap（石けん）を使うという指示から考える。また，直後の先生の to dry them（それら（＝手）を乾かすための）とあることから，hands（両手）という語も使って，「石けんで手を洗うべきだ」という内容を入れる。

④直後の先生の発言中に「私たちの体育館は小さすぎる」とあるので，「体育館には生徒全員のための十分なスペースがない」という内容を入れる。enough は，形容詞・副詞を修飾するときはその後ろに置く（例：large enough「十分に大きい」）が，「十分なスペース」のように名詞を修飾するときは enough space の語順にするのが普通。there isn't enough space for all the students in the gym でもよい。

⑤直前の文が「（インターネット上の）一部の情報は本当ではない」という内容だから，「ネット上に書いてあることを全部信じてはいけない」という内容を入れる。everything の代わりに all (the) information（すべての情報）を使ってもよい。

Q&A

Q 正解例の文（We should not believe everything on the Internet.）は，「インターネット上のことはすべて［1つも］信じてはいけない」という意味になりませんか？

A いいえ。次の点を覚えておきましょう。

暗記 not の後ろに all，every など「全部」を意味する語を置くと，「全部が～なわけではない」（部分否定）の意味になる。

・I don't know **everything** about him.（私は彼についてすべてのことを知っているわけではない［知らないこともある］）

＊「私は彼のことを何も知らない」は，I don't know anything about him. と表現する。

・**Not all** (of) the members came to the meeting.（メンバー全員が会合に来たわけではない［来なかったメンバーもいる］）

＊「メンバーは全員［誰も］会合に来なかった」は，None of the members came to the meeting. と表現する。

全訳　（正解例を入れて完成した会話）

先生：今日は，私たちの日常生活の中で，新型コロナウイルス感染症から身を守るための方法について話し合います。最初に，外出するときにするべき大切なことがあります。それが何かわかりますか。

生徒A：①私たちは忘れずにマスクをつけておかねばなりません。

先生：そのとおり。食べるときだけそれを外すべきです。次に，私たちの教室について考えましょう。私たちは，いつでも確実にたくさんの新鮮な空気を入れる必要があります。どのようにしてそれができますか。

生徒B：②私たちは窓を開けたままにしておくべきだと思います。

先生：そうです。もしそうすれば，空気があちこちに動くことができます。次に，昼食時間の話に移りましょう。私たちは食べる前に何をすべきですか。

生徒C：③私たちは石けんで(注意深く)手を洗うべきです。

先生：そうです。それから，手を乾かすために清潔なタオルを使うことを忘れないように。また，私たちはたいてい体育館で大きな集会や式典を行いますが，今年度はそれらをすべて中止しました。なぜだかわかりますか。

生徒D：私たちはお互いに近づきすぎて立ってはいけませんが，④体育館には全生徒のための十分なスペースがありません。

先生：そうです。残念ながら，私たちの体育館は小さすぎます。最後に，新型コロナウイルス感染症やその他のことについての多くの情報がインターネット上にあります。しかし一部の情報は本当ではありません。だから，⑤私たちはインターネット上のすべてのことを信じるべきではありません。皆さん，安全で健康なままでいてください。

語句

protect O from ～「O を～から守る」
Exactly.「そのとおり」
take ～ off「～を脱ぐ，外す」
make sure (that) ...「確実に…する」
towel「タオル」 gym「体育館」
cancel「～を中止する」 close to ～「～の近くに」
unfortunately「残念なことに」
stay C「C のままでいる」

040 ① **wishes that he could travel around the world and visit many famous**
② **to understand my turtle's feelings because she has never made a sound**
③ 例 **Didn't you wish for anything when[while] the star was shooting?**
④ **That's because I'm happy with my life now.**

解説 ①仮定法過去を使った次の形がポイント。

暗記 〈S **wish(es)** ＋仮定法過去〉「(今)～ならよいのに(が実際にはそうでないのが残念だ)とSは思う」

・I **wish** my family were richer.
　　　　　　　　　　仮定法過去
(私の家族がもっと金持ちならいいのに(実際にはそうでないのが残念だ))

＊仮定法過去のbe動詞は，主語が何であってもwereを使うのが原則。

この問いの完成した文は，「彼は世界一周旅行をして多くの有名な場所を訪れることができればいいのにと願っている」という意味。He wishes he could .... のcouldは，canを仮定法過去にしたもの。

②文の意味は全訳を参照。make a soundは「音を立てる」の意味で，ここでは「(自分のカメが)言葉を話したことがない」と言おうとしている。

③(1)の絵に「何かお願いしましょう」とあり，(4)の絵でカレンがNo, I didn't. と答えていることから，この空所には「あなたは何もお願いしなかったの？」という内容が入ると考えられる。この日本語はDidn't you wish for anything? と英訳できるが，「10語で」という条件を満たすにはあと5語必要なので，when[while] the star was shooting(星が流れているとき[間に])を加える。shootは「(星が)流れる」の意味の動詞で，a shooting starは「流れ(てい)る星→流れ星」。

文法 否定疑問文

notを含む疑問文を，否定疑問文と言う。否定疑問文は「イエス」の答えを期待して使う。

・**Don't** you know this song?
（この歌を知らないの？）
この質問には，「君はこの歌を知っているよね？」という気持ちがこめられている。返答は次のようになる。
・**Yes, I do.**（いや，知っているよ）
・**No, I don't.**（うん，知らないよ）
下線部に注意。not を含まない質問(Do you know this song?) に答えるときと同様に，知っていれば Yes, I do. で，知らなければ No, I don't. で答えればよい。×Yes, I don't. ／ No, I do. という答え方は誤り。

④「それは～だからだ」は，**That is[That's, It's] because ～.** で表す。「～に満足している」は，**be happy[satisfied, content] with ～**。

注意！ **Because ～.** だけの文は原則として誤り。
英作文で，次のような誤った書き方が非常によく見られる。
「私は動物園で働きたい。動物が大好きだからだ」
→×I want to work at a zoo. Because I love animals.
下線部が誤りなのは，これだけでは文の形として不完全だから。because（…なので）は接続詞だから，次のように２つの節（SV を含む意味のかたまり）を結びつける形で使うのが正しい。
(1) I want to work at a zoo **because** I love animals.
（I = S，want = V；I = S，love = V）
（私は動物が大好きなので，動物園で働きたい）
(2) I want to work at a zoo. That is **because** I love animals.
（That = S，is = V；I = S，love = V）
（私は動物園で働きたい。それは，私が動物が大好きだからだ）
［参考］ただし Why ～？という疑問文に対しては，Because ～. という答え方ができる。

全訳 （正解例を入れて完成した会話）
(1)「ほら，あれを見て！」
「わあ，君の誕生日に流れ星だよ，カレン！」
「急いで，何かお願いしましょう！」
(3)「(ア)私の（飼っている）カメはこれまで一度も口をきいたことがないから，そのカメの気持ちを理解したいわ」
(4)「君はなぜそんなに静かなの，カレン？」
「(イ)星が流れているとき何もお願いしなかったの？」
「ええ，そうよ」
(5)「なぜ?! お金持ちになりたいとか，もっと物がほしいとか思わないの？」
(6)「ええ，思わないわ。(ウ)それは今の生活に満足しているからだよ」
(7)「なるほど！ じゃあ，このプレゼントは必要なさそうね」
「待って…。何?! いや！」

041 例 ① **you[we] can buy many kinds of things from these machines**
② **Put some money into the machine and push the button (of the drink you want).**

解説 ①自動販売機の説明となる言葉を入れる。
【別解】you can find a lot of machines like these on the street. You can get drinks or other things without having to go to a store（これらのような多くの機械を路上で見つけることができます。お店に行かなくても飲み物やその他のものを買うことができます）
②自動販売機の使い方の説明を入れる。
【別解】Choose the drink you want and put some coins here. These drinks are 120 yen or 150 yen. Then push the button for the drink you want. It comes out here.（あなたがほしい飲み物を選んで，ここに硬貨を入れてください。これらの飲み物は120円または150円です。それから，自分がほしい飲み物のボタンを押してください。ここに出てきます）

全訳 （正解例を入れて完成した会話）
旅行者：すみません。これらは何ですか。
あなた：ああ，自動販売機ですよ。
旅行者：自動販売機とは何ですか。
あなた：日本では，①これらの機械から多くの種類の物を買うことができます。
旅行者：わあ！ それはとても便利ですね。じゃあ，いくつか飲み物を買ってみます。この機械の使い方を教えてもらえますか。
あなた：いいですよ。②機械にお金を入れて，（自分がほしい飲み物の）ボタンを押してください。
旅行者：簡単そうですね。ありがとうございます。
あなた：どういたしまして。日本の旅を楽しんでください！

第3回 実力テスト

1 例① **How is the weather in Kyoto?**
② **Where are you going (to go) today?**
③ **What time will you leave Kyoto?**

解説 全訳を参照。①は，how（どんな様子で）を使って質問する。②はレオの今日の予定を尋ねている。Where are you going to visit today?（今日はどこを訪ねる予定なの？）などでもよい。③はレオが「2時に」と答えていることから考える。will you leaveの代わりにare you going to leaveやare you leavingを使ってもよい。

［参考］ 与えられた5つの疑問詞の中からそれぞれ1語を使用するという条件がなければ，②はWhat will you do today?（今日は何をするつもりなの？），③はWhen are you going to leave Kyoto?（いつ京都を発つ予定なの？）などでもよい。

文法 howの3つの意味
(1)「どんな様子で」
・**How's** your family?（ご家族はお元気ですか）
＊How is[are] ～？の形で使うことが多い。How are you?（元気かい）のhowや，この問いの①のhowも同様。
(2)「どのようにして，どんな方法で」
・**How** did you get that ticket?
（そのチケットはどうやって手に入れたの？）
(3)「どのくらい～，どの程度～」
・**How long** did you study yesterday?
（昨日はどのくらい（の時間）勉強したの？）
＊この意味のhowは，後ろに形容詞・副詞を置いて使う。

全訳 （正解例を入れて完成した会話）
タクヤ：①京都の天気はどう？
レオ：こちらは晴れているよ。旅行には最高の天気だ。
タクヤ：ああ，君はとても運がいいね。②今日はどこへ行く予定なの？
レオ：今日はお城と有名な寺を訪ねる予定だよ。
タクヤ：それは楽しそうだ。明日帰って来るよね？③何時に京都を発つの？
レオ：2時だよ。新幹線で4時間くらいかかるだろう。だから6時ごろ家に着くよ。

2 例① **What time does it start**
② **What[Which] kind of movies do you like**
③ **Let's have dinner there before the show**

解説 ①絵とユカの返答から考えて，ジェニーは映画が始まる時刻を尋ねている。暦や時刻表などで確定している予定は，未来のことでも現在形で表すのが普通。
【別解】What time does the movie start in the afternoon
（映画は午後は何時に始まるの）
②絵とジェニーの返答から考えて，ユカは彼女にどんな映画が好きかを尋ねている。
【別解】What are your favorite kinds of movies（あなたの一番好きな種類の映画は何）
③絵と会話の流れから考えて，ユカは映画館の隣のレストランで食事をとってから映画を見ようとジェニーを誘っている。**How about** having dinner ...?（…夕食をとるのはどう？），**Shall we** have dinner ...?（…夕食をとりましょうか）などの形も使える。
【別解】The food there is really delicious（そこの料理は本当においしいわ），We can eat a delicious meal together（一緒においしい料理を食べられるわ）

全訳 （正解例を入れて完成した会話）
ユカ：来週映画を見に行くの。あなたも来る？
ジェニー：ええ，もちろん。いつ行きたいの？
ユカ：火曜日よ。いいアクション映画があるの。
ジェニー：わかったわ。①何時に始まるの？
ユカ：3時15分よ。
ジェニー：ああ，ごめんなさい。最後の授業が4時に終わるの。夜の上映は何かある？
ユカ：ええ，少しね。7時ごろ始まるわ。②あなたはどんな種類の映画が好きなの？
ジェニー：私は恋愛ものが好きよ。
ユカ：まあ，７時15分にいいのがあるわ。「大阪ラブストーリー」よ。
ジェニー：いいわね！ それを見ましょう。ところで，映画の前に食事ができる？
ユカ：ええ。映画館の隣にすてきなレストランがあるわ。③上映の前にそこで夕食をとりましょう。
ジェニー：わかったわ。じゃあまた。

4 与えられた情報を使って英文を書く問題

042 ① **How do you study English**
② A イ　B エ　C ア　D ウ

解説 ①英文の内容から考えて，このグラフはクラスの生徒たちの自宅での英語の学習方法を尋ねた結果を示している。したがって，「あなたはどのようにして英語を勉強していますか」という内容を入れるのが適切。

②英文の内容から考える。「多くの生徒が家で英語の本を読んだり英語を書いたりしている」「英語の本を読む生徒が最も多い」とあるので，A はイ，B はエ。英語の CD を聞く生徒の数は英語の本を読む生徒の３分の１だから，C はア。「英語で話す生徒はあまり多くない」とあるので，D はウ。

全訳（正解例を入れて完成した文章）
英語の授業で ALT の先生が私たちに質問しました。彼女は「家ではどのように英語を勉強していますか」と尋ねました。私たちの回答についてお話しします。
グラフを見てください。多くの生徒が，家で英語の本を読んだり，英語で何かを書いたりすることによって英語を勉強しています。英語の本を読む生徒の数が一番多いです。その数は，英語の CD を聞く生徒の数の３倍です。私はよく家族と英語で話をします。しかし，それをしている生徒はあまり多くありません。それ以外の方法をする生徒は２人だけです。
ALT の先生は「聞くこと，読むこと，話すこと，書くことはすべて大切です。いろいろな方法で英語を勉強してください」と言いました。

043 **How long did it take to**（６語）

解説 C でユキコが Two hours. と答えている。これは It took (me) two hours to get there.（そこへ着くのに（電車とバスで）２時間かかった）を短く表現したものと考えられる（〈**It takes** (**X**［人］)＋時間＋ **to** ***do*.**〉「（X が）～するのに…（の時間が）かかる」）。この下線部を How long で尋ねる疑問文は，**How long did it take** (you) to get there? となる。

［参考］ この状況では，you は言わなくてもわかるので省けばよい。また，How many hours ...? はユキコが２時間以上電車とバスに乗ったことを想定した質問であり，実際の所要時間は１時間以下だったかもしれないから，how long を使って尋ねる方がよい。

全訳（正解例を入れて完成した文章）
A　ユキコは「私は先週の日曜日に祖父を訪ねました。祖父はかもめ村に住んでいます」と言った。レイカは「私はその村には一度も行ったことがありません。どのようにしてそこへ行ったのですか」と言った。
B　ユキコは「祖父の家へはたいてい家族と一緒に車で行きます。でも今回は，私ひとりで電車とバスで行きました」と言った。レイカは「電車とバスを使ったとき，そこへ行くのにどのくらい時間がかかりましたか」と尋ねた。
C　ユキコは「２時間です。バスの窓からきれいな山々を見て楽しみました。祖父と私の旅の話をしました。今度は，一緒にかもめ村を訪ねることができます」と言った。レイカは，「まあ，行きたいです！」と言った。

044 ① **most popular**
② **wants us to have［eat］**（４語）

解説 ①「これはこのレストランでナンバーワンの料理です」を，「これはこのレストランで最も人気のある料理です」と言い換える。
②「それはシェフ Rui が今日私たちに食べてほしいと思っている料理です」と表現する。**want** O **to** ***do*** は「O に～してほしい」（→ 002 -④）。

［参考］ would like は want のていねいな表現だが，I'd like ～., Would you like ～? のように相手に向かって使う。この文のような客観的な説明には，want を使えばよい。

Q&A
Q「食べる」は，eat と have のどちらを使ってもよいのですか？

A はい。ただし一般的に言えば，「X［飲食物］をとる」の意味では **have** を使う方がよいでしょう。

・I **have** toast and coffee for breakfast.
（私の朝食はトーストとコーヒーです）

この文では，have を「食べる」「飲む」の両方の意味で使っています。have を使わなければ I eat toast and drink coffee for breakfast. と言わねばならないので，have を使う方がシンプルです。

・What would you like to **have** for lunch?
（昼食は何を食べたい？）

この文では eat も使えますが，have の方が上品に響きます。また，日本語でも「昼食を食べる」の代わりに「昼食をとる」と言いますね。これは「昼食を食べる」では意味の重複が感じられるからです。英語でも eat lunch より have lunch の方が好まれます。

045 例 ① **It takes about forty minutes to walk there (from Tamahama Station)** （8［11］語）

② **we won't (have to) go to the park** （6［8］語）

解説 ①メール1で，マークは玉浜駅からブルーパークまで歩いて行く場合の所要時間を尋ねている。広告には「玉浜駅から徒歩で約40分」とあるので，「(玉浜駅から)歩くと約40分かかる，だから長い道のりだ」と答えればよい。

【別解】You have［need］to walk (for) about forty minutes
（君は約40分歩かねばならない［歩く必要がある］）

②広告によれば，雨天の場合はボランティア活動は行われない。したがって「雨が降ったら公園へは行かない［行く必要はない］」と答える。

【別解】we won't do the volunteer work at the park（ぼくたちは公園でボランティア活動を行わない）（9語），the volunteer work at the park will be canceled（公園でのボランティア活動は中止される）（9語）

全訳 （正解例を入れて完成した文章）

【メール1】やあ，健司。ブルーパークでのボランティア活動について君に尋ねたいんだ。君は公園までバスに乗ればいいとぼくに教えてくれたけど，玉浜駅からそこまで歩いて行くと，どのくらい時間がかかるの？ もし晴れていたら，歩きたいんだ。雨が降ったらバスに乗るよ。　マーク

【メール2】やあ，マーク。君の質問に答えるよ。①そこまで歩いて行くと約40分かかるから，長い距離だ。それにもし雨が降れば，②ぼくたちは公園には行かない［行く必要がない］(ことになる)。玉浜駅ホールで海の動物についての勉強をするんだ。駅の近くだよ！　健司

046 例 **How are you (doing)? Next month, I am going to sing English songs for some［the］children who are learning English. Can［Could］you come to my room and play the piano (for me［them］)?**

解説 正解例の英文を1つずつ確認しよう。

◆How are you (doing)?（元気ですか？）

・あいさつの決まり文句。省いてもよい。

◆Next month, I am going to sing English songs for some［the］children who are learning English.（来月，私は英語を学んでいる子どもたちに英語の歌を歌ってあげるつもりです）

・時を表す副詞(句)は文末に置くのが基本だが，この文で next month を文末に置くと，next month が are learning を修飾して「来月英語を学ぶ」ように感じられるので，最初に置くのがよい。

・I will sing とも言えるが，「～する予定だ」は be going to で表すと覚えておこう。

・learn English（英語を習得する）は，学習の過程や結果に重点を置いた言い方。たとえば I'm learning English. は「私は英語を習得しつつある」ということ。一方 I'm studying English. は「(学校で教科として)英語を勉強している」と言っているだけで，英語の力がついているかどうかはわからない。小さな子どもが英語の歌を聞いたりして英語学習をする場合は，learn English を使う方がよい。

Q&A

Q 正解例で，some children と the children とは意味が違いますか？

A はい。the children は「(あなたも知っている)その子どもたち」ということです。由美のメールにある「英語を勉強している子どもたち」のことをルーシーも知っているなら，the children を使います。一方，その子どもたちのことをルーシーが知らないときは，(the が使えないので代わりに) some children を使います。some は省くこともできますが，入れる方が普通です。次の例も同じように考えることができます。

(1) There is a cat in the park.
　(公園に1匹のネコがいる)

(2) There are some cats in the park.
　(公園に何匹かのネコがいる)

この2つの文の間には，〈a＋単数名詞〉〈some＋複数名詞〉という関係があります。a[an] を「不定冠詞」，the を「定冠詞」と言いますが，(2)の some は(1)の a に相当する(いわば「複数形の前に置く不定冠詞」の)働きをしています。(2)で some を省いた場合，「公園には(他の動物ではなく)ネコがいる」という響きになります。

◆Can[Could] you come to my room and play the piano (for them[me])?

・友人同士なら I want you to come ....(あなたに来てほしい)を使ってもよいが，これだと相手に選択権を与えない(押しつけがましい)言い方になりかねない。相手が断る可能性を考えて，Can[Could] you 〜?(〜してくれませんか)という疑問文を使う方がよい。for me は「私のために」，for them は「子どもたちのために」。これらは省いてもよい。

047 例 ① **I like sending an e-mail better.**
② **First(ly), it is cheaper than talking on the phone. Second(ly), e-mails are more convenient because they can be read anytime.** (20語)

解説 ①「メールを送るのと電話で話すのと，あなたはどちらの方が好きですか」という質問。**Which do you like better, A or B?** という質問に対しては，**I like A better.** または **I like B better.** と答える。正解例では「メールを送る方が好きだ」と答えている。それに「私は2つの理由を持っている」と続けて，②にその2つの理由を入れる。

②正解例は，「第1に，それ[メールを送ること]の方が電話で話すよりも安い。第2に，メールはいつでも読めるのでメールの方が便利だ」。2つの理由を並べるには，次のような表現を使ってもよい。

・**One[The first] reason is that .... The other[second] reason is ....** (1つ[第1]の理由は…ということだ。もう1つ[第2]の理由は…ということだ)

048 例 ① イ
② **The tourists can enjoy the view of the sea and go to the souvenir shop on the way to the hotel, too.** (22語)

解説 地図を見ると，距離的にはアもイも同じだが，アの方が多くのみやげ物店を回れる。一方イは，海の眺めを楽しめる。正解例ではイを選び，その理由として「その観光客たちは海の眺めを楽しめて，ホテルへ行く途中のみやげ物店へ行くこともできる」の意味。

【別解】(アを選んだ場合)They can visit a number of souvenir shops. Also, there is a sushi restaurant on the way to the hotel. (彼らはより多くのみやげ物店を訪ねることができる。また，ホテルへ行く途中にすし屋もある)(20語)

049 ① **river** ② **sun** ③ **clouds**

解説 イラストを見て，下の意味の文章を完成する。cloud(雲)は可算名詞であり無冠詞単数形では使えないので，③には clouds(複数形)を入れる点に注意。

全訳

この絵は水がめぐる様子を示している。山に雨が降ると，水は①川に流れ込み，それから海へ出る。②太陽が(海)水を温めると，それは空気中に上る。その後，水は③雲になる。その雲から，再び雨が降る。

050〉例 It will be held on February twenty-fifth. Twelve students will take part. Could you be one of the judges for the contest? (22語)

解説 英文の意味は全訳を参照。「コンテストに参加する」は，**take part in** the contest。take part(参加する) + in the contest(コンテストに)という形だから，下線部は(言わなくてもわかることとして)省略してよい。

注意！ 英作文では，同じ言葉のくり返しをできるだけ避けることが大切。正解例の英文中には，contest という名詞は1回しか出てこない。これを The contest will be held.... Twelve students will take part in the contest. Could you ... for the contest? のように同じ名詞をくり返して書くと，ぎこちない文章になる。

【別解】The date of the contest is February twenty-fifth. Twelve students will take part in it. If you are available, we would like you to be one of the judges. (コンテストの日付は2月25日です。12人の生徒がそれに参加する予定です。もしご都合がつくようなら，審査員の1人になっていただきたいのですが)(29語)(available「(人の)都合がつく，予定が空いている」)

全訳 (正解例を入れて完成した文章)
拝啓 ジョーンズ様
お元気ですか。私たちは岡山白陵中学校で英語のスピーチコンテストを開く予定です。それは2月25日に開かれます。12人の生徒が参加します。コンテストの審査員の1人になっていただけますか。
よいご返事をお待ちしております。
敬具
(あなたの名前)

051〉例 (I think) the automatic door (is convenient.) We don't have to use our hands to open it. (10語)

解説 正解例の意味は全訳を参照。

【別解】I think the elevator is convenient. It helps older or disabled people to go upstairs easily. (私はエレベーターが便利だと思います。エレベーターはお年寄りや体の不自由な人たちが簡単に上の階へ上がるのを手助けしてくれるからです)(10語)(disabled people「体の不自由な人たち，障がい者」)/I think the shopping cart is convenient. It is easy to carry a lot of things in it. (私はショッピングカートが便利だと思います。たくさんの物をそれに入れて運びやすいからです)(11語)

全訳 (正解例を入れて完成した会話)
メアリー：このショッピングセンターでは，たくさんの物が便利だと思うわ。
あなた：ええ。あれを見て。私は自動ドアが便利だと思う。開けるのに手を使わなくてもいいから。
メアリー：私もそう思うわ。もっと見つけましょう。

052〉例 ① What is your (3語)
② give me gifts for the wrong team (7語)

解説 ①「何歳ですか」と尋ねるときは，How old are you? または What is your age? (あなたの年齢はいくつですか)を使う。May[Can] I have your age? (あなたの年齢を聞いてもいいですか)も可。

注意！ How old is your age? とは言わない。たとえば My age is thirty.(私の年齢は30(歳)です)の下線部(名詞)を What で尋ねる形。次の例も同様。
・What is the height of that mountain?
(あの山の高さはいくら[何メートル]ですか)
＊下線部を How high[much] とは言わない。

全訳 (正解例を入れて完成した会話)
A：あなたは何歳ですか。
B：ごめんなさい。それについてはあなたに言いたくありません。
A：では，推測しなければなりません…。45歳ですか。
B：いいえ！ まだほんの30歳です！

②正解例を入れて完成した文章の意味は全訳を参照。誕生日に「私」が悲しいのはなぜかを考える。I am sad が現在形なので，空所に入る動詞も現在形にする点に注意。正解例は，「家族は私の誕生日に毎年大阪タイガースの関連グッズをプレゼ

ントしてくれる」ということ。

【別解】take me to Osaka Tigers games（私を大阪タイガースの試合に連れて行く）（6語）

全訳（正解例を入れて完成した文章）

父，母，兄[弟]は大阪タイガースのファンで，彼らは私も大阪タイガースのファンだと思っているが，私は東京ライオンズを応援している。私は（みんなと）違っていると見られたくないので，それを誰にも示したことがない。私のチームが勝つと私はうれしいということを誰も知らない。私は私のチームのポスターを寝室の壁に貼ることができない。誕生日に家族は私に間違ったチームのプレゼントをくれるので，私は悲しい。

053 例 **(You should buy) X (because) it is bigger, so you can carry more things in it. Also, if it's raining and you don't have an umbrella, the things you put in X won't get wet.**（30語）

解説 Lindaは「こんにちは！ 私はかばんを買いたいと思っています。XとYのどちらを買うべきですか。あなたの助言をください！」と相談している。カタログからは次のことがわかる。

(1) Yの方が安い。

(2) Xは50%引きの値段である。

(3) Xは防水である。

(4) Yの方が軽い。

(5) Xの方が容量が大きい。

Xを選ぶなら(2)(3)(5)のどれか2つを，Yを選ぶなら(1)(4)の理由を書くとよい。正解例ではXを選び，because以下は「それ[X]の方が大きいので，より多くの物をそれに入れて持ち運べる。また，もし雨が降っていて傘を持っていなくても，Xに入れたものはぬれない」という意味（waterproof「防水の」という形容詞も知っておくとよい）。

なお，次のような言い方をまとめて覚えておこう。

「このシャツはかっこいいし，値段も高くない」

→・This shirt is cool, and it's **also** inexpensive.

・This shirt is cool, and it's inexpensive, **too**.

・This shirt is cool and inexpensive **as well**.

・This shirt is cool. **Besides**, it's inexpensive.

・This shirt is cool. **In addition**, it's inexpensive.

【別解】though X is more expensive, it is 50 percent off, so I think it is a good chance for you to get a quality bag.（Xの方が高いけれど，50%オフなので，あなたが高品質のバッグを手に入れるよいチャンスだと思います）（25語）

054 ① **Many people have thought [think] that one of the best parts of traveling is eating.**

② **There is something special about enjoying food with local people on a trip.**

[A] 例 **these days the main purpose of many people's trips may not be to eat local food.**（16語）

解説 ①「醍醐味」をどう英訳するかを考える。正解例の意味は「旅（すること）の最高の部分の1つは食べることだ，と多くの人々が考えてきた」。

【別解】A lot of people have thought [think] that food is one of the main pleasures of traveling.（食べ物が旅の主な楽しみの1つだと多くの人々が考えてきた）

②正解例の意味は「旅行中に地元の人々と一緒に料理を楽しむことには何か特別なものがある」。英訳が難しいときは，人間を主語にして書いてみるのもよい（→029-④）。

【別解】I really enjoy eating together with local people when I travel.（私は旅行するとき地元の人々と一緒に食事をするのが本当に楽しい）

[A]正解例の意味は「（ところが，）近ごろでは多くの人々の旅行の主な目的は，地元の料理を食べることではないかもしれない」。この後の文に「今や家にいても日本中から食べ物のお取り寄せが可

能だ」という文があるので，これと重複する内容（例：「今では自宅で日本中の料理が食べられる」）を入れないように。

【別解】fewer people go out on a trip just to enjoy local food.（地元の料理を食べるだけのために旅行に出かける人は減っている）(12語)

注意！ travel は基本的に動詞。名詞としては不可算なので，a travel，travels は誤り。したがって travel を使って「旅行」の意味を表すには，**traveling**（旅行すること）を使う。また，travel は主に海外旅行をする場合に使い，国内の小旅行は **a trip** で表す（trip は可算名詞）ことが多い。

055 例 **As it is cooler, you can enjoy walking outdoors. The leaves on the trees turn red and yellow, so you can enjoy beautiful sights as you walk.**

(27語)

解説 スミス先生が「秋に外出するとき私は何を楽しむことができますか」と尋ねているので，その答えとなるよう「あなたは～を楽しむことができます」という内容を入れる。「外出するとき」という条件があるので，「秋は食べ物がおいしい」のような（外出と直接関係のない）内容は不可。正解例の as you walk は「歩くとき，歩きながら」の意味（この as は when に近い意味を表す）。while (you are) walking とも言える。

全訳（正解例を入れて完成した会話）

スミス先生：今は日本はとても暑いけれど，日本には他の季節もあることは知っています。誰か私に，日本の季節について教えてくれますか。

ケンタ：はい。ぼくが次の季節についてお話しします。秋です。秋は外出するのにいい季節です。

スミス先生：よろしい。秋に外出すると，私は何を楽しむことができますか。

ケンタ：（夏よりも）涼しいので，屋外を歩くのを楽しめます。木の葉が赤や黄色に変わるので，歩きながら美しい景色を楽しめます。

スミス先生：ありがとう。日本で秋に外出するのが楽しみです！

056 例 ① **It takes a little less than an hour to get there from central Tokyo** (14語)

② **I would like you to enjoy the beautiful nature that changes from season to season** (15語)

解説 ①〈**It takes** ＋時間＋ **to *do*.**〉（～するのに…（の時間が）かかる）の形を利用する。「1時間弱」の表し方については，まず次の2つの表現を覚えよう。

暗記 〈**more than** ＋数字〉「～より多い」

暗記 〈**less than** ＋数字〉「～より少ない」

- **More than** 50 people came to the party.（50人より多くの人々[50人以上]がパーティーに来た）
- I slept (for) **less than** three hours last night.
（ゆうべは3時間未満しか眠らなかった）

これらの表現の前に a little（少し）を加えると，「～より少し多い[少ない]」という意味になる。

- We moved here **a little more than** a year ago.（私たちは1年ちょっと前にここに引っ越しました）

この問いでは，「1時間弱」を **a little less than** an hour（1時間より少し少ない（時間））で表す。

【別解】You can get there in a little less than an hour from downtown Tokyo（東京の中心街から1時間足らずでそこに着くことができる）(14語)

②「5）四季折々に変化する美しい自然を味わってほしい」に相当する内容を入れる。正解例の目的語が you なのは，次の文の ... you can see ... と形をそろえるため。**would like O to *do*** は「O に～してもらいたい」（want よりも would like の方がていねいな言い方）。「～ごとに，～に応じて」は，**from A to A** の形で表す。「季節ごとに」は from season to season。この形では，A が可算名詞であっても無冠詞単数形にする。

- Laws differ **from country to country.**
（法律は国ごとに異なる）

全訳 (正解例を入れて完成した文章)

高尾山について話したいと思います。①都心から電車で1時間弱でそこに着きます。高尾山は，2009年にミシュラン旅行ガイドで3つ星を獲得して以来，世界中の人々にとても人気になりました。260万人以上の観光客が毎年その山を訪れます。高尾山は，猿園，野生植物園，1,000年以上の歴史を持つ薬王院などの見どころが豊富で，子どもだけでなく大人にも魅力的です。また高尾山は，桜，スミレ，その他の多くの種類の花を見るのによい場所でもあります。②私はあなたたちに，季節ごとに変化する美しい自然を楽しんでほしいと思います。天気がよいときは，山頂から富士山の素晴らしい眺めが見られます。高尾山を訪ねてみませんか。

語句

become popular with ～「～に人気になる」
receive「～を受け(取)る」
be full of ～「～でいっぱいだ」
amazing「驚異的な，見事な」
such as ～「たとえば～のような」 wild「野生の」
plant「植物」 temple「寺」
attract「～を引きつける，魅了する」
cherry blossoms「桜(の花)」 violet「スミレ」
view「眺め」
Why don't you ～?「～してはどうですか」

057 例 **According to the chart, about a quarter of the city's population are children under the age of 12. A playground for children would be helpful for them and their parents. On the other hand, there are also a lot of elderly people over 65 in this city. The problem with this plan is that there is no place[are few places] for them to enjoy themselves.** (63語)

解説 「施設」はfacilityと言うが，この語を知らなければ別の言葉を使う必要がある。計画によれば，この施設にはスポーツをするスペースと子ども用の遊び場が作られる。その両方について説明してもよいし，片方だけを取り上げてもかまわない。

それらの施設が「よい」理由は，「グラフによれば，それらの施設が役に立つ年齢層の人々が一定数いるから」という方向で説明する。単に「若者がスポーツを楽しめるから」「子どもが遊べるから」ではグラフとの関連性がわからないので，完全な答えにはならない。

一方，「問題となる点」は，「これらの施設は市の人口の多くを占める高齢者向きではない」という点を，自分の書ける英語で説明すればよい。正解例の全訳は次のとおり。

「グラフによれば，この市の人口のうち約4分の1は12歳以下の子どもである。子ども用の遊び場を作れば，その子どもたちと親たちにとって役立つだろう。一方，この市には65歳以上の高齢者もたくさんいる。この計画の問題は，彼らが楽しめる場所がない[ほとんどない]ことである」

正解例の英文を1つずつ見ながら，重要表現を確認しよう。

◆ According to the chart, about a quarter of the city's population are children under the age of 12.

・**According to the chart, ...**(グラフによれば…) = **The chart shows (that) ....**(グラフは…ということを示している)

・**a quarter of** ～「～の4分の1」。25 percent of ～(～の25%)とも表現できる。「2分の1」はa half,「3分の1」はa[one] third,「3分の2」はtwo thirds。

・children (who are) under the age of 12は，厳密には「12歳未満の子ども」の意味だが，「12歳以下の子ども(children (who are) 12 or[and] under)」の意味で使うこともある。

◆ A playground for children would be helpful for them and their parents.

・**would**は仮定法過去の助動詞。この計画は決定しているわけではないと考えられることから,「もし(仮に)この施設を作ったら」という意味で仮定法過去を使っている。

[参考] willだと，計画が決定済みであるように響く。

・be helpful for ～「～にとって役に立つ」。helpfulの代わりにuseful(役に立つ)，convenient(便利な)なども使える。

◆ On the other hand, there are also a

lot of elderly people over 65 in this city.

・**on the other hand**「他方では」。2つのことを対比して述べるときによく使われるフレーズ。however(しかし)などでもよい。

・elderly people over 65は，厳密には「65歳を超える高齢者」だが，「65歳以上の高齢者(elder people (who are) 65 or[and] over)」の意味で使うこともある。

◆The problem with this plan is that there is no place for them to enjoy themselves.

・the problem with ～「～に関する問題」。文全体は **The problem is that ....** (問題は…ということだ)という形。

・enjoy oneself「楽しむ，楽しい時を過ごす」(have a good time)

第4回 実力テスト

1 例 **You should take an airplane to the island. It is much faster than a ship. Also, you won't have to get up early in the morning if you take an airplane because it leaves three times a day.**

解説「ジョシュ先生，あなたに旅行のための助言をしたいと思います」に続く内容を答える。最後の文は「あなたが旅行を楽しむことを願っています！」の意味。

まず，[2]の指示に従って，飛行機と船のどちらかを勧める。「(交通機関)を利用する」は **take** で表す。飛行機を勧める場合は「所要時間が短い」「便数が多い」という2つの理由が考えられる。船を勧める場合は「運賃が安い」の他に(図には書かれていない)もう1つの理由を考える必要があるが，「きれいな海を見られる」などが考えられる。

正解例の意味は次のとおり。

「あなたは飛行機を利用して島へ行くべきです。その方が船よりもずっと速いです。また，飛行機は1日に3回出るので，飛行機に乗るなら早起きする必要はありません」

【別解】I think you should choose a trip by ship. One reason is that it is much cheaper than an airplane. Besides, you can enjoy seeing the beautiful sea on the way to the island. (あなたは船による旅を選ぶべきだと思います。1つの理由は，その方が飛行機よりずっと安いことです。それに加えて，島へ行く途中で美しい海を見て楽しめます)

2 例 ① **He took some pictures of it[the bird]** (6語)

② **You don't have to be afraid** (6語)

③ **I want to enjoy swimming** (5語)

解説 正解例を入れて完成した文章の意味は，全訳を参照。

【別解】① He was taking its picture(父はその(鳥の)写真を撮っていました)

② Don't worry[be afraid]. That bird is not dangerous(心配しない[怖がらない]で。あの鳥は危険じゃないわ)

③ I've never swum in the sea(私は海で泳いだことが一度もない), I like fishing in the sea(私は海で釣りをするのが好きだ)

全訳 (正解例を入れて完成した文章)

私の家族の写真についてお話しします。私は昨年，家族と一緒に熊本のある山へ行きました。これを見てください。このとき，私たちは空を飛んでいる大きな鳥を見て，父はとても興奮していました。父はバードウォッチングが好きなので，①その鳥の写真を撮りました。しかし，妹はその鳥を見て泣き出しました。母は妹の世話をして，「②怖がらなくていいのよ」と言いました。その後，私たちは山の頂上で昼食をとりました。とても楽しいひと時でした。

今年は，③私は泳ぎを楽しみたいから，海へ行くつもりです。

ご清聴ありがとうございました。

5 自分の考えを英語で書く問題

058 例 **I want to have a clock in my room. I want to put it on the wall next to my bed. Then I can check the time when I get up in the morning.**

解説 必ずしも(1)(2)(3)を1つの文で書く必要はない。正解例の意味は次のとおり。
「私は自分の部屋に時計がほしい。それをベッドの隣の壁にかけたい。そうすれば，朝起きたとき時間を確認することができる」

【別解】I would like to have a computer on my desk. That[This] is because I want to watch online videos to study English. I have a smartphone, but the screen is too small and watching it for a long time is bad for my eyes. (私は机の上にパソコンがほしい。それは，英語を勉強するためにオンラインの動画を見たいからだ。私はスマートフォンを持っているが，画面が小さすぎて長時間見るのは目に悪い)

注意！ 下線部をBecauseと書かないこと！
(→040－④)

［参考］「パソコン」はa personal computer，a PCではなく，単にa computerと言うのが一般的。a laptop (computer)(ノートパソコン)と区別したいときは，a desktop (computer)(デスクトップコンピューター)を使う。

059
① **use our own bags**
② **as much paper as**
③ **repair broken things**
④ 例 **we should use trains or buses, not cars.**

解説 正解例を入れて完成した文章の意味は，全訳を参照。

① our own bagsは「私たち自身のバッグ」。日本語ではマイバッグと言うが，この文でuse my bagと言うと「私[スピーチをしている本人]のバッグ」という意味になるので誤り。

② **as ～ as possible**(できるだけ～)の形を利用する。paper(紙)は不可算名詞である点に注意する。many papersだと「多くの新聞紙(newspapers)」と解釈される。

③ brokenは「壊れた(状態の)」の意味の形容詞。「この腕時計は壊れている」はThis watch is broken.と言う。

④他にwe should plant more trees(より多くの木を植えるべきだ)，we should use less electricity(使う電気を減らすべきだ)などを入れてもよい。

全訳 (正解例を入れて完成した文章)

地球を救うために私たちに何ができるか？

今では地球上に多くの環境問題があります。その1つはゴミです。ゴミを減らすための最も簡単な方法は，買い物に行くとき①自分のバッグを使うことです。②できるだけ多くの紙をリサイクルするのはよいことです。③壊れた物を修理することは，別のよい方法です。また私は，二酸化炭素を減らすために何かをすべきだと思います。たとえば，④私たちは車ではなく電車やバスを利用すべきです。

1人では小さなことしかできませんが，私たちが一緒にしてみれば，大きなことをすることができます。地球を救うために，私はみんなにこのことを覚えておいてほしいと思います。

060 例
① **I want to join the light music club because I like playing the guitar.** (14語)
② **I want to be a professional e-sports player because I love playing video games.** (14語)
③ **(Because) I can use English to communicate with people in other countries when I travel abroad.** (16語)

解説 ①「あなたは高校時代に何をしたいですか。それはなぜですか」という問い。正解例は「私はギターを弾くのが好きなので，軽音楽部に入りたいです」。I want .... Because ....のようにbecause以下を独立した文にしないように。

【別解】I want to pass Eiken Grade 2 because I will have a better chance to get a good job if I am good at English.

（私は英検２級に合格したい，なぜなら英語が得意ならよい仕事につく機会が増えそうだからです）(25語)

②「あなたは将来何になりたいですか。それはなぜですか」という問い。正解例は「私はビデオゲームをするのが大好きなので，Ｅスポーツのプロ選手になりたいです」。

【別解】I want to be a YouTuber. That is because I want to make a living by doing what I love.（私はユーチューバーになりたい。それは，自分が大好きなことをすることで暮らしを立てたいからです）(20語)

③「あなたはなぜ英語を勉強したいのですか」という問い。正解例は「(なぜなら)私は海外旅行をするとき英語を使って他の国の人々とコミュニケーションをとることができるからです」。Why ～？という質問に対しては，Because .... と答えてもよい。Because は省略することもできる。

【別解】(Because) I can work as a volunteer guide for foreign tourists if I can speak English.（もし英語を話せれば，外国人観光客のためにボランティアのガイドとして働くことができるからです）(16語)

061〉 例 **The most important person for me is my brother. He is a good soccer player, and I want to be as good as he is. He always practices with me and helps me to improve my skills.** (37語)

解説 ボブの質問はメールの最後の２文なので，「自分にとって最も大切な人」と「その理由」を答える。正解例の訳は次のとおり。

「私にとって最も大切な人は，私の兄です。彼はサッカーが上手で，私は彼と同じくらい上手になりたいと思っています。彼はいつも私と一緒に練習して，私の技術が向上するのを手助けしてくれます」

全訳（ボブからのメール）

こんにちは。先週の水曜日に英語のグリーン先生が，生徒たちに「あなたたちにとって最も大切な人は誰ですか」と質問しました。最初に，先生は自分のことを話しました。彼女にとって最も大切な人は，彼女の祖父です。彼も英語の先生で，何年も前に日本で働いていました。彼女は小さいころに彼の話を何度も聞き，日本で英語教師として働くことに興味を持ちました。彼の話は彼女の人生に大きな影響を与えました。ぼくにとって最も大切な人は，ぼくのギターの先生です。ぼくはミュージシャンになりたいと思っていて，彼女のレッスンと支援はぼくにとってとても大切です。君にとって最も大切な人は誰ですか。そして君は，なぜそう思うのですか。

062〉 ① **I have been interested in**

② **read books to children at [in] the library**

③ 例 **A, I walk to school through the park every day and I want to make it cleaner** (16語)

解説 ①導入の２つ目の該当箇所を英語に直す。

②活動内容のＡかＢの該当箇所を英語に直す。read は SVOO の形で使うことができるので，「子どもたちに本を読んであげる」は read children books または read books to children で表す(→001〉-⑥)。

③正解例はＡを選んだ場合(全訳を参照)。Ｂを選んだ場合の正解例は次のとおり。

(... because) I like small children and love reading books to them（私は小さな子どもが好きで，彼らに本を読んであげるのが大好きだから）(10語)

全訳（正解例を入れて完成した文章）

先週，私はボランティア活動についてのポスターを見ました。私は長い間ずっとボランティア活動①に興味があったので，その１つに参加したいと思っています。

ポスターで，私はＡとＢという２つの異なる活動を見つけました。もしＡを選べば，私は公園でゴミを拾うことになります。もしＢを選べば，私は②図書館で子どもたちに本を読むことになります。③私は毎日その公園を通って学校まで歩いており，そこをもっときれいにしたいので，Ａに参加したいです。

あなたも私と一緒に参加しませんか。

063 ① ウ

② 例 (B) **I'm interested in Lecture B the most.**

(C) **Because I believe that all children should have a chance to study at school. Studying is necessary for everyone to live happily.**

解説 ①オリバーの発言内容と講義の紹介を合わせて考える。

②(B)には，直前のオリバーの質問を利用して，I'm interested in X the most. という形を作り，Xの位置にLecture A・B・C・Dのどれかを入れる。(C)には自分の考えを書く。正解例を入れた英文の意味は，全訳を参照。

【(C)の別解】(B)にLecture Aを入れた場合：According to the table, I think that getting clean and safe water for everyone is the biggest global problem.（表によれば，みんなにきれいで安全な水を手に入れることが最大の世界的な問題だと思う）

(B)にLecture Cを入れた場合：I think I can do something to solve this problem and want to learn what I should do.（ぼくはこの問題を解決するために何かできると思うし，自分が何をすべきかを学びたい）

(B)にLecture Dを入れた場合：I'm interested in global warming. If many forests are lost, it will become a more serious problem.（ぼくは地球温暖化に関心がある。もし多くの森林が失われたら，それはより深刻な問題になるだろう）

全訳（正解例を入れて完成した文章）

【案内】

講義A：すべての人のための安全な水	約22億の人々がきれいで安全な水を飲むことができず，彼らの多くは病気になる。安全な水はその人々の健康的な生活に必要だ。
講義B：学校で勉強すること	約16億人の子どもが学校へ通っていない。その多くは読み書きや計算のしかたを学んで自分の生活を改善したいと願っている。
講義C：食べ物を無駄にしてはいけない	約20億の人々が十分な食事をとれていないが，世界の食料の30％以上が無駄にされている。私たちは食料の浪費をどのようにして止めることができるだろうか。
講義D：森が失われるだろう	2030年までに，アマゾンの熱帯雨林の60％が失われるかもしれない。そうなれば，そこに住む多くの動植物は住みかを失うだろう。

【会話】

＊＊＊：わあ！ 全部の講義が面白そうだ。君はどれを聞くの？

オリバー：ぼくは講義Cを聞くよ。母さんがレストランで働いていて，大量の食べ物が無駄にされているとよく言うんだ。ぼくはそれを止める方法を学びたい。君はどう？ 君はどの講義に一番興味があるの？

＊＊＊：ぼくは講義Bに一番興味があるよ。

オリバー：なぜそれを聞きたいの？

＊＊＊：すべての子どもが学校で勉強する機会を持つべきだと信じているからだよ。勉強することは誰にとっても幸福に生きるために必要だ。

064 例 **(I would choose) B. If I could travel to the future, I would meet myself at the age of thirty or forty. If he didn't have a happy life, I would ask him what I should do while I'm young.**（36語）

解説 マイケル先生の質問の意味は次のとおり。

「【A】と【B】は2つの願いです。もしどちらか1つの願いを持てるとしたら，どちらを選びますか。そして，なぜそれを選ぶのですか。それについて書いてください」

【A】は「歴史上の有名な人に会う」，【B】は「未来へ旅行する」という願い。質問文に仮定法過去の助動詞（could，would）が使われている点に注意。どちらの願いも実際にかなえることはできないので，この問いでは仮定法過去を使って書くことが求められている。正解例の意味は次のとおり。

「ぼくはBを選びます。もし未来へ旅行できるなら，ぼくは30歳か40歳の自分に会います。もし彼が幸福な生活を送っていなければ，ぼくは若いときに何をすべきかと彼に尋ねます」

【別解】(I would choose) A. I would like to meet Osamu Tezuka because I want to be a cartoonist. If I could meet him, I would ask him how to draw good manga.（私はAを選びます。私は漫画家になりたいので，手塚治虫に会いたいです。もし彼に会えたら，よい漫画の描き方を尋ねるつもりです）(28語)

065 例 **Before entering high school, I want to join a volunteer group and make many friends. I think it is important to have friends outside of school. It will make my life more enjoyable.** (33語)

解説 正解例の意味は次のとおり。

「高校に入る前に，私はボランティア団体に入って多くの友人を作りたい。学校の外で友人を持つことは大切だと思う。それによって私の生活は，もっと楽しくなるだろう」

「何をやりたいか」「その理由は何か」の２つの内容を入れるのが基本。正解例では下線部の情報を含めているが，語数が多くなるようなら省いてもよい。

Q&A

Q 「30語程度で書け」という指示がある場合，どのくらいの語数が許容されますか？

A 学校の採点方針によっても異なりますが，目安としては制限語数プラスマイナス２割程度と考えておきましょう。制限語数が30語なら，24〜36語程度が許容範囲でしょう。

066 例 ①(1) **Can you help me**

(2) **What are you going to make**

② **I feel "mottainai" when I buy paper books. To reduce paper waste, I can read e-books instead of paper books.** (20語)

解説 ①(1)ナンシーのSure. という返答は，相手に何かを頼まれて「わかりました，いいですよ」と答える場合などに使う。状況から，ホストファーザーは「手伝ってほしい」と頼んでいると考えられる。

(2)絵４のホストファーザーの返答から考えて，ナンシーは「何を作るつもりですか」と尋ねていると考えられる。

②「もったいないと感じるのはいつか」「それについて何ができるか」を20語程度の英文で書く。正解例の意味は次のとおり。

「私は紙の本を買うとき『もったいない』と感じる。紙のゴミを減らすために，私は紙の本の代わりに電子書籍を読むことができる」

全訳 （正解例を入れて完成した会話）

絵１「ただいま！ おなかがぺこぺこ…」

「おかえり，ナンシー。もうすぐ夕食の準備ができるよ。(1)手伝ってくれるかい？」

絵２「いいわ。何をすればいいの？」

「たまねぎを３個と，にんじんを２本切ってくれ」

「わかった」

絵３「これらの野菜くずはここに捨ててもいいの？」

「だめだよ。それはゴミじゃない。それを使ってもう１皿作るつもりなんだ」

「本当に？ (2)何を作るの？」

絵４「野菜スープを作るつもりだ。健康にいいし，ゴミも減らせるからね」

「それはいい考えね」

【スピーチ】

今日は，私の一番好きな日本語について話したいと思います。それは「もったいない」です。私はこの言葉を，ホストファーザーと一緒に料理をしているときに習いました。英語にはそのような言葉はありませんが，この言葉は大切だと私は思います。たとえば，コンビニエンスストアやスーパーマーケットやレストランで，毎日多くの食べ物が捨てられています。それに私たちは食べ物をたくさん買いすぎることがよくあります。食べ物を無駄にするのは本当に「もったいない」ことであり，今世界中で大きな問題になっています。しかし私たちの日常生活の中には，他にも「もったいない」問題があります。あなたはいつ「もったいない」と感じ，その問題について何をすることができますか。

067 例 **(I) like listening to music(.) I feel happy when I listen to my favorite music before going to bed, even if something bad happened during the day.** (22語)

解説 次の形は覚えておくとよい。

暗記 **spend O 〜ing**「〜して O[時間]を過ごす」

・I usually **spend** Sundays **reading** books.
（私はたいてい日曜日は本を読んで過ごす）

この問いでは必ずしも spend を使う必要はなく，最初の文は I like[enjoy] 〜ing.（私は〜が好きだ[を楽しむ]）などでもかまわない。それに続けて，そうすることが好きな理由を書く。正解例の意味は次のとおり。

「私は音楽を聞くのが好きです。たとえ昼間によくないことがあっても，寝る前に大好きな音楽を聞くと楽しい気分になります」

068 例 **(Answer A)**

② **As a member of the soccer club, I have learned the importance of teamwork**

③ **I have made many friends in my club**

④ **They make my school life more exciting**

解説 質問は，「クラブ活動はあなたの学校生活の中で重要だと思いますか」。解答 A は，「クラブ活動は私の学校生活の中で重要だと思います。2 つの理由があります」に続けて，「第 1 に，私はクラブ活動から多くのことを学ぶことができます。(②)。第 2 に(③④)。これらの理由から，私はクラブ活動のない学校生活は考えられません」という文章を完成する。正解例の意味は次のとおり。

②サッカー部員として，私はチームワークの大切さを学びました

③私は自分のクラブで多くの友人ができました

④彼らは私の学校生活をより刺激的にしてくれます

解答 B は，「クラブ活動は私の学校生活の中で重要ではないと思います。2 つの理由があります」に続けて，「第 1 に，学校の外には私の技能を向上させるための別の場所があります。(②)。第 2 に(③④)。これらの理由から，クラブ活動は私の学校生活にとって必要な一部ではないと思います」という文章を完成する。こちらを選んだ場合の解答例は次のとおり。

② Instead of joining a school club, I take guitar lessons after school.（学校のクラブに入る代わりに，私は放課後にギターのレッスンを受けています）

③ I like doing things alone.
（私は一人で何かをするのが好きです）

④ I don't think people like me need to join a club at school.（私のような人は，学校のクラブに入る必要はないと思います）

注意！ 全く同じ文をくり返して使うのはよくない。

この問いの文章は，「(1)結論＋(2)具体的な説明（理由など）＋(3)結び（結論の確認）」という典型的な構成になっている。この場合，(1)と(3)に全く同じ文を置くのは避ける方がよい。たとえば Answer A では，(1) I think club activity is important in my school life. という文がある。一方(3)では，For these reasons, I can't think of my school life without club activity. という（言いたいことは同じだが）形の違う文を使って(1)の結論を確認している。(3)で For these reasons, I think club activity is important in my school life. のように(1)と全く同じ文を使うのは，（日本語で書く場合と同様に）文章として好ましくない。

なお，この問いに関連して，次の言い方を知っておこう。

暗記 「〜ではないと思う」は，I don't think .... で表す。

次の 2 つの文が表す意味は同じである。

(1) I don't think club activity is important in my school life.（クラブ活動は私の学校生活の中で重要だとは思わない）

(2) I think club activity isn't important in my school life.（クラブ活動は私の学校生活の中で重要ではないと思う）

しかし，普通は(1)を使う。それには2つの理由がある。まず，英語では否定語(**not**，**no** など)をなるべく前に置く傾向がある。

(a) I have **no** money with me now.

(b) I don't have **any** money with me now.

（今はお金を全く持ち合わせていない）

〈**no＝not＋any**〉という関係があるので，(a)と(b)は同じ意味である。どちらを使ってもよいが，(b)がよく使われる((a)は「全くない」ことを強調した言い方で，no を強く読む)。

また，(2)は「重要ではない」と断定しているように響く。一方(1)は「(他の人がどう思うかは知らないが)私は～ではないと思う」という意味だから，(2)よりも言葉の響きが穏やかになる。

069〉 例 **I sometimes go shopping at the supermarket. I try to choose and buy foods with short expiration dates. By doing so, I think I can help reduce food loss.** (29語)

解説 正解例の意味は次のとおり。

「私は時々スーパーマーケットへ買い物に行く。私は賞味期限の短い食べ物を選んで買うようにしている。そうすることで私は食品ロスを減らす手助けができると思う」

正解例を見ながら，重要な語いや表現を確認しよう。

- **go shopping at** the supermarket [convenience store]「スーパーマーケット［コンビニエンスストア］へ買い物に行く」。at の代わりに to を使うのは誤り。「スーパーマーケットで買い物をする＋行く」と考える。
- **expiration date**「(食品の)賞味期限」。「期限切れ(expiration)の日付(date)」ということ。**best-before date** とも言う。「賞味期限が切れそうな食品」は **short-dated** food。
- by doing so「そうすることによって」。**by ～ing** は「～することによって」の意味。
- **help (to)** ***do***「～するのを助ける，～するのに役立つ」。to は省略できる。
- **reduce** food loss「食品ロスを減らす」

環境問題に関しては，次のような表現も覚えておくとよい。

- **recycle plastic bottles**「ペットボトルをリサイクルする」(pet bottle とは言わない)
- **reuse** glass bottles「ガラスびんを再利用する」
- **eco-friendly goods**「環境に優しい商品」
- **save energy[electricity]**「エネルギー［電気］を節約する」
- **electric car**「電気自動車」
- **global warming**「地球温暖化」
- **climate change**「気候変動」
- **cause environmental pollution**「環境汚染を引き起こす」

070〉 ① **studied for the exam [examination, test] last Sunday** (6語)

② 例 **From the graph, I can imagine that last Sunday was just before the exam. I wonder if the students who did not study for the exam got good grades.**

解説 ①グラフから，このクラスの生徒数は40人であり，40人の25%を計算すると10となり，17人とある試験勉強が該当するとわかる。よって「25%を超える生徒たちが，先週の日曜日に試験［テスト］(のために)勉強をした」という文を完成する。

②内容は自由に考えてよい。正解例の意味は次のとおり。

「グラフから，先週の日曜日は試験の直前だったと想像できる。試験勉強をしなかった生徒たちは，よい成績を取れただろうか」

Q&A

Q ①の英文で，the students や the exam の the は必要ですか？

A はい，必要です。次のルールを思い出してください。

暗記 可算名詞は，原則として無冠詞単数形では使えない。(→019〉-⑤)

student(生徒)や exam(試験)は可算名詞(数えられる名詞)です。このような名詞を文中で使う場合，たとえば student(無冠詞単数形)という形は誤り。a student, the student, students, the students のどれかを使う必要があります。

正解例を入れて完成した文を見てみましょう。

More than 25 percent of the students studied for the exam last Sunday.

students や exam に the がついているのは，「特定の生徒たち」「特定の試験」を表すからです。「特定の」とは，「あなたも知っている(例の)」ということ。つまり，「何を指すかが相手にはわかるはずだ」と自分が思う名詞の前には **the** をつけます。

別の例で考えてみましょう。

・Close **the** door.（ドアを閉めなさい）

＊door の前に the をつけるのは，この文を口に出した人[話し手]が，どの(特定の1つの)ドアを閉めてほしいかが相手[聞き手]に伝わると思っているから。door は可算名詞だから，Close door. は誤り。Close a door. だと「どれでもいいから1つのドアを閉めなさい」という不自然な意味になる。

・He lives in **a** town by the sea. **The** town's name is Izumi.（彼は海辺の(ある)町に住んでいます。その町の名前はイズミです）

＊第1文を発した時点では，話し手は「どの(特定の)町のことかが聞き手にはわからない」と思っている。だから the ではなく a を使う。第2文で the を使うのは，(日本語からもわかるとおり)聞き手が「the town＝彼が住んでいる町」と特定できる(と話し手が考えている)から。

・He lives in **the** town by the sea.
（彼は海辺のその町に住んでいる）

＊「海辺のその町」のことはすでに話題に出ており，どの町を指すのかが聞き手にはわかっている。そういう状況でない限り，この文は使わない。

071〉 例 **I respect my uncle the most. He wanted to go to college, but his family was poor. So he worked hard to make money after finishing high school and entered college when he was 26.** (35語)

解説 「あなたが最も尊敬する人は誰ですか。(それは)なぜですか。会ったことのある人についてでもない人についてでも書くことができます」という問い。まず，I respect X the most.（私はXを最も尊敬している）と書き，その後に理由を続ける。何度もくり返すが，I respect X the most. Because .... と書かないこと(→ 040 -④)。正解例の意味は次のとおり。

「私はおじを最も尊敬しています。彼は大学へ行きたかったけれど，家族は貧しかったのです。だから彼は高校を出た後お金をかせぐために熱心に働き，26歳のとき大学に入りました」

Q&A

Q 実際に自分が尊敬している人について書くのが(個人的な情報を開示したくないなど)難しい場合，架空の人物を使って書いてもよいのですか？

A はい。正解例はその1つの例として示しました。実際には自分におじがいなくても，このように書いてかまいません。この問いに限らず，英語の試験は英語力を判定するのが目的ですから，基本的に書いてある内容は(問題の指示に反していない限り)判定の対象になりません。

072〉 例 **I agree with Miki. Typing messages is easier than handwriting because you can change them just by typing on the keyboard. When you write by hand, you have to use an eraser to rewrite.** (30語)

解説 (1)の指示に従って，まず I agree with Yuto [Miki]. または I agree with Yuto's [Miki's] opinion. という文を書く(**agree with** ～「～に賛成する」)。2文目 because ... の主語は I や we を使ってもよいが，「一般の人」は **you** で表すとよい(→第2回実力テスト 3 -②)。正解例の意味は次のとおり。

「私はミキさんに賛成です。メッセージをタイプする方が手で書くより簡単です，なぜならキーボードを打つだけでそれら[メッセージ]を変えることができるからです。手で書くときは，書き直すために消しゴムを使わねばなりません」

全訳

先生：近ごろ，私たち教師はたいていパソコンを使い，手書きの機会は多くありません。しかし生徒の皆さんは，ふだんノートに多くのことを書いています。手書きすることは大切だと思いますか。

ユウトさん：手で書くことで，誰がそのメッセージを書いたかがわかります。手紙のサインを見ると，にせ物ではなくそれを書いた人からの本物の手紙だと信頼できます。だから手書きすることは大切です。
ミキさん：私はそう は思いません。メッセージをタイプすることは…
先生：ありがとう，ユウトさん，ミキさん。2人の意見を支持するさらに多くのよい理由がありそうです。あなたはどう思いますか。

073 例 **To improve my English, I would like to try to write e-mails in English. I'm afraid speaking English is too difficult for me. Writing e-mails would be easier because I have enough time to think about what to write.** (39語)

解説 Bに書かれている4つのアイデアのうち1つを選び，下線部の質問に合わせて，I would like to (try to) *do*.（私は〜し(てみ)たい）という形を最初に置く。その後に理由を続ける。正解例の意味は次のとおり。
「英語(力)を向上させるために，私は英語でメールを書いてみたいです。英語で話すのは私には難しすぎるのではないかと思います。メールを書く方が，何を書くかを考える時間が十分にあるので簡単でしょう」
正解例の重要表現を確認しよう。

- **I'm afraid (that) ....** 「残念ながら[申し訳ないが]…」。好ましくないことを語る場合に，I think の代わりに使える表現。
- Writing e-mails **would be** easier（メールを書く方が簡単だろう）：下線部は is でもよいが，「もしメールを書くとしたら，その方が簡単だろう」という意味をこめて，仮定法過去を使っている。結果的に，is を使うよりも言葉の響きが柔らかくなる。

全訳
A「英語学習の方法について話し合いましょう。英語(力)を向上させるために私たちは何ができますか。よい方法を何か知っていますか」
B「ぼくは時々英語の歌を聞きます」
「英語でメールを書くのはどうですか。私はそれがよいと思います」
「英語の本を読むのは本当によいことです」
「ぼくは ALT の先生とよく話します」
C「アイデアを共有してくれてありがとうございます。私たちは今4つのアイデアを持っており，それらは全部よい考えだと私は思います！ あなたは自分の英語(力)を向上させるためにどのアイデアを一番試したいですか。それはなぜですか」

074 例 **It is a restaurant near my house named Miami. This restaurant is famous for its "katsudon." "Katsudon" is a very popular food in Japan. If you have never had it, please try it.** (33語)

解説 「こんにちは，今日は私のお気に入りの場所についてお話しします」という文に続けて書く。071で説明したとおり，必ずしも自分が実際に住んでいる町や自分の知っている場所について書く必要はない。正解例の意味は次のとおり。マイアミは架空の店である。
「それは，私の家の近くのマイアミという名の食堂です。この店は『かつ丼』で有名です。『かつ丼』は日本ではとても人気のある料理です。もし一度も食べたことがなければ，ぜひ食べてみてください」

Q&A
Q 正解例で，katsudon に引用符(" ")がついているのはなぜですか？
A katsudon は，英語の単語ではありません。このように日本語をそのままローマ字で書く場合は，引用符をつけるのが基本です。

- My brother is an "aniota." He watches anime programs on TV every day.（兄[弟]は「アニオタ」です。毎日テレビでアニメ番組を見ています）

＊**what is called**（いわゆる）を使って，My brother is what is called an "aniota." と言うこともできる。aniota は数えられる名詞なので，前に an を入れ忘れないように。なお，文末にピリオドと引用符を置く場合，アメリカ英語ではピリオドを引用符の内側に置く。

[参考] anime（アニメ），kimono（着物），sushi（すし）などは，英英辞典にも載っている。otaku（おたく）もその

うち英語として認められるかもしれない。

075〉 例 **There is a large park near our school. In spring many people visit there to see the cherry blossoms. I think your friend can take beautiful pictures there!** (28語)

解説 「写真家である私のアメリカ人の友人が，春に滋賀を訪ねます。彼女を滋賀のすてきな場所へ連れて行って写真を撮らせてあげたいと思っていますが，どこへ行くべきかわかりません。私によい助言をもらえますか」という問いかけに答える。琵琶湖(Lake Biwa)について書くこともできるが，正解例では架空の場所を挙げている。正解例の意味は次のとおり(cherry blossoms「桜の花」)。

「私たちの学校の近くに大きな公園があります。春には多くの人が桜の花を見るためにそこを訪れます。あなたの友人はそこで美しい写真を撮ることができると思います！」

［参考］ 正解例の cherry blossoms の前に the がついているのは，前の文の内容から考えて「特定の[その公園の]桜の花」であることが読み手に伝わるはずだ，と書き手が考えているから。The の代わりに its を使ってもよい。

076〉 例① **Animals in zoos are kept in small cages. I don't think they are healthy because they don't get enough exercise. Maybe they would live longer if they lived in the wild.** (31語)

② **It is very important for children to see real animals with their own eyes. It helps them to like animals more and understand the importance of life.** (27語)

解説 「動物園は是か非か」というテーマは，自由英作文ではしばしば見られる。このように賛否が分かれるテーマに関しては，どんな内容を書くかをあらかじめ考えておくとよい。巻末の「英作文の勉強の仕方」を参照。正解例を入れて完成した会話の意味は全訳を参照。

注意！ 名詞の前に「何となく」**the** をつけてはいけない。

021〉-②で説明したとおり，the は「(相手が)1つに特定できるもの」の前に置く。したがって「私はネコ(という動物一般)が好きだ」は I like cats. と言い，the は使わない。正解例の次の文も同様。

・① Aminals in zoos are kept in ② small cages.

①は「動物園の動物たち一般」という意味だから，the をつけない。the をつけると「動物園にいる(あなたも知っている)その(特定の)動物たち」という意味になる。②の small cages も同様。このような場合に，深く考えずに「何となく」the をつける誤りがよく見られる。「**X** 一般」の意味を表すときは **X** の前に **the** をつけないという点を頭に入れておこう。

全訳 (正解例を入れて完成した会話)

裕二：昨日友だちと動物園へ行ったんだ。そこでたくさんの動物を見たよ。とても楽しかった。

マーク：それはよかった。ぼくは動物園が好きだけれど，動物園で動物を飼うのはよくないと思う。①動物園の動物は，狭いおりの中で飼われている。それらは十分な運動をしないので不健康だと思う。野生で暮らせば，たぶんもっと長生きするだろう。

裕二：なるほど。動物は時々悲しそうに見えるから，その考えは理解できるよ。

絵美：マーク，あなたの言うことは正しいかもしれないけれど，動物園にはいい点もあるわ。②子どもが実物の動物を自分の目で見ることはとても大切よ。それは子どもが動物をもっと好きになって，命の大切さを知るのに役立つわ。

裕二：ああ，それは本当だ。動物園に行くのは楽しいけれど，君のおかげでぼくは動物園の別のいい点を学んだよ。

077 例 **(I think living in) a city (is better). I like listening to music. But I have no chance to listen to live music because I live in a small town. If I lived in a city, I would often go to concerts. So I want to live in a city.**

解説 「4つの英文を書くこと」という条件は，次のような文章構成を想定して，(2)〜(5)の文を書くことが求められていると考えられる。

(1)導入(結論の提示)

(2)(3)(4)本論(結論の理由など具体的な説明)

(5)結び(結論の確認)

正解例の意味は次のとおり。

「私は都会に住む方がよいと思う。私は音楽を聞くのが好きだ。しかし私は小さな町に住んでいるので，生の音楽を聞くチャンスが全くない。もし都会に住んでいたら，私はしばしばコンサートに行くだろう。だから私は都会に住みたい」

正解例の英文では，I would often go to concerts. の下線部が無冠詞複数形である点を確認しよう。

×go to concert：concert は可算名詞だから，無冠詞単数形では使えない(→019-⑤)。

×go to the concert：「その(あなたも知っている特定の1つの)コンサートに行く」の意味。

×go to the concerts：「その(あなたも知っている特定の複数の)コンサートに行く」の意味。

×go to a concert：「(あなたの知らない)あるコンサートに行く」という意味。

したがって，「コンサートというもの(一般)に行く」は，go to concerts で表す。「私はネコが好きだ」を I like cats. と言うのと同じ(→021-②)。

Q&A

Q 問題文に，「田舎＝the country，都会＝a city」とあります。このtheとaの違いは何ですか？

A ある種の名詞(**X**)は，「〜というもの(一般)」の意味を〈**the＋X**〉の形で表します。**the country** の **the** はその例です。

では，どのような名詞の前にtheをつけるのでしょう？ 基本的には次のように考えてください。

暗記 みんなが同じイメージを持てるものは，「**X**一般」の意味を〈**the＋X**〉で表す(ことができる)。

次の例で考えてみましょう。

(1)I like playing the guitar.
(私はギターを弾くのが好きだ)

(2)I like playing tennis.
(私はテニスをするのが好きだ)

(1)でguitarの前にtheがついているのは，「ギター」と言えば誰でも同じ形の楽器を思い浮かべる(はずだと話し手が考えている)からです。一方，「テニス」と聞いて思い浮かべるイメージは人によって違うでしょう。だからtennisにはtheをつけません。別の言い方をすれば，この用法のtheは「ほら，あれですよ。あなたにもわかるでしょう」と1つのものを指し示す働きをしています(「総称のthe」とも呼ばれます)。

guitarなどの楽器名の他に，street(通り)，train(電車)，bus(バス)，convenience store(コンビニエンスストア)など，日常生活と深いかかわりを持つものを表す名詞の前には，この用法のtheを置くことができます。

・Don't use your smartphone on the train.
(電車の中でスマートフォンを使ってはいけない)

この文のthe trainは「電車という乗り物」の意味に解釈できます(「その(特定の1本の)電車」の意味にも解釈できます)。下線部はa trainも可能ですが，the trainの方が普通の言い方です。

またこのtheには「Xを同種の他のものと対比して指し示す」という働きもあります。on the train[bus] のtheには，電車やバスを他の乗り物との対比が意識されているとも言えます。同様にin the summer(夏に)，in the east(東に)では，他の季節や方角との対比が意識されています。

live in the country(田舎に住む)も理屈は同じです。このtheは「典型的にイメージできる(はずの)田舎という場所」を表しており，それとの対比で言えばlive in the city(都会に住む)という表現も可能です。一方，live in a cityは「ある(不特定のどれか1つの)都市に住む」という意味です。cityの場合にはtheもaも使えますが，live in a countryだと「ある国に住む」と解釈されるので，「田舎に住む」はlive in the countryと表現しなければなりません。

078 例 **I love the comic "One Piece." It teaches me the importance of hard work and friendship. When I have difficulties to achieve a goal, I read "One Piece." It helps me believe that I can do anything if I work hard.**

解説 問題文の意味は次のとおり。

「次の文章を読んで，あなたの答えを英語で書きなさい。

　達成すべき目標は持っているけれど，その目標を達成するためには困難な点があると考えなさい。そのような場合，誰または何が，あなたがそれらの難点を克服するのに役立ちますか。誰または何であるかを書き，それに続けて，自分の経験または例から，なぜそう思うのかを説明しなさい」

who or what helps you ...（誰または何があなたを助けるか）の helps が現在形になっている点に注意が必要。この現在形は「習慣」を表しており，「自分が困難に突き当たったときはいつでも助けてくれる」ような人やものについて書くことが求められている。したがって「以前～が私を助けてくれた」のように過去の経験を書くだけでは不十分である。抽象的なことを書こうとすると表現が難しいので，who or what という問いへの答えとしては，家族や本などを挙げるとよいだろう。正解例の意味は次のとおり。

「私は『ワンピース』という漫画が大好きだ。この作品は私に努力や友情の大切さを教えてくれる。目標を達成するのに苦労しているとき，私は『ワンピース』を読む。それは努力すれば何でもできると私に信じる手助けをしてくれる」

079 例 **I don't agree with you. I think you need to stay longer to learn the culture and customs of a country. What you learn in just a few days might be wrong.** (32語)

解説 テーマは「外国の文化や習慣を学ぶための効果的な方法」。陽子は「数日でも外国を訪れることが，外国の文化や習慣を学ぶための効果的な方法だと私は思います。あなたは私に賛成しますか」と発言している。この問いに対しては，(Yes,) I agree (with you). または (No,) I don't agree (with you). とまず答える。正解例の意味は次のとおり。

「私はあなたに賛成しません。ある国の文化や習慣を知るためには，もっと長く滞在する必要があると思います。わずか数日で学んだことは，間違っているかもしれません」

注意! 問題文をよく読むこと。

　「あなたは…陽子と英語で意見交換をしている」という設定なので，I agree with her[Yoko]. と書いてはいけない。

文法 関係代名詞の what

what には関係代名詞としての用法がある。この what は「何」の意味ではなく，「～する[である]こと[もの]」という意味を表す。**what = the thing(s) that** と考えることができる。高校の学習範囲だが，英作文に利用できるので知っておくとよい。what 以下は名詞のかたまり[名詞節]であり，文中で S・O・C などの働きをする。前置詞の後ろにも置ける。

・**What we need** is more time.
　S: What we need　V: is　C: more time
（私たちが必要とするものは，より多くの時間だ）

・I can't believe **what he said.**
　S: I　V: can't believe　O: what he said
（私は彼の言ったことが信じられない）

・I'm sorry for **what I did.**
　前置詞: for
（私のしたことを申し訳なく思います）

正解例の文で確認しよう。

What you learn in just a few days might be wrong.
　S: What you learn in just a few days　V: might be　C: wrong
（あなたがわずか数日で学んだことは，間違っているかもしれない）

080 例 **Yes, I think so. You can keep all your books in one small tablet, so it is easier to carry. And you don't have to go out to buy new books, either.** (32語)

解説「今日では，スマートフォンとタブレットを使って，紙の本の代わりに電子書籍を読む人々がいます。あなたは紙の本よりも電子書籍の方がよいと思いますか。それはなぜですか」という問い。これもよく問われるテーマである。電子書籍には，「軽い(ので持ち運びに便利だ)」「スペースをとらない」「知らない言葉があっても，アプリを使って意味を簡単に調べられる」などの利点がある。紙の本には「書き込みがしやすい」「目が疲れにくい」などの利点があり，「紙の本でないと本を読んだ気がしない」という人もいるだろう。正解例の意味は次のとおり。
「はい，私はそう思います。すべての本を1台の小さなタブレットの中に保管できるので，より簡単に持ち運ぶことができます。それに，新しい本を買いに出かける必要もありません」

081 例 **I think online lessons are better for three reasons. First, they save you the time it takes to go to school. Second, you can take lessons even when the weather is bad or you are not feeling very well. Third, by recording, you can watch the same lesson over and over again.**
(52語)

解説「教室での通常の授業とオンライン授業とでは，どちらの方がよいと思いますか。2つまたは3つの理由を添えて，あなたの意見を私たちに伝えなさい。英語で書き，約50語を使いなさい。語数を書いてください」という問い。正解例の意味は次のとおり。
「私は3つの理由でオンライン授業の方がよいと思います。第1に，通学時間を省くことができます。第2に，悪天候のときやあまり体調がよくないときでも授業を受けることができます。第3に，録画することによって，同じ授業をくり返して見ることができます」
正解例の英文に含まれる重要表現を確認しよう。

◆ **... for three reasons.**「3つの理由のために…」。第1文の最後にこのフレーズを置き，それに続けてFirst, ... Second .... Third [Finally] .... と3つの理由を説明すれば，文章の流れがスムーズになる。

◆ **save** O_1 O_2「O_1[人]のO_2[時間・労力など]を節約する，省く」

◆ **even when ...**「(たとえ)…するときでさえ」。**even if ...**(たとえ…しても)と合わせて覚えておこう。

・**Even if** it rains tomorrow, I will go fishing with my friends.(たとえ明日雨が降っても，私は友人たちと釣りに行きます)

Q&A

Q「導入＋本論＋結び」という基本的な構成(→077)のうち，「結び」はなくてもよいのですか？

A はい。「結び」は最初に述べた結論を確認するのが目的です。正解例では，I think online lessons are better for three reasons. の下線部は結論に当たります。語数制限がなければ，最後にFor these reasons, I think online lessons are better than regular lessons in classrooms.(これらの理由から，私はオンライン授業の方が教室での通常の授業よりもよいと思います)という結びの1文を入れることができます。しかし語数がオーバーするときは，この結びを省いてもかまいません。

082 例 **I'll use both my tablet and books for my research. First, I'll use my tablet to collect information on the Internet. Some of it might be wrong. So I'll read some books from the school library to make sure that I can believe all the information I have gotten online.** (50語)

解説「スピーチや発表をすることは，理解を深めるために効果的です。スピーチや発表をするとき，もっと知りたいと思うことを発見するかもしれません。より多くのことを知るためには，調査をする必要があるでしょう。たとえば，学校ではこれを多くの方法で行うことができます。学校の図書室やタブレット型のコンピューターも助けになります。あなたは自分の調査のために図書館やコンピューターなどのものをどのように使いますか」

という問い。図書館とコンピューターは調べものをするときに使う手段の例にすぎないが，実際に自分が何かを調べようとすればこの２つを使うのが普通だろう。この問いでは，下線部の質問に対して，「どのように使うか」「なぜその使い方をするのか」という２つの答えを求めている。正解例の意味は次のとおり。

「私は自分の調査のためにタブレットと本の両方を使います。最初に，タブレットを使ってインターネットの情報を集めます。(しかし)一部の情報は間違っているかもしれません。だから，自分がオンラインで得たすべての情報が信じられることを確かめるために，学校の図書室で借りた本を読みます」

文法「つなぎ言葉」の活用

内容的なまとまりのある文章を書くには，次のような「つなぎ言葉」(文と文との論理関係などを表す言葉)を使うとよい。以下の語句のうち最初が大文字のものは，しばしば文頭で使う。

◆理由・結果などを表す語句

because ...(…なので)，**because of ...**(…の(理由の)ために)，**so ...**(だから…)，**That[This] is why ....**(そう[こう]いうわけで…)，**For this reason[these reasons] ....**(この[これらの]理由のために…)，**As a result, ...**(その結果…)

◆逆接・対比などを表す語句

but ...(しかし…)，**However, ...**(しかし…)，**On the other hand, ...**(一方では…)，**Actually, ...**((ところが)実際は…)，**instead of ...**(…の代わりに)

◆例示・追加などを表す語句

For example, ...(たとえば…)，**A such as B**(たとえばBのようなA)，**Also, ...**(また…)，**Besides[In addition], ...**(そのうえ…)，**... as well**(同様に[加えて]…も)，**In other words, ...**(言い換えれば…)

◆その他

First (of all), ...((まず)第1に…)，**at least ...**(少なくとも…)，**A, especially B**(A，特にB)，**In short, ...**(要するに…)

083 例 **I want to go to school in school uniform. The first reason is that I don't have money to buy casual clothes. The second reason is that I want to be proud of my school and show people that I'm a student there.** (43語)

解説 最初に「私は制服[私服]で登校したい」という文を入れ，その後に理由を２つ書く。正解例の意味は次のとおり。

「私は制服を着て登校したい。第１の理由は，私服を買うお金がないということだ。第２の理由は，自分の学校に誇りを持ち，私がそこの生徒だと人々に示したいということだ」

なお，私服を選ぶ場合は，「何を着るべきかを決めるのは楽しい(it is fun to decide what to wear)」「ファッション感覚が高められる(improve my sense of fashion)」などの理由が考えられる。

084 例 **I agree with this idea. More and more workers and tourists are coming to Japan from other countries. We can probably communicate with many of them if we speak English. But some of them may not speak English. So we should learn English and another foreign language to communicate with various people from around the world.** (56語)

解説「２つの外国語を学ぶことは日本の高校生にとってよい考えだろうと考える人々がいます。あなたはこの考えに賛成ですか。それについて50～60語の英語で書きなさい。自分の考えを支持するための(いくつかの)理由と例を挙げなさい」という問い。some reasons and examples と指示されているが，理由と例の数にこだわる必要はない。まとまった内容の文章を書くことが大切である。正解例の意味は次のとおり。

「私はこの考えに賛成です。他の国々からますます多くの労働者や観光客が日本へ来ています。私たちは，英語を話せばおそらく彼らの多くとコミュニケーションをとることができます。しかし中には英語を話さない人々がいるかもしれません。だから私たちは，世界中からやって来るさまざまな人々とコミュニケーションをとるために，英語ともう1つ別の言語を学ぶべきです」

正解例中の次の重要表現を確認しよう。

◆ **More and more** workers and tourists **are coming** to Japan（日本へ来る労働者や観光客がますます増えている）：次の形を覚えておくとよい。

暗記 **〈More (and more)** S＋V[現在進行形]**....〉**「～するSが(どんどん)増えつつある」

この more は「より多くの」の意味。現在完了進行形(have been coming)を使ってもよい。

085 例 **I'm not sure what "wellness" means, but I think it's the opposite of "illness." In other words, wellness probably means that someone is in good health. So I think the most important thing to keep a good level of wellness is to eat well and get enough sleep.**

解説 「『ウェルネス』という英単語は，世界中でますます使われつつあります。この語は何を意味すると思うか，またよいレベルのウェルネスを保つのに最も大切なものは何かについて，英語で書きなさい」という問い。

下線部からわかるとおり，この問いは必ずしも wellness(健康な状態)という語の意味を知っているかどうかを尋ねているわけではない。正解例の意味は次のとおり。

「wellness が何を意味するか私はよくわかりませんが，それは illness(病気)の反意語だと思います。言い換えれば，wellness とはおそらく，誰かが健康だということを意味します。だから，よいレベルの wellness を保つために最も大切なことは，よく食べて十分な睡眠をとることだと私は思います」

なお，問題文に複雑な形の英文が使われているので，文法的な確認をしておこう。

◆ is being used（使われつつある）：**〈be動詞＋being＋過去分詞〉**は進行形と受動態を組み合わせた形で，「～されつつある」という意味を表す。次のように考えるとよい。

(1)進行形(be動詞＋[～ing])「～しつつある」

(2)受動態([be動詞]＋過去分詞)「～される」

(1)と(2)を組み合わせると，[　]の部分が1つになって，being(be 動詞の ing 形)に変わる。

◆ ... about what you think this word means（この語が何を意味するとあなたは思うかについて…）：下線部は間接疑問で，元の疑問文は次のとおり。

・What do you think this word means?
（この語は何を意味するとあなたは思いますか）
この下線部も間接疑問であり，次のように考える。

(1) Do you think＋〈What does this word mean?〉?

(2) Do you think＋〈what this word means〉?

(3)〈What〉＋do you think＋〈this word means〉?

(1)の〈　〉の疑問文を間接疑問にすると，(2)になる。そこから，質問の焦点である what を文頭に出すと，(3)ができる(→013-①)。

086 例 **I want to live a busy life in the future. I plan to work as hard as I can when I am young. That is because I want to save enough money to get married and have a family. I will be busier and busier if I have children. It will make me even happier.** (55語)

解説 「あなたは将来忙しい生活を送りたいですか。あなたの計画は何ですか」という問い。**live [lead] a ～ life** は「～な生活を送る」の意味。最初の問いは Yes か No かで答える形だが，

Yes / No は入れなくてもよい。正解例の意味は次のとおり。
「私は将来忙しい生活を送りたい。私は若いときにできるだけ熱心に仕事をすることを計画している。それは，結婚して家族を持てるだけの貯金をしたいからだ。子どもを持てば私はますます忙しくなるだろう。それは私をさらに幸福にしてくれるだろう」
なお，「私は忙しい生活を送りたくない」という方向で書くときは，「好きなことをする十分な時間がほしい(I want enough time to do what I like)」「仕事のしすぎは体に悪い(working too much would be bad for my health)」などの内容が考えられる。

087 例 **First, we should also learn many things outside of school. For example, we can do volunteer activities if we don't have homework. Second, we are old enough to think about what we should do for ourselves. Most students will decide to start studying before they are told to by teachers.** (50語)

解説 「先生たちは，長期休暇の間に私たちに宿題を与える[出す]べきではない。私には２つの理由がある」という文に続けて，２つの理由を具体的に書く。これまでの問いと同様に，First, ... Second, ... という書き出しを使えばよい。正解例の意味は次のとおり。
「第１に，私たちは学校の外でも多くのことを学ぶべきだ。たとえば，もし宿題がなければ私たちはボランティア活動をすることができる。第２に，私たちは自分がすべきことについて自分で考えられる年齢だ。ほとんどの生徒は先生に言われる前に勉強し始めることに決めるだろう」

第 5 回　実力テスト

1 例 **(I will choose) A(.)　I think many boys like sports better than cooking.　I'm going to ask Sam which he likes better, soccer or baseball.　If he likes either or both of them, I want to take him to see a game.**
(38語)

解説 問題の指示と【条件】をよく読むことが大切。問題には「A・Bのどちらかの案を選び」とあるので，両方を含む計画(たとえば「スポーツ観戦をして，その後一緒に料理を作る」「スポーツ観戦に行くつもりだが，雨が降ったら一緒に料理を作る」)は不可。また，【条件】の(2)に「２つの案について触れながら」とあるので，A・Bのどちらを選ぶにせよ，もう一方の行動にも触れる必要がある。正解例の意味は次のとおり。
「私はAを選ぶ。多くの男子は料理よりもスポーツの方が好きだと思う。サッカーと野球のどちらがより好きかをサムに尋ねるつもりだ。もしそのどちらかまたは両方が好きなら，彼を試合を見に連れて行きたい」

2 例 **I want to go to Kyoto. First, Kyoto has many famous temples and shrines.　I have never been there, so I want to see them.　Also, Kyoto is famous for "matcha."　It is my favorite tea.　I hope I can go soon.** (42語)

解説 比較的書きやすいテーマ。40語程度の文章を書く場合，文の数は３～５文程度になる。「私は～へ行きたい」とまず書き，その場所の具体的な説明を２～４文で表現すればよい。正解例の意味は次のとおり。
「私は京都へ行きたい。第１に，京都には多くの有名な寺や神社がある。私はそこへ一度も行ったことがないので，それらを見てみたい。また，京都は抹茶で有名だ。それは私の大好きなお茶だ。早く行ければいいと思う」

【別解】I want to travel around Hokkaido. In summer, it is cool there. I dislike hot weather. In addition, one of the three famous night views in Japan can be enjoyed in Hakodate. I have seen the other two, and want to visit the third.（私は北海道一周旅行をしたい。夏には，そこは涼しい。私は暑い天候が好きではない。それに加えて，函館では日本の３つの有名な夜景のうちの１つを楽しむことができる。私は他の２つを見たことがあり，３つ目を訪ねたい）(44語)

3 例 **I think students should spend some time abroad. I went to China when I was in elementary school. I saw a lot of things that could not be found in Japan. I think traveling abroad is a good way to increase our experience and knowledge.**

(45語)

解説 指示に従って，最初の文は I think [I don't think] (that) students should spend some time abroad. とする。「30語以上」という指示については，語数が増えるのはかまわないが，解答欄に収まる分量にすること。これまでにも説明したとおり，自分自身が一度も外国へ行ったことがなくても，正解例のように書いてかまわない。正解例の意味は次のとおり。

「生徒は外国で時間を過ごすべきだと私は思います。私は小学生のころに中国へ行きました。そこで私は，日本にはない多くのものを見ました。外国旅行は自分の経験と知識を増やすためのよい方法だと思います」

なお，I don't think で文を始めるなら，「外国には危険な場所が多い(there are many dangerous places in foreign countries)」「多くの学生は外国旅行できるほどのお金を持っていない(many students don't have enough money to travel abroad)」などの理由が考えられる。

全訳

スミス先生：ミサキさん，今年の冬に何をする予定ですか。

ミサキ：今年の冬ですか。そうですね，たぶん宿題をして，テニスクラブへ行くだけです。

スミス先生：はは，それはそれでいいですね。でも，あなたはもっと多くのことができると思います。この学校の多くの生徒が，休暇中に外国へ行くそうです。

ミサキ：ええ，でもよくわかりません…。それはいい考えですか。生徒は外国で時間を過ごすべきだと思いますか。

スミス先生：ああ，それはいい質問です。次の英語の授業でこの話題を話し合いましょう。

英作文の勉強の仕方

和文英訳の勉強の仕方

日本語を英語に直す問いでは，自分が書いた英文が文法的に正しいかどうかを誰かに判断してもらう必要がある。学校の先生に添削してもらえればそれが一番よいが，今日ではAIを使って英文を添削してくれる無料のサービスがインターネット上で利用できる。

たとえばDeepL Writeというサイトでは，左側のウインドウに自分の書いた英文を入れれば，瞬時に添削されて右側の窓に正しい英文が表示される。このようなツールを使って，自分が書いた英文中の間違いと正しい英文を確認する習慣をつければ，英作文(および英会話)の力は飛躍的に向上するだろう。

自由英作文の勉強の仕方

自分自身について語るような問いなら，実際には経験していないことを書いてもかまわない。しかし，たとえば「動物園のよい点と悪い点を答えなさい」のような問いでは(→*p.072* 076)，自分が書きたい内容を英語で表現するための語い力と表現力が必要になる。そのような問いを解くための力をつけるには，たとえば次のような方法が考えられる。

❶ 試験でよく問われるテーマ(賛否の意見を求めるものなど)を箇条書きにする。たとえば，学校の制服，厳しい校則の是非，ボランティア活動，英語学習の方法や必要性など。
❷ それらのテーマについて，自分の意見を日本語で書いてみる。
❸ その日本語を，インターネット上の翻訳サイトを使って英語に直す。
❹ その英文中に自分の知らない単語や表現があれば，それを１つずつ覚えていく。

たとえば，「動物園のよい点と悪い点」というテーマについて考えてみよう。

1 書く内容を考える。

〇よい点「子どもが実物の動物を間近で見ることは教育上の効果が高い」「希少動物を動物園で保護し，繁殖させることで，密猟者から動物を守ったり種の絶滅を防いだりすることができる」など。

DeepL Write　https://www.deepl.com/ja/write
DeepL 翻訳　https://www.deepl.com/ja/translator
ChatGPT　https://openai.com/blog/chatgpt

×悪い点「動物園の動物は狭いおりの中に入れられており，かわいそう[動物虐待]だ」など。

2 上の日本語を，DeepL 翻訳というサイトで英訳する（インターネット上で無料で利用できる）。

3 そこに表示された英文を見れば，「動物園というテーマについて英語を書くときは，こんな表現を使えばいいのか」とわかる。そのようにして，さまざまなテーマに関する表現力を高めていこう。

なおインターネット上では，AIがどんな質問にも答えてくれる無料のサービスが利用できる。たとえばChatGPTというサイトに「動物園のよい点と悪い点をいくつか挙げてください」という質問を入れれば，左に挙げたような説明が箇条書きで表示される。また，こんな質問もできる。

> 次の英文は正しいですか？　I think to go to America someday.

これに対しては，次の答えが返ってくる。

> The sentence is grammatically correct, but it could be improved by changing “think to” to “hope to” or “plan to” to make the intention clearer. For example: “I hope to go to America someday” or “I plan to go to America someday.”
>
> （その文は文法的には正しいけれど，意図をより明確にするために，think toをhope toまたはplan toに変えることによって改善できます。たとえば，I hope to go to America someday. あるいはI plan to go to America someday. です）

このように，質問は日本語でもできる。回答の英文を読むことは，リーディングの力の向上にも役立つ。英文の意味がわからないときは，その文をDeepL翻訳にコピー＆ペーストすれば日本語訳が表示される。

以上のように，インターネット上でAIが翻訳，添削，質問への回答などを提供するサイトを利用すれば，英語の表現力を効率的に高めることができる。

⚠ 注意　ここで紹介したインターネット上のサービスやツール等をご利用の際は，あらかじめご家庭内で話し合って使い方のルールなどを決め，大人の監督下でご活用いただくことをお勧めいたします。

暗記用例文100

音声を聞く
スマートフォンでアクセスしよう

以下の英文は英作文での利用価値が高い表現を含むので，暗記しておくとよい。

1	I want to be a comedian.	私はお笑い芸人になりたい。
2	My dream is to study abroad.	私の夢は留学することだ。
3	There are many places to visit in my town.	私の町には訪ねるべき場所がたくさんある。
4	I want something hot to drink.	何か温かい飲み物がほしい。
5	I'm saving money to buy a new smartphone.	私は新しいスマートフォンを買うために貯金している。
6	I want someone to take care of my dog.	誰かに私の犬の世話をしてもらいたい。
7	Our coach told us to practice every day.	コーチは私たちに毎日練習するように言った。
8	This map will help you to find good restaurants.	この地図はあなたがよいレストランを見つけるのに役立ちます。
9	I didn't know what to do.	私は何をすればよいのかわからなかった。
10	Do you know how to make an apple pie?	アップルパイの作り方を知っていますか。
11	It takes ten minutes to walk to the beach.	ビーチまで歩いて10分かかる。
12	How long did it take you to cook this?	これを作るのにあなたはどのくらい時間がかかりましたか。
13	It is important for everyone to save energy.	エネルギーを節約することはみんなにとって大切だ。
14	It's kind of you to help me.	私を手伝ってくれるとはあなたは親切ですね。
15	This table is too heavy for me to carry.	このテーブルは私が運ぶには重すぎる。
16	This apartment is large enough for us to live in.	このアパートは私たちが住めるくらいの広さがある。
17	All you have to do is push this button.	あなたはこのボタンを押すだけでよい。
18	Let me know your new e-mail address.	あなたの新しいメールアドレスを私に教えてください。
19	Playing video games is fun.	ビデオゲームをするのは楽しい。
20	I'm interested in doing volunteer work.	私はボランティアの仕事をすることに興味がある。
21	I'm looking forward to seeing you again.	あなたにまた会えるのを楽しみにしています。
22	I'm not used to making a speech in English.	私は英語でスピーチをすることに慣れていない。
23	He left the room without saying goodbye.	彼はさよならも言わずに部屋を出た。
24	Kyoto is a famous city visited by many foreign tourists.	京都は多くの外国人観光客によって訪問される有名な都市だ。
25	The boys playing soccer are my classmates.	サッカーをしている男の子たちは私のクラスメイトです。
26	I saw some boys playing soccer in the park.	公園で何人かの男の子がサッカーをしているのが見えた。
27	I have already finished reading the book.	私はもうその本を読み終えた。
28	Have you finished your homework yet?	もう宿題は終わりましたか。
29	I haven't written the report yet.	私はまだレポートを書いていない。
30	Have you ever seen a French movie?	フランス映画を見たことがありますか。
31	I have never been to China.	私は中国へは一度も行ったことがない。
32	I have known her since we were children.	私は子どものころからずっと彼女と知り合いだ。
33	I've been looking for the key for more than 30 minutes.	私はそのカギを30分以上探し続けている。
34	It has been three months since we moved here.	私たちがここに引っ越してから3か月になる。
35	This book is read by many people around the world.	この本は世界中の多くの人に読まれている。
36	What is this flower called in English?	この花は英語で何と呼ばれますか。
37	This song is known to most young people in Japan.	この歌は日本のほとんどの若者に知られている。
38	I was spoken to by a stranger on the street.	私は通りで知らない人に話しかけられた。
39	If it rains tomorrow, we won't go shopping.	明日もし雨が降れば，私たちは買い物に行かないだろう。
40	If I were you, I would buy this dictionary.	もし私があなたなら，この辞書を買うだろう。
41	I wish I could speak English well.	英語を上手に話せればいいのに。
42	Could you tell me the way to the station?	駅へ行く道を教えてもらえますか。
43	We might not be able to catch the train.	私たちは電車に間に合わないかもしれない。
44	We had to give up the plan.	私たちはその計画をあきらめなければならなかった。
45	You don't have to do the work by yourself.	あなたはその仕事を一人[自分]でする必要はありません。
46	Shall I help you with your homework?	あなたの宿題を手伝いましょうか。
47	Shall we take a short break?	短い休憩をとりましょうか。
48	Do you know who that man is?	あの男性が誰だか知っていますか。

49	Who do you think that man is?	あの男性は誰だと思いますか。
50	What is your new teacher like?	あなたの新しい先生はどんな人ですか。
51	What kind of music do you like?	あなたはどんな種類の音楽が好きですか。
52	Where are you going to visit in Kyoto?	京都ではどこを訪ねる予定ですか。
53	How do I look in this dress?	このドレスは私に似合いますか。
54	How can I get to the station?	駅へはどのようにして行けばいいですか。
55	How about going to the movies?	映画に行くのはどうですか。
56	How far is it from here to the station?	ここから駅までの距離はどのくらいですか。
57	There is an old hotel in front of the station.	駅の前に１軒の古いホテルがある。
58	The restaurant is near the station.	そのレストランは駅の近くにある。
59	You look happy, don't you?	うれしそうですね。
60	"Aren't you tired?" "No, I'm not."	「疲れていませんか」「ええ（疲れていません）」
61	Be careful when you cross the street.	通りを横切るときは気をつけなさい。
62	My father gave me an interesting book.	父は私に面白い本をくれた。
63	I asked him where he was going.	私は彼にどこへ行くのかと尋ねた。
64	My mother always keeps the kitchen clean.	母はいつも台所をきれいに保っている。
65	This novel has made her a popular writer.	この小説は彼女を人気作家にした。
66	What made her so angry?	なぜ彼女はそんなに怒ったのですか。
67	What has made you change your mind?	あなたはなぜ決心を変えたのですか。
68	This photo reminds me of my childhood.	この写真を見ると私は子どものころを思い出す。
69	My room isn't as large as this room.	私の部屋はこの部屋ほど広くない。
70	It is not as cold today as it was yesterday.	今日は昨日ほど寒くない。
71	Nothing is as important as health.	健康ほど大切なものはない。
72	My sister has as many comic books as I do.	姉[妹]は私と同じくらいの数の漫画本を持っている。
73	This room is about three times as large as my room.	この部屋は私の部屋の約３倍の広さだ。
74	I'll get up as early as I can tomorrow morning.	明日の朝はできるだけ早く起きます。
75	The population of Tokyo is much larger than that of Osaka.	東京の人口は大阪の人口よりもずっと多い。
76	I like basketball better than soccer.	私はサッカーよりバスケットボールの方が好きだ。
77	More and more workers are coming to Japan from other countries.	外国から日本へ来る労働者がますます増えている。
78	The more you practice, the better you can play.	練習すればするほど，上手にプレーできます。
79	No other player in my club is taller than Shota is.	私のクラブの他のどの選手も，ショウタほど背が高くない。
80	Ken is the tallest of the five players.	ケンはその５人の選手のうちで一番背が高い。
81	This is the most beautiful picture I've ever seen.	これは私が今までに見た一番美しい絵です。
82	I've never read such an exciting novel.	こんなにわくわくする小説は今まで読んだことがない。
83	Yokohama is the second largest city in Japan.	横浜は日本で２番目に大きい都市だ。
84	The student who got the highest score was Nami.	最高点を取った生徒はナミだった。
85	This is a picture I took in Hawaii.	これは私がハワイで撮った写真だ。
86	The subject I like the best is math.	私が一番好きな科目は数学だ。
87	I had a cold, so I didn't go to the concert.	私は風邪をひいていたので，コンサートに行かなかった。
88	I didn't go to the concert because I had a cold.	私は風邪をひいていたので，コンサートに行かなかった。
89	Can you call me when he comes back?	彼が戻って来たら，私に電話してもらえますか。
90	Leave the door open so that the cat can come in.	そのネコが入れるように，ドアを開けておきなさい。
91	I like the way this announcer speaks.	私はこのアナウンサーの話し方が好きだ。
92	Hurry up, or you'll miss the bus.	急ぎなさい，さもないとバスに乗り遅れますよ。
93	I was so tired that I fell asleep.	私はとても疲れていたので寝てしまった。
94	It was such a funny story that I couldn't stop laughing.	それはとてもゆかいな話だったので，私は笑うのをやめられなかった。
95	She never comes to my house without giving me a present.	彼女は私の家に来るときはいつも私にプレゼントをくれる。
96	This book is different from the one I ordered.	この本は私が注文したのと違う。
97	She goes to the gym twice a week.	彼女は週に２回ジムに通っている。
98	I don't have any money with me now.	私は今お金を少しも持ち合わせていない。
99	According to the newspaper, it will snow tomorrow.	新聞によれば，明日は雪が降るだろう。
100	I agree with his opinion for two reasons.	私は２つの理由で彼の意見に賛成だ。